Managing
Classrooms
to Facilitate
Learning

Managing Classrooms to Facilitate Learning

ANNE M. BAUER
REGINA H. SAPONA

University of Cincinnati

Prentice Hall, Englewood Cliffs, NJ 07632

Library of Congress Cataloging-in-Publication Data

Bauer, Anne M.
    Managing classrooms to facilitate learning / Anne M. Bauer, Regina H. Sapona.
        p.   cm.
    Includes bibliographical references.
    ISBN 0-13-543315-0
    1. Classroom management.   I. Sapona, Regina H.   II. Title.
LB3013.B36   1991
371.1'02—dc20

90-30421
CIP

Editorial/production supervision
  and interior design: **June Sanns**
Page makeup: **June Sanns**
Cover designer: **Ben Santora**
Prepress buyer: **Debra Kesar**
Manufacturing buyer: **Marianne Gloriande**

Printed in the United States of America

10 9 8 7 6 5 4 3 2 1

ISBN 0-13-543315-0

PRENTICE-HALL INTERNATIONAL (UK) LIMITED, *London*
PRENTICE-HALL OF AUSTRALIA PTY. LIMITED, *Sydney*
PRENTICE-HALL CANADA INC., *Toronto*
PRENTICE-HALL HISPANOAMERICANA, S.A., *Mexico*
PRENTICE-HALL OF INDIA PRIVATE LIMITED, *New Delhi*
PRENTICE-HALL OF JAPAN, INC., *Tokyo*
SIMON & SCHUSTER ASIA PTE. LTD., *Singapore*
EDITORA PRENTICE-HALL DO BRASIL, LTDA., *Rio de Janeiro*

Dedicated
to
Riley, Demian, Tara, and Christopher
and
Regina, Christe, Ingrid, and Sonia

Contents

Preface

University supervisor:	There seemed to be a lot of disruptive behavior during your lesson. It's hard for me to evaluate your lesson plan in view of the students' behavior.
Student teacher:	I know. I'm still learning how to get them under control so I can teach.

*   *   *

Teacher preparation and certification programs usually require introductory coursework in classroom management. This course is frequently an introduction to behavior modification, applied behavior analysis, or the use of specific, recipe-like strategies to manage students and eliminate undesirable behavior. Classroom management coursework generally includes an emphasis on discipline, "controlling" student behavior, and typically employs a single perspective (usually behavioral). The total picture, that of structuring a classroom to facilitate student learning, is often neglected. Yet the view of teachers as professional practitioners, working in a complex environment, has been gaining more attention in the professional literature. The study and education of teachers as thinking, interacting professionals has been recommended by both the Holmes Group and the Carnegie Commissions on reforming teacher preparation.

Managing Classrooms to Facilitate Learning reflects this new emphasis on developing successful, professional practitioners. As such, it reflects a dramatic shift from the traditional discipline/control perspective. The emphasis is creating and managing environments that invite students to learn. "Controlling" or "reducing" behaviors is not addressed. Rather, the consideration of a complex classroom context is presented through the use of a framework for developing an agenda for classroom management. Through the use of this framework, components of the physical, social, and personal context of the student and classroom are studied, and questions are generated for further study. Teachers may then design more effective ways to enhance conventional means of communication, develop socially appropriate behaviors, and facilitate self-regulated learning. Through this proactive perspective, the goal of this text is to help you develop strategies to "manage classrooms to facilitate learning."

Rather than teacher educators who "should know," our perspective is that of classroom observers, teacher collaborators, and students of classroom interaction. Our research and review of others' work have shown us that skills deemed essential and emphasized in teacher preparation programs, such as writing lesson plans, may not occur in actual practice. Yet in actual practice, our studies of expert teachers have demonstrated different issues, such as recognizing the complexity of the classroom context, the teacher's communicative competence and match with students, the communication and application of routines, which frequently receive little attention in coursework in classroom management.

Our experience in classrooms and reviews of the literature have taught us that there are no simple answers and no single way of responding to students and situations. Unlike books which present problems and solutions, we offer no recipes for instant student compliance, cooperation, and agreeability. Rather than observing nonproductive and unsuccessful interactions and positing answers in an "all you need to do..." tone, we observe those interactions and respond, "Wow—Look at everything to be considered in this situation!"

As teachers, we are concerned that this be considered a teaching text. As such, we have opened each chapter with scripts of interactions from our observations in classrooms. These scripts serve as running examples throughout the chapter. In addition, each chapter includes a self-evaluation, key words, objectives, a summary, and application activities to provide an opportunity for practicing and integrating the chapter content.

Managing Classrooms to Facilitate Learning opens with an overview of managing classrooms to facilitate learning. In the chapters of this section, classroom management and the many roles assumed by teachers in managing classrooms are discussed. The importance of teacher stance and the impact of teacher interactions on student behavior and learning are described. Section One concludes with the description of a framework for teachers to use in developing management strategies for the total class and individual students.

Section Two, "Managing Classrooms Through Structuring the Context," provides insight into a large part of the framework, that of working with the physical and social context of the classroom. In this section, noninstructional variables, such as the physical environment, scheduling, material selection, and grouping are discussed. The impact of these variables on managing classrooms is described.

The following sections of the book describe "Managing Classrooms Through Patterns of Interactions" (Sections Three through Five). In our work in classrooms and through our research, three patterns of interactions have emerged. These patterns provide the framework for discussion of management strategies and techniques. Teacher-focused activities, such as mastery learning, direct instruction, and behavioral management techniques are presented, as are student-focused activities, such as group meeting models and nondirective interviews, and activities that focus on the data, material, or problem, such as inquiry or cooperative learning. In Section Six, examples of developing a classroom agenda and applications of patterns to practice are presented.

This is a book about facilitating learning, and, as such, we must thank those who have facilitated our learning about classrooms and working with children as learners. We'd like to thank Sue Murphy, Lisa Webb, Linda Phillips, Cindy Miller, and John Brengelmann and their students for collaborating with us in and around classrooms. This book would not have been possible without the assistance of these expert teachers. We'd like to thank Richard Kretschmer and Roberta Truax for keeping us on track with teacher preparation rather than teacher training and Ellen Lynch for reviewing sometimes rough forms of the manuscript. We would also like to thank the Prentice Hall reviewers: Richard M. Brandt, Department of Educational Studies, University of Virginia; and Marian Alice Simmons, Department of Teacher Education, University of Missouri at Kansas City. And we'd like to thank our families for permitting us to grow and change.

Annie Bauer

Regina Sapona

To the Reader

This textbook was developed with the intent of helping pre-service and inservice teachers increase their knowledge and skills in managing classrooms. To fulfill this intent, it includes a variety of pedagogical aides and uses a standard format for chapters. And, as teachers who should model appropriate behavior and attempt to apply research to their teaching, we are explicit in our organizational format (related to increased student achievement by Kallison, 1986).*

Each chapter will begin with situations recorded from our observations and participation in classrooms. Following these scripts, self-evaluation items are provided to stimulate thinking and serve as readiness activities for the content. These self-evaluation items are followed by key words, that are also defined in the glossary. Chapter objectives, which are then further explored through narrative, follow. Each chapter concludes with a summary, review questions, and application activities that are designed to clarify and amplify the essential issues presented in the chapter.

---

*Kallison, J. M. (1986). Effects of lesson organization on achievement. *American Educational Research Journal, 23*, 337–347.

Managing Classrooms to Facilitate Learning

CHAPTER ONE

Classroom Management and Managing Behaviors

SITUATIONS

Setting: A junior high school American history class, sixth period.

Students are slumped in their desks; three young women are in the back, writing notes and comparing doodles; others are playing with pencils, drawing, reading paperbacks inside their history books; and so on.

Teacher: Class, sit up.   It's time we start today.   Come on, get up [some general shifting of positions occurs].   There are both economic and social reasons for the American Civil War.   First, we'll describe the five economic reasons.   The first of these... [turns to write on board].

Student: [While the teacher's back is turned, faces the class and mouths the lecture.   A second student throws a paperwad at him.   He looks insulted and taps on the book.]

Teacher: [Turns around, looks insulted, taps on the book. Students laugh.] This is important material. It will be on the test. You are responsible for knowing it. If I have to stop again, you will be responsible for the remainder of the chapter yourselves [turns back to board to write second reason].

Student:. Ms. S., I can't see the board while you're writing on it.

Teacher: Then wait until I'm finished writing.

Student: By then you'll be going on to something else and I'll never get it down. And this material will be on the test. I will be responsible for knowing it.

Teacher: I have had it with your smart mouths. Get out your books. Turn to Chapter Six and read. There will be a quiz on this material tomorrow.

Students: Aw, c'mon. What? I'm not reading this ——.

Teacher: Quiet. Get to work.

*   *   *

Setting: Third grade classroom; half the group is having reading instruction with the teacher, the other half is doing seatwork.

Student: [Waving her arm] Ms. T., Ms. T., I need to sharpen my pencil.

Teacher: Go ahead, Elizabeth, but do so quietly.

Student: [Leaves seat, walks by windows, and gazes outside, watching students on the playground; goes by record player, giving the turntable a spin or two; walks by gerbil cage, talks to gerbil, and tries to get it to eat a part of a carrot; goes through cloakroom and makes sure lunch is in lunch box; finally reaches pencil sharpener and sharpens pencil; begins "grand tour" on the way back to her seat.]

Teacher: Elizabeth, why are you out of your seat?

Student: I'm just sharpening my pencil.

*   *   *

These two interactions are representative of those which may occur in regular education classrooms. Although they vary in the number, ages, and responses of students involved, both interfere with learning. Teachers must be able to deal with a wide range of behaviors in ways that enhance rather than deter student learning. Teachers must be able to structure the classroom in ways that allow students to develop as self-regulating learners.

This first section of the book presents a view of classrooms as places in which teachers, students, and subject matter interact. Classrooms are viewed as highly interactive, complex environments. Managing this environment requires an understanding of classroom communicative processes and the development of a personal stance to guide teachers' roles in the interactional process. Chapters One through Three present information relating to a stance we believe is most effective in creating environments that facilitate student development. In addition, we suggest that a teacher's agenda for classroom management emanates from his or her stance. To assist teachers in developing their agendas for classroom management, we offer a four-phase framework to be applied to challenging situations involving student participation in the learning process.

In keeping with our proactive stance toward behavior management, we will present information that addresses initial classroom management concerns (e.g., establishing effective routines, developing schedules, designing physical space). The reader will note that variables mentioned in the context of our discussion of the framework (i.e., teacher, student, task, and setting variables) play a key role in Section Two in structuring classrooms to prevent breakdowns in the learning process. Sections Three through Five continue to build on the previous sections through a presentation of patterns that teachers may use to design instructional activities.

In this chapter, classroom management is examined from a proactive perspective. That is, the emphasis will be on how to create a successful, interactive classroom environment. The teacher's role as an improvising problem solver and data gatherer is described. The relationship between "effective teaching" research and classroom management will be explored. The chapter concludes with a description of the format of this book and ways to use it effectively.

SELF-EVALUATION

To stimulate thinking about the content, each of the chapters of this book begins with a self-evaluation. Complete them candidly; they serve as readiness activities, points for discussion, and probes into your present level of understanding of the information provided.

Please indicate whether you agree or disagree to each of the items below.

1. Classroom management is synonymous with classroom discipline.
2. The teacher's role in the classroom is to have a positive, valued relationship with students.
3. Knowing why to use a teaching technique is not as important as knowing a wide range of techniques.

4. The teacher's role is to structure the classroom so that behavior problems do not occur.
5. The teacher's role is to manage students' behaviors so that the students can profit from instruction and social interaction.
6. Teachers should be able to describe their rationale for choosing to interact with students in a particular way.
7. The teacher's role is to provide daily, positive social interaction among students and between students and teacher.
8. Most of the inappropriate behaviors in classrooms are attention seeking.

KEY WORDS

classroom management

stance

in-flight decisions

interactive decisions

if-then statements

routines

OBJECTIVES

After completing this chapter, you will be able to:

1. Describe classroom management.
2. Describe the relationship between student learning and classroom management.
3. Describe the relationship between teacher activities and roles and classroom management.
4. Describe the relationship between classroom communication and classroom management.

Objective One: *To Describe Classroom Management*

The last twenty years have represented dramatic changes in classroom management. Jones (1986) suggests that during the mid-1960s, a counseling approach was used with students who were considered disruptive, with removal and individual interventions for problems. This period was followed by the use of behavioral methods which emphasized control. During this period teachers learned to state clear behavioral expectations, quietly and consistently intervene with disruptive students (usually in less than positive ways), and provide group reinforcement for appropriate behavior. An emphasis on teacher organization and management skills has emerged within the literature on teacher effectiveness. In striving to increase instruction, teachers were provided with simple, usually control-oriented classroom management methods. The teacher was deemed responsible for developing instructional and management skills (Jones, 1986).

Increased teacher responsibility for instructional and management skills has not been paired with greater emphasis in research and training. Brophy and Rohrkemper (1981) state that "there has been little research on methods of dealing with problem students, and in particular, very little research focusing on techniques that may be feasible and effective for the ordinary classroom teacher" (p. 295). Teachers are often presented with superficial methods for dealing with instructional and management problems, and are not provided training in effective teaching and management methods (Jones, 1986).

Classroom Management: Dealing with Complexity. Superficial methods, however, cannot address the complexity of managing classrooms. Classroom management refers to the steps and procedures necessary to establish and maintain an environment in which instruction and learning occur (Doyle, 1979). Effective classroom management is the "ability to establish, maintain, and (when necessary) restore the classroom as an effective environment for teaching and learning" (Brophy, 1986, p. 182). Most beginning teachers, however, equate classroom management with discipline. It is more a matter of group management and problem prevention than disciplinary responses to misbehavior (Brophy, 1986).

Tattum (1986) describes the complexity of classroom management, including "the allocation of time and space, the distribution of materials, and careful record-keeping, as well as coping with pupil behavior" (p. 62). He suggests that the alternative to an effective classroom management style is an unsystematic "bag of tricks," which is developed over time and through the rigors of experience. This "bag of tricks" approach has no real rhyme or reason, but contains a wide range of "whatever works."

Classroom management is enmeshed with effective teaching, teacher activities, and communication in the classroom (Doyle, 1986). Rosenshine (1983) states that "instruction cannot be effective if the students are not managed" (p. 348). The tasks of instruction and order, the result of classroom management, are intertwined: Doyle (1986) indicates that orderliness is necessary for instruction to occur and lessons must be so constructed as to capture and maintain attention. Order within a classroom means that students are, within acceptable limits, "following the program of action necessary for a particular classroom event to be realized in the situation" (Doyle, 1986, p. 396). The teacher's management task is to establish and maintain an effective learning environment for classroom groups rather than spotting and punishing misbehavior. In the junior high school problem situation presented at the beginning of this chapter, the classroom was not in order. The program of action necessary for instruction in American history was not being followed. Rather than creating and maintaining an interesting, interactive learning environment, the teacher was reacting to misbehavior and finally abandoned her course of action completely.

Effective management emerges from clearly established classroom structures, routines, and teacher roles. After reviewing the literature, Doyle (1986) suggested that classroom structures are successfully established when rules and procedures are announced, demonstrated, enforced, and routinized. By applying rules and procedures, teachers communicate an awareness of what can happen in the classroom and demonstrate a commitment to completing work (Brooks, 1985). In the elementary classroom situation presented at the beginning of the chapter, a working rule regarding performing a task and returning promptly to one's seat would have mitigated Elizabeth's "grand tour." Yet managing students and mastering routine activities are not easy; Shefelbine and Hollingsworth (1987) found that these activities were difficult for teacher interns and distracted them from making decisions about instruction.

Objective Two: *To Describe the Relationship Between Student Learning and Classroom Management Style*

Teachers' beliefs and behavior effect student learning. These beliefs and behavior influence not only activities in the classroom but students' behavior, perceptions of schooling, and self-perceptions (Halperin, 1976). Rohrkemper (1984) contrasted two management styles: behavior modification and inductive teaching. Behavior modification–style teachers relied on reward-based contingency programs, using contracts to maintain classroom organization, emphasizing the more tangible consequences of behavior. For example, in preparation for a fire drill, a behavior modification–style teacher may state that students who are quiet during the fire drill will earn five minutes of additional free time. Inductive teachers communicated extensively and provided rationales for behavioral demands, hoping to promote student insight into the reasons underlying behaviors and consequences. The inductive teacher would prepare for the same fire drill by telling students that quiet is necessary for student safety, so that they can move quickly and be sure to hear any directions that may be given by teachers, firefighters, or other adults. Rohrkemper interviewed students to obtain interpretations of their teacher's responses to problems depicted in vignettes of classroom events. She found that the teachers' management style was consistently related to the students' prediction and interpretation of teacher behavior. Students in inductive classrooms were more likely to describe a teacher's rationale for reaction to a behavior, whereas students in behavior modification classrooms focused more on global, negative teacher reactions. Students in inductive classrooms were more active in describing reasons for behavior unlike students in behavior modification classrooms who reported authority-based morality. This study suggests that more than achievement is influenced by teacher style.

A recognizable style or "stance" is the particular orientation or position which guides the improvising practitioner (Bruner, 1986). This stance includes attitude toward self and others that guides interactions (McGee, Menolascino, Hobbs, and Menousek, 1987). McGee and associates suggest that this stance differs from, but includes, theoretical orientation and techniques. For example, a teacher may profess a theoretical orientation and use behavior modification techniques, yet project warm relationships with students, flexibility, and a recognition of context which are not assumed by that theoretical framework or those techniques. If a teacher can define his or her stance, he or she can judge effects of interactions and the impact those interactions have on students' development. The notion of stance is critically important and will be discussed in later chapters.

Objective Three: *To Describe the Relationship Between Teacher Activities and Classroom Management*

As classroom managers, teachers undertake several activities and fulfill several roles. Through these activities and roles, they determine if, when, and how to provide support to maintain the flow of an activity, or interrupt the flow to repair order, stop competing activities, and return the class to task. Although interventions can repair temporary disturbances, they cannot establish order when no primary activity is operating (Doyle, 1986). The need to intervene is a sign that the mechanisms through which order is established and maintained are not working. Effective teachers decide whether their action will disrupt order and how to intervene in inconspicuous ways to cut off the path to disorder. In the elementary school problem situation, the teacher may have averted Elizabeth's grand tour in an inconspicuous way by providing limits with the permission. Sharpening the pencil quietly was not an adequate limit. The teacher may have prevented Elizabeth's roaming by stating, "Do so quickly—right to the pencil sharpener, and then to your seat."

Teachers as Decision Makers. Shavelson and Stern (1981) suggest that teachers are thinking professionals who make decisions in complex environments. Shavelson (1973) maintains that decision making is "the basic teaching skill." Teachers have reasons for their decisions. Their decisions are based in the simplified model of reality which they construct while teaching. Shavelson and Stern suggest that teachers are active agents with many instructional techniques at their disposal to help students reach some goal; in order to choose from this repertoire, teachers must integrate a large amount of information about students from a variety of sources and combine this information with their own beliefs and goals, the nature of the task at hand, and the constraints of the situation.

Teachers make two kinds of decisions, "in-flight reactions" and planned decisions (Shefelbine and Hollingsworth, 1987). In-flight decisions are made during the activity itself, whereas planned decisions are conscious and occur before the activity takes place. For example, if students are responding to an open-ended question, the teacher may make an inflight decision to write responses on the chalkboard when students begin to repeat other students' reponses. The open-ended question itself, however, may be the result of a planned decision, decided upon when the teacher prepared the lesson. In their study of interns involved in reading instruction, Shefelbine and Hollingsworth found that "in-flight reactions," which called for immediate, complex decisions, were more difficult. These decisions did not present within a specific format. Easier decisions involved advanced planning and required fewer minute-by-minute changes and variations.

Critics of the "decision maker" model of teaching suggest that conscious decision making may occur in only 25 percent of a teacher's reported thoughts (Yinger, 1986). Parker and Gehrke (1986) emphasize the importance of the "in-flight" decision, a process they describe as "interactive decision making." These decisions result from the interaction of the student, teacher, and materials or content. Parker (1984) indicates that interactive decision making is "the cognitive activity that results in teachers' on the spot selection of instructional behaviors." Instructional behaviors may include moving toward or away from students, demonstrating, providing a verbal prompt, providing a visual prompt such as writing on the chalkboard, or repeating an explanation which seems to be causing difficulty for the students.

Parker (1984) maintains that if formal decision making is one of the most frequently practiced professional skills of teaching, it seems to occur less frequently than it might and when it does occur, it often occurs without consideration or weighing of alternatives. Through a treatment involving guided reflection and role taking, Parker sought to increase the sophistication of the interactive decisions made by teachers and decrease the amount of decisions made while teachers were on "automatic pilot," making decisions in the process of the activity, with little consideration of alternatives. Throughout the training, teachers made more comments concerning weighing the alternatives and "triggers" of decisions. In further studies of interactive decision making, Parker and Gehrke (1986) found that interactive decisions are a property of the learning activities underway rather than the lesson objective. The primary intention of the teacher's decisions is to move the learning activity forward to completion; the decision rules are if-then statements concerned about completing activities. The teacher considers, for example, "If I speed up the rate at which I'm asking for responses, I may increase Joey and Jill's attention."

Doyle (1986) argues that the decision to intervene, that is, to interrupt an activity and take a specific action, is risky. Interventions are, by their very nature, reactive. Because they are provoked by unplanned behaviors, they are by nature unplanned, their timing is difficult to control, and their form must be decided on the spot. Pittman (1985) suggests that decisions to intervene are based on information about whether the behavior was serious and distracting and decisions about the intensity of the intervention depend on the student's past behavior. In the junior high school situation that opens this chapter, one can assume that the class has a history of lack of participation through analysis of the teacher's reaction. By terminating the instructional activity early in her presentation, she may be reacting to experience that less serious reactions do not stop the disruptions. However, had the teacher restructured the activity to involve the students more actively, participation may have increased, and the disruptions decreased.

Teacher as Design Professional. The teacher–decision maker model may, however, be constrictive. Yinger (1986) suggests that teachers are, rather, design professionals, who plan, theorize, problem solve, craft, and improvise. Yinger suggests that teachers are involved in "design," defined by Simon (1981) as actions aimed at bringing about desired states of affairs in practical contexts. Rather than making a series of decisions within routine actions, design is described as an ongoing dialogue involving construction of a new theory of the unique case, searching for adequate specifications of the situation, defining means and ends interactively, and remaking and reevaluating concerns as one proceeds. Schon (1983) describes this experience as "feeling one's way through the situation."

Teachers as Improvisors. Yinger (1987) has generated propositions regarding improvisational performance in a practical context which relate to teaching. He describes the teacher as an actor in a three way conversation between teacher, students, and problems. As in theatrical improvisation, there is no real "problem" to solve, but action and meaning to be developed. Rather than an analytic process, teacher improvisations emerge from current actions, progressing in ways that "feel right," but may not be analytically appropriate. Yinger further describes the "working method of improvisation... as using patterns from past action to order future action" (p. 16). Later chapters will present information and examples of patterns of interaction which teachers should consider as they structure their classrooms to facilitate student learning.

Teacher as Researcher. Bissex (1986) suggests that the teacher as researcher is an observer, questioner, learner, and more complete teacher. As researchers, teachers continue to build their own knowledge in such a way that they can develop their understanding of their students and learning (McConaghy, 1986). If one views research as primarily a process of discovery, each lesson could be considered a form of inquiry (Britton, 1987).

Teacher as Master Planner. Leinhardt and Greeno (1986) perceive teaching as a cognitive skill. Implicit in the activity of teaching is an agenda or master plan which is used to organize the action segments of lessons. These action segments may be routines (shared, cooperative, social scripts which automize and facilitate the activity by reducing the cognitive complexity of the classroom). Expert teachers' lessons are perceived as an action agenda, consisting of a series of action segments. Each segment has an independent goal and structure to be completed. Through using routines, the teacher frees himself or herself to attend to more important elements of the information to be taught or to the students.

Leinhardt, Weidman, and Hammond (1987) have found considerable use of routines among successful teachers. They depict the teacher as choreographing management routines (housekeeping, discipline, maintenance, and movement routines), support routines (distributing and collecting papers, getting materials ready), and exchange routines (interactive behaviors which permit the teaching-learning exchange to occur) as the stage directions and steps to the dance, culminating in the pas de deux.

Objective Four: *To Describe the Relationship Between Classroom Communication and Classroom Management*

Spoken language is the medium for most teaching and most student demonstrations of what they have learned (Cazden, 1986). Cazden suggests that it is essential to consider classroom communication systems as media which may pose problems for teachers and students.

After reviewing a series of published and unpublished studies funded by the National Institute of Education, Green (1983) provided a series of assumptions about classroom communication. She suggested that interaction between teachers and students and among students is governed by context specific rules. The rules themselves are implicit, conveyed and learned through interaction itself. In addition, meaning is context specific; all instances of a behavior may not serve the same purpose, and behaviors may have multiple meanings. Frames of reference for classrooms evolve over time and impact on student participation. She concludes that complex communicative demands are placed on both teachers and students by the diversity of classroom communicative structures, and teachers evaluate student ability from observing communicative performance (Green, 1983).

Creaghead and Tattershall (1985) suggest that a wide range of communicative skills are required in school. These communicative skills involve nonverbal, verbal, and written communicative activities (see Table 1.1).

Classroom communication problems are not created and maintained by students alone. Grice (1975) contends that communication is accomplished through the cooperative efforts of participants to achieve a transmission of meaning. These cooperative efforts are based on mutual adherence to a set of communication rules. If either participant fails to adhere to the rules, communication may break down. He maintains that four areas of difficulty may be described using this cooperative principle. There may be a problem in the *quantity* of information provided or the *quality* or accuracy of the message. *Relations* describes problems with relevance, maintaining topic, and making appropriate remarks. The final category, *manner,* describes problems with "not what you say but how you say it."

Nelson (1985) further describes the need for a match between teacher and student communication strategies. She describes informal assessment which may be used to increase teachers' awareness of the match between teacher talk and student listening. Some of the areas which have an impact on classroom management and instruction include

- ❖ The complexity and level of abstraction of the message
- ❖ The students' background and experience with the content of the message
- ❖ The students' understanding of classroom interactions and routines
- ❖ Teacher and student awareness of nonverbal communication
- ❖ Preparation of teachers to switch from thinking about language as a mode of communication to viewing it as an object of discussion
- ❖ The cognitive organization teachers provide before launching into specific content
- ❖ The quality of the listening environment

TABLE 1.1 Communicative Skills Required in School

Knowledge About the School Routine

- ❖ Knows routines for activities such as beginning the day, lunch, bus time
- ❖ Knows routine for lesson participation, that is, when and how to ask questions, transitions between lessons
- ❖ Can deviate from the routine when necessary
- ❖ Can determine the teacher's cues for a given routine
- ❖ Participates in routines with peers

Knowledge About Communicative Routines

- ❖ Knows when to talk
- ❖ Can take turns appropriately in the conversation
- ❖ Initiates conversations appropriately
- ❖ Can adjust interaction style with partners

Ability to Use Format to Comprehend Written Language

- ❖ Recognizes written material by format, for example, textbook versus leisure reading
- ❖ Predicts workbook directions on the basis of page format
- ❖ Predicts contents on the basis of title, headings, illustrations
- ❖ Confirms or modifies predictions after reading content

Giving and Following Oral Directions

As a speaker, the student

- ❖ Clearly identifies pertinent objects
- ❖ Specifies locations
- ❖ Checks for comprehension
- ❖ Revises directions when necessary
- ❖ Takes responsibility when directions do not work

As a listener, the student

- ❖ Follows directions exactly
- ❖ Follows general direction, but proceeds further on presumed information
- ❖ Requests clarification

Giving and Following Written Directions:

When writing directions, the student

- ❖ States objectives in topic sentences
- ❖ Uses a single direction per sentence
- ❖ Sequences directions appropriately
- ❖ Gives adequate but not too much information

When reading directions, the student

- ❖ Follows multiple directions
- ❖ Notes unpredictable procedures in an otherwise predictable set of directions
- ❖ Notes unpredictable directions

TABLE 1.1 Continued

Comprehension and Use of Figurative Language

❖ Restates figurative meanings of similes, metaphors, and idioms
❖ Draws pictures to illustrate figurative meanings
❖ Uses idiomatic expressions that are used by peers
❖ Comprehends material involving figurative language
❖ Determines the meaning of unknown figurative expressions when given appropriate context

Source note: This table is an adaptation of Appendix 4–1 from N. A. Creaghead and S. S. Tattershall, "Observation and Assessment of Classroom Pragmatic Skills," in *Communication Skills and Classroom Success: Assessment of Language-Learning Disabled Students,* Charlann S. Simon, editor (pp. 129–131). Boston: College-Hill Press, 1985. Used with permission of the publisher.

Just as teachers evaluate students by observing their communicative performance, students form their impressions about the teacher and about the teacher's competence through interactions with teachers (Brooks, 1985). Brooks found that on the first day of class, effective teachers select and sequence activities that communicate competence. Effective teachers communicate their expectations clearly to their students.

The recent literature has continued to explore the relationships between communicative problems and school and behavior problems. Cantwell and Baker (1985) found that about half of the six hundred students in their sample referred and evaluated for communication problems had diagnosable psychiatric disorders (i.e. behavioral disorders, anxiety, depression, autism, mental retardation). In addition, students with learning problems demonstrated a high rate of language disorders. Hasenstab (1985) found a relationship between spoken language problems and oral reading behaviors which further illustrates the relationship between communicative problems and instructional problems.

SUMMARY

Classrooms are complex environments in which teachers, students, and the subject matter interact. This interaction is facilitated by effective classroom management and structures. The teacher's management task is to establish and maintain an interesting, flexible learning environment for classroom groups rather than spotting and punishing misbehavior. Furthermore, as Rohrkemper (1984) suggests, task success is not the goal of a well-managed and well-structured classroom. Rather, adaptive behaviors including approaching a task, maintaining task involvement, and if necessary, regaining task involvement is the goal. Success in the classroom is perceived as adaptive learning: marshalling resources to recover from frustration, learning from errors, and correcting errors when necessary.

Managing a complex, highly interactive environment such as the classroom is a serious responsibility. Teachers assume many roles as they attempt to create and maintain environments which invite students to learn. Teachers act as researchers, decision makers, master planners, and design professionals who observe, question, and plan activities. In addition, they are improvisers who engage in three-way conversations between themselves, students, and instructional problems. These conversations occur within continuously changing contexts. Finally, teachers must consider the relationship between classroom communication and classroom management. We hope that a further exploration of the ideas contained in this chapter will help teachers develop their personal "stance" which will guide their interactions within the dynamic environment of the classroom.

REVIEW QUESTIONS

1. Describe the dramatic changes which have occurred in classroom management strategies since the 1960s. Relate these changes to your personal experience and through observations of teachers who were prepared at varying times during the decade.

2. Define effective classroom management. What are some of the variables that are involved in management?

3. Describe the role of teacher socialization style or stance on student behavior. Describe your personal stance, and reflect on how it may impact on potential students.

4. Contrast the roles of teachers. In which role or roles do you feel most comfortable at this time? What roles do you perceive emerging as you interact with students?

5. In what ways can communication impact on classroom management?

APPLICATION ACTIVITY

Each of us has experienced effective (and less than effective) teachers. As individual learners, we have also each experienced some task which was difficult for us to learn. In this application activity you will use personal experience to gain insight into the impact of teacher stance, role, and management activities on your learning.

Describe two tasks that were difficult for you to learn to accomplish successfully. The first task should be one which was eventually learned with the assistance of an effective teacher. The second task should be one for which instruction was provided by a less than effective teacher. These tasks may include any activity from learning to drive a stick shift to physical chemistry class, to knowing how to bake a souffle. Comment on these points:

❖ What was the stance of each of the teachers? What attitudes and expectancies were projected by each of the teachers?

❖ What roles did each teacher assume in the teaching-learning experience?

❖ What language and communication techniques were used by each of the teachers (verbal, nonverbal, written, kinesthetic, demonstration, etc.)?

❖ What was the greatest difference between the two teachers? In what ways were they similar?

❖ Besides the teachers and communication, what contributed to the differences between those learning experiences?

Summarize your response by describing your reasons for selecting these two experiences. Suggest how these experiences may have an impact on your developing teacher behavior.

REFERENCES

BISSEX, G. (1986). On becoming teacher experts: What's a teacher-researcher? *Language Arts, 63*, 482–484.

BRITTON, J. (1987). A quiet form of research. In D. Goswami & P. R. Stillman (Eds.), *Reclaiming the classroom: Teacher research as an agency for change* (pp. 13–19). Upper Montclair, NJ: Boynton/Cook.

BROOKS, D. M. (1985). The teacher's communicative competence: The first day of school. *Theory into Practice, 24*, 63–70.

BROPHY, J. (1986). Classroom management techniques. *Education and Urban Society, 18*, 182–184.

BROPHY, J. E., & ROHRKEMPER, M. M. (1981). The influence of problem ownership on teacher's perceptions of and strategies for coping with problem students. *Journal of Educational Psychology, 73*, 295–311.

BRUNER, J. (1986). *Actual minds, possible worlds*. Cambridge, MA: Harvard University Press.

CANTWELL, D. P., & BAKER, L. (1985). Interrelationship of communication, learning, and psychiatric disorders in children. In C. Simon, (Ed.), *Communication skills and classroom success* (pp. 43–64). San Diego, CA: College Hill Press.

CAZDEN, C. B. (1986). Classroom discourse. In M. C. Wittrock, *Handbook of research on teaching* (3rd ed., pp. 432–463). New York: Macmillan.

CREAGHEAD, N. A., & TATTERSHALL, S. S. (1985). Observation and assessment of classroom pragmatic skills. In C. S. Simon, *Communication skills and classroom success* (pp. 105–131). San Diego, CA: College Hill Press.

DOYLE, W. **(1979).** Making managerial decisions in classrooms. In D. L. Duke (Ed.), *Classroom management.* Chicago: University of Chicago Press.

———. **(1986).** Classroom organization and management. In M. C. Wittrock, *Handbook of research on teaching* (3rd ed., pp. 392–431). New York: Macmillan.

GREEN, J. L. **(1983).** Research on teaching as a linguistic process: A state of the art. In E. W. Gordon (Ed.), *Review of research in education* (Vol. 10, pp. 152–252). Washington, DC: American Educational Research Association.

GRICE, H. P. **(1975).** Logic and conversation. In P. Cole & J. Morgan (Eds.), *Studies in syntax and semantics: Speech acts* (Vol. 3, pp. 41–58). New York: Academic Press.

HALPERIN, M. **(1976).** First grade teachers'and children's developing perceptions of school. *Journal of Educational Psychology, 68,* 636–648.

HASENSTAB, M. S. **(1985).** Reading evaluation: A psychosocio-linguistic approach. In C. Simon (Ed.), *Communication skills and classroom success* (pp. 339–374). San Diego, CA: College Hill Press.

JONES, V. **(1986).** Classroom management in the United States: Trends and critical issues. In D. P. Tattum (Ed.), *Management of disruptive pupil behavior in schools* (pp. 69– 90). Chichester, England: John Wiley.

LEINHARDT, G., & GREENO, J. G. **(1986).** The cognitive skill of teaching. *Journal of Educational Psychology, 78* (2), 75–95.

LEINHARDT, G., WEIDMAN, C., & HAMMOND, K. M. **(1987).** Introduction and integration of classroom routines by expert teachers. *Curriculum Inquiry, 17*(2), 135–176.

MCCONAGHY, J. **(1986).** On becoming teacher experts: Research as a way of knowing. *Language Arts, 63,* 724–728.

MCGEE, J. J., MENOLASCINO, F. J., HOBBS, D. C., & MENOUSEK, P. E. **(1987).** *Gentle teaching: A non-aversive approach to helping persons with mental retardation.* New York: Human Sciences Press.

NELSON, N. W. **(1985).** Teacher talk and child-listening—Fostering a better match. In C. Simon (Ed.), *Communication skills and classroom success* (pp. 65–104). San Diego, CA: College Hill Press.

PARKER, W. C. **(1984).** Developing teachers' decision making. *Journal of Experimental Education, 52,* 220–226.

PARKER, W. C., & GEHRKE, N. J. **(1986).** Learning activities and teachers' decision making: Some grounded hypotheses. *American Educational Research Journal, 23,* 227–242.

PITTMAN, S. I. **(1985).** A cognitive ethnography and quantification of a first-grade teacher's selection routines for classroom management. *Elementary School Journal, 85,* 541–557.

ROHRKEMPER, M. M. **(1984).** The influence of teacher socialization style on students' social cognition and reported interpersonal classroom behavior. *The Elementary School Journal, 85,* 245–275.

ROSENSHINE, B. **(1983).** Teaching functions in instructional programs. *The Elementary School Journal, 83,* 335–351.

SCHON, D. **(1983).** *The reflective practitioner: How professionals think in action.* New York: Basic Books.

SHAVELSON, R. J. (1973). What is the basic teaching skill? *Journal of Teacher Education, 14,* 144–151.

SHAVELSON, R. J., & STERN, P. (1981). Research on teachers' pedagogical thoughts, judgments, decisions, and behavior. *Review of Educational Research, 51,* 455–498.

SHEFELBINE, J. L., & HOLLINGSWORTH, S. (1987). The instructional decisions of preservice teachers during a reading practicum. *Journal of Teacher Education, 38*(1), 36–42.

SIMON, H. A. (1981). *The sciences of the artificial* (2nd ed.). Cambridge, MA: MIT Press.

TATTUM, D. P. (1986). Consistency management—School and classroom concerns and issues. In D. P. Tattum (Ed.), *Management of disruptive pupil behavior in schools* (pp. 51–68). Chichester, England: John Wiley.

YINGER, R. J. (1986). Examining thought in action: A theoretical and methodological critique of research on interactive teaching. *Teaching and Teacher Education, 2*(3), 263–282.

———. (1987). *The conversation of practice.* Paper presented at the Reflective Inquiry Conference, College of Education, University of Houston, Houston, TX.

CHAPTER TWO

Managing Behaviors and Enhancing Communication

SITUATIONS

Setting: Second grade language arts activity.

Teacher: Class, we've completed three examples together. I'm going to leave the work we did at the board up for you to remind you of some of the trickier things about the worksheet. As soon as we've completed this activity, we'll be ready to share our books from silent reading time. [Students begin to work.]

Student: [Raises hand] Ms. S., should we complete both sides of the worksheet?

Teacher: Yes [showing paper, and pointing to problems on both sides]. You'll need to have both sides completed. [Students begin working.]

Student: [Raises hand] Ms. S., I have a question on this one. [Ms. S. goes to student, reviews work.]

Teacher: Looks good to me, Sarah! [Student returns to worksheet. After completing another item, again raises hand.]

Student: Ms. S., could you help me?

Teacher: [Turning paper and reviewing it] Sarah, this one is correct, too. What's the problem? We learned how to do these at the board, and we did three examples on the worksheet.

Student: But you didn't tell me how to do these!

*   *   *

Setting: Secondary high school language arts class; the bell rings indicating the beginning of class; students stop talking and face the teacher who is standing at the board.

Teacher: Mark, you've had enough time to talk to your friends between classes. Besides, I've got a lot to cover today. Yesterday I suggested that the play *Cyrano de Bergerac* was like a soap opera. I gave you three key points of comparison between *Cyrano* and most daytime soaps. Toni, do you remember where we left off yesterday [waits a few seconds]? We don't have all day, Toni [waits a few more seconds].

Toni: [Scrambling to find her copy of *Cyrano de Bergerac*] You said something about comparing Cyrano to a soap opera.

Teacher: [Annoyed, walks over to another student] Oh, Mark, you finally found your book. Toni wasn't paying attention yesterday. Let's see if you were. What is one way that this play is like a soap opera?

Mark: He couldn't get the girl at first. I saw the movie on TV. You know, Steve Martin had this long nose and he couldn't get it fixed. My cousin had this scar on his face he got in an accident. No one would go out with him he looked so bad. [Other kids laugh, some say "I saw that movie, too."]

Teacher: [Moves to her desk, pages through her plan book, then walks to the front of the room, points to the board, and speaks in a harsh tone] Mark, you always talk about your family and make remarks that have nothing to do with the lesson. [Sarcastically] Does anyone else have comments about friends or relatives who have scars that they'd like to share with the class [glares around the room]? You kids have

got an exam next week, and I've got to finish these
activities today [pointing to the list on the board].

*   *   *

These interactions represent two examples of breakdowns in the
communicative processes involved in teaching and learning. These
breakdowns not only interfere with the teachers' goals for the activities, but also have an impact on the interpersonal relationships between the teacher and students. Positive interpersonal relationships
are critical to the development of classroom environments which
"invite" students to learn.

In this chapter, the relationship between communication and
behavior will be described, with an emphasis on a discussion of student-teacher interactions. Building upon the notion of "stance" introduced in Chapter One, the impact of a teacher's stance on classroom
interactions will be discussed. Specifically, two styles of interaction
will be contrasted: directive and facilitative. A discussion of professional considerations in classroom management will be presented to
stimulate thinking about the impact of teachers' decisions on the
learning environment. The chapter concludes with a brief examination
of the impact of cultural diversity and community influences on issues
related to communicative interactions and classroom management.

SELF-EVALUATION

Please indicate whether you agree or disagree with each of the items
listed below.

1. An effective teacher remains "true" with lesson plans and
   permits limited student influence on the planned instructional activity.
2. Interpersonal relationships have some influence on classroom
   management but little impact on the student's learning of academic content.
3. Continuous questioning about work assignments indicates lack
   of understanding of the content of the assignment.
4. One means for coping with the complexity of the classroom is
   through the teacher's development of a "stance" that supports
   classroom interactions and activities.
5. Most management problems may be traced to student behavior
   that violates the rules of the classroom.
6. To succeed in school, students must learn classroom rules for participation and interaction, no matter how different those interactional
   patterns may be from their home and community experiences.

KEY WORDS

communicative competence

order

directive

facilitative

OBJECTIVES

After completing this chapter, you will be able to:

1. Describe the relationship of communication to behavior and student-teacher interactions in the classroom.
2. Describe the impact of teacher's stance on classroom interactions.
3. Contrast directive and facilitative teaching.
4. Discuss professional considerations in classroom management.
5. Recognize the role of cultural diversity in perceived differences among students.

Objective One: *To Describe the Relationship of Communication to Behavior and Student-Teacher Interactions in the Classroom*

Teaching and learning in classrooms is a communicative process (Puro and Bloome, 1987). In this way, classroom communication, classroom instruction, and teacher-student interaction are inherently linked. Puro and Bloome suggest that learning in classrooms occurs through, and is inseparable from, interpersonal communication between teacher and students and among students. With each interaction, a communicative context is constructed against which actions and utterances are interpreted. They state

> for educators, the implications of a communicative view of classroom learning are profound. What students learn in classrooms is how to conceptualize what is happening in a classroom, their own behavior, others' behavior, academic tasks, and classroom texts in terms of the communicative context...The communicative context of the classroom becomes a frame through which students interpret and redefine classroom academic learning. (pp. 29–30)

In classrooms, communication is both explicit and implicit. Teacher and student messages may be interpreted in terms of the context in which they occur rather than the explicit meaning of the words spoken. This context is constructed by teachers and students in their interactions among each other, and as Puro and Bloome describe, includes both explicit and implicit messages communicated through verbal and nonverbal communication, activities, and the setting itself.

Puro and Bloome conclude that as teachers and students jointly determine this communication context, norms and standards of behavior are determined. They mutually negotiate the meaning of events and interactions. Teachers are proactive designers of social interaction through their instructional activities (Yinger, 1987).

In these activities which they design, teachers present not only the content of the lesson, but communicate and manage how and which students can participate. The teacher's management of how students gain the opportunity to participate in classroom activities is communicated both verbally and nonverbally, explicitly and implicitly, through academic instruction. Through classroom activities, students learn both content and appropriate ways to participate and communicate (Evertson, 1987).

Teachers can facilitate student learning, then, through facilitating the development of students' communicative competence. Shultz, Florio, and Erickson (1982) define communicative competence as "all the kinds of communicative knowledge that individual members of a cultural group need to possess to be able to interact with one another in ways that are both socially appropriate and strategically effective." Carr and Durand (1985) explicitly describe a linkage between communicative development and the management of student behaviors. They maintain that the literature on normal development suggests that increases in communicative competence are correlated with decreases in a variety of behavior problems. Behavior problems, then, are communicative in nature. Carr and Durand suggest that working with students on their communicative strategies could have the effect of replacing behavior problems.

The elementary school situation at the beginning of this chapter depicts a student using an ineffective communicative strategy. The student's constant asking for affirmation may serve a variety of purposes: she may be concerned about making errors, she may have questions about the process that she is unable to formulate, she may be seeking positive reinforcement for correct responses, or she may simply be looking for teacher attention. Because the teacher is unable to describe concisely the reason and goal of the behavior, it is not an effective communicative strategy: it leaves the teacher guessing about the desired response. More appropriate communicative attempts would include requesting help, requesting a "check," asking specific questions about the process, or perhaps making a positive social comment or compliment to gain teacher attention. If the student were a more effective communicator, she wouldn't be "annoying" the teacher.

Objective Two: *To Describe the Impact of the Teacher's Stance on Classroom Interactions*

The teacher's stance encompasses his or her personal posture toward self and others, as well as theoretical orientation and instructional and management techniques (McGee, Menolascino, Hobbs, and Menousek, 1987). Recall from Chapter One that a teacher's stance guides interactions with others. In classrooms, teacher stance is related to productive interactions with students. Through our classroom observations and research, we have seen clear illustrations of how a teacher's stance may inhibit students' opportunity to participate, which, in turn, is likely to have a significant impact on student learning.

Mour (1977) contends that it is inappropriate to assume that teacher behaviors are all productive and contribute to student learning. Rather, teachers may demonstrate counterproductive behaviors. Productive teacher behaviors require continual efforts to understand each student, a willingness to share with students, and fair treatment of and respect for each student. These productive behaviors require a stance which involves listening, trusting, and respecting, rather than lecturing and admonishing. Mour describes counterproductive behaviors to include forcing students to comply, using punishment or threats of punishment, or shaming and belittling students. The stance related to these counterproductive behaviors is controlling and projects that learning is not a cooperative effort. Mour suggests that teachers only have power to create a classroom climate conducive to learning or to modify an existing environment to become supportive rather than having power over student learning.

Teacher stance has a significant effect on students' social perceptions of their teacher, their classmates, and themselves. As we discussed in Chapter One, Rohrkemper (1984) contrasted teachers with two socialization styles or stances: inductive and behavior modification. Inductive-style teachers approached student socialization with a concern for extensive communication. These teachers frequently provided students with rationales for behavioral demands. Their intent was to promote student insight into the responses underlying behavior and its consequences. In contrast, behavior modification–style teachers relied primarily on reward-based contingency programs involving shaping procedures or contracts to maintain classroom organization and to promote student behavior change. Whereas inductive teachers focused on causes of behaviors, behavior modification teachers focused on tangible consequences. In the first situation which opens this chapter, an inductive-style teacher would explain to the student that it is important to work independently and self-evaluate responses, because of the need for the skill or the inability of the teacher to always be there. A behavior modification–style teacher would give the student a contingency, such as awarding a sticker for a paper completed independently. All teachers in Rohrkemper's study were judged outstanding in their ability to manage difficult students by principals, observers, and interviewers.

Three vignettes depicting problematic classroom events were shown to students who are asked to predict and role play their teachers' responses to those problems. The teachers' stance was consistently related to the students' prediction of teacher behavior, their understanding of and reaction to a fictional student's behavior, and students' role play. Students in inductive classrooms discussed more rules when predicting teachers' responses to behaviors and focused on teacher rationale for behavior demands. Students in behavior modification classrooms were more likely to discuss teacher evaluations of students that were behavior rather than student specific. They focused on lower level, primarily negative teacher evaluations, unlike inductive students who perceived teachers as functioning within the role of teacher.

Barnes (1982) describes two behaviors related to teacher stance, "reply" and "assess." Teachers who "reply," by implication, take the students' perceptions about the subject matter seriously though they may extend and modify it. The student and teacher are in a collaborative relationship, which leads to increased student confidence in actively interacting with the subject matter. A teacher who replies would make comments such as, "That's one strategy" or "Could you tell me more about that?" Teachers who "assess" distance themselves from students' perceptions and apply external standards which may devalue the students' construction of the task at hand. A teacher who assesses would make comments such as "Good job" or "No, that's not what the book said." The reply, or understanding, strategy places responsibility for learning in the student's hands, reinforcing student contributions to the generation of meaning. The assessment, or judging, strategy maintains teacher responsibility and places the negotiation of criteria of correct responses outside the student's reach.

Teacher stance does, then, impact on students' interpersonal behavior. In response to the power of teacher stance, we suggest facilitative rather than directive strategies, replying rather than assessing. The high school situation at the beginning of the chapter depicts a teacher stance that is highly directive and results in student behavior which seems to be unrelated to the learning activity. The teacher attempted to spark student interest in the academic content by referring to television shows. However, through her selection of the topic for comparison (e.g., soap operas), she preempted student opportunities for initiating topics of their choice. She lectured the students on the need to keep pace with the planned lesson and seemed annoyed with personal comments made by one student. In contrast, a teacher who has a facilitative stance would listen to students' contributions to the discussion, acknowledge those contributions, and carefully bring the students back to the planned activity. This teacher would show respect for students' opinions through her comments, tone of voice, and general demeanor. She would also provide students with a rationale for moving them back to the discussion of the play. In some instances, she might even abandon her plans and provide students with opportunities to discuss issues more pertinent to their needs. She might also prepare activities which require greater student involvement. In the situation at the beginning of the chapter, rather than ask students to recall a list of teacher-generated points of comparison, the teacher could have designed activities which require students to discuss their views of the conflicts within the play.

Objective Three: *To Contrast Directive and Facilitative Teaching*

Order in a classroom means that students are, within acceptable limits, following the program necessary for a classroom event to be realized (Doyle, 1986). Teachers, when generating order in classrooms, may do so either through a facilitative or directive stance. This order is generated through a considerable amount of interaction. When order becomes unstable, teachers intervene, or take actions to repair that order. In that the teacher takes the action, intervention is directive.

Rogers, Waller, and Perrin (1987) described the interactions of an "excellent" facilitative teacher as characterized by extended conversations with her students. The teacher attempted to elicit significantly fewer right-or-wrong answers than teachers described in other studies; questions posed were real requests for information. The facilitative teacher's interactions were described as natural, spontaneous, sensitive, and individualized. Through facilitation, a teacher becomes less constraining and monitors the student's responses more carefully. In this way, he or she is able to provide input for the student which is more finely tuned to the student's behavior and interests at the moment.

To clarify differences between directive and facilitative teaching, Mirenda and Donnellan (1986) describe specific conversational behaviors. Facilitative adults initiate fewer topics and initiate those topics through indirect questions, statements, or comments. Direct questions are rarely used to extend topics; statements, encouragements, and expansions are used. Facilitative interactions are marked by requests for clarification and long periods of waiting for responses (30 seconds). The contrast between directive and facilitative interaction in conversation is summarized in Table 2.1.

In a study of facilitative teachers of students who are gifted and talented (Story, 1985), additional categories of behaviors emerged. Facilitative teachers provided for positive and close physical relationships, being on the same eye level when discussion ensues with students, and

TABLE 2.1   The Contrast of Facilitative and Directive Conversational Behavior

	FACILITATIVE	DIRECTIVE
Topic Initiation	Initiate no more than two topics during a ten-minute conversation	Initiate at least four topics during a ten-minute conversation
Initiation of Conversation	No direct questions Indirect questions Statements	Direct questions at least five times during a ten-minute conversations
Topic Continuation	Few direct questions Direct statements Encouragements Expansion questions	Direct questions at least six times in ten-minute conversation
Clarification	Direct clarification statements	Clarification not requested
Silences	Lags up to 30 seconds	Lags not allowed to occur

Source note: This table is an adaptation of the Appendix (p. 141) from P. Mirenda, and A. Donnellan, "Effects of Adult Interaction Style versus Conversational Behavior in Students with Severe Communication Problems," in *Language, Speech, and Hearing Services in the Schools, 17,* 126–141, 1986. Reprinted with permission of the authors and the American Speech-Language-Hearing Association.

touching the student to emphasize enthusiasm or encouragement. Verbal interactions were marked by encouragement, humor, and clarification strategies to help the student focus on his or her work.

Facilitative teachers were flexible with their use of time, allowing varied response time, shifting the control of time and talk during work periods to students, and permitting alterations in schedules. Facilitative teachers were process oriented and based work on the students' interests. They encouraged responsibility and maintained records of each student's progress. Facilitative teachers built into their lessons an awareness of the interrelationships of various topics and ideas but referring back to earlier topics or content. In the classroom, they provided appropriate supports, including many and varied resources, physical and human. Finally, they modeled these facilitative behaviors in interactions for their students, waiting, listening, and making comments rather than asking questions. Facilitative teachers accepted their own limitations, admitting that they were also learning, and became personally involved with students. Although creative in developing curricula and activities, facilitative teachers felt isolated from professional peers.

Perhaps these facilitative behaviors can best be described through an example. During a group discussion, for example, a facilitative teacher would sit in a chair in the circle of students. Rather than asking questions, he or she would converse, making comments rather than evaluative statements. A facilitative teacher would allow the students to initiate discussion points. In modeling behaviors for the students, a facilitative teacher would actively listen, allow the student plenty of time to respond, and wait for other students to comment. A facilitative teacher would recognize when he or she had not considered a point, or when they weren't able to understand the content or comments.

Objective Four: *To Describe Professional Considerations in Classroom Management*

Organizing and maintaining a classroom environment that facilitates student learning requires numerous decisions to be made by the teacher. Donnellan (1984) suggests employing a "criterion of the least dangerous assumption" when making decisions concerning students. This criterion posits that in the absence of conclusive data, educational decisions ought to be based on assumptions which, if incorrect, will have the least dangerous effect on the likelihood that students will be able to function independently as adults. In making decisions concerning management, teachers must ask themselves, "Which action will have the least dangerous effect on the likelihood that the goal will be attained?" For example, in the elementary school situation which opened this chapter, the teacher needs to assess her goal of the activity. If that goal is independent practice, she must determine which of many alternative actions will enhance Sarah's development of self-regulated practice. Responding to each request for help or affirmation may only contribute to Sarah's dependence. Reprimanding interruptions without dealing with the reason for the behavior may only contribute to Sarah's withdrawal or acting out. By viewing the interruptions as meeting some need that Sarah has, and developing/generating/improvising a response that meets those needs in a more acceptable way, a strategy with the least dangerous effect on Sarah's educational success is developed. For example, the teacher may say, "Sarah, you seem unsure of these problems. When you finish five more, I'll come over and see how you are doing." If the five problems are completed accurately, the teacher could again be proactive and say, "Now, I'll check on your work when you've completed the page," and continue to fade support.

As a professional, a teacher shares ownership of problems when management and instruction are less than successful. However, when problems occur, assessment of the situation usually occurs outside of the classroom context and focuses on the learner. Englemann, Granzin, and Severson (1979) provide an "equation" to help teachers more professionally and ethically determine the nature of management and instructional concerns.

Englemann and associates (1979) suggest that in our classrooms the learner's behavior is influenced by two major factors: his or her predisposition and instruction. Typically, we infer that if our management or instruction fails, the problem is solely related to the student. Instead, we need to ascertain which aspects of our management and instruction are inadequate for that student. Through this questioning, we can determine how best to change our behavior to correct the inadequacies. The teacher in the high school situation blamed the failure of instruction on students who did not pay attention to the lesson rather than consider that her instruction did not maintain student interest.

In addition, Englemann and associates caution teachers to make a "minimum knowledge assumption." This assumption asserts that the learner uses the least possible knowledge required to produce the various behaviors we observe. For example, if a model is provided on a mathematics worksheet, we can't assume that the student is able to work problems without that model present. If we as teachers fail to make the minimum knowledge assumption, then we fail to test the possibility that students are responding to messages other than the ones which we intended.

Teachers, then, need to be aware of the potential impact of their actions on long term educational goals. In addition, Pinnell and Galloway (1987) pose a series of position statements supportive of the professional, facilitative stance of teachers described in this text. They suggest, first, that teachers should recognize the learner's contribution to the educational process. Teachers should recognize that students actively participate and think, generating their own meanings of classroom management and instructional activities. Students' learning occurs when there is a need to learn, and, as teachers, we must create activities that invite students to engage in varied forms of spoken and written skills. In creating those activities, teachers should recognize that students need many opportunities to talk, read, and write, so that they can form their own theories and understandings about the content.

Pinnell and Galloway also posit several considerations specific to teachers. They suggest that teachers must recognize the power of the social context in all learning. In addition to aspects of the learning environment such as teacher-student and peer interactional patterns, teachers must consider cultural and community influences on student learning. Pinnell and Galloway contend that it is the teacher's role to create school contexts that use and reinforce students' previous knowledge while building on their experience. As professionals, teachers should develop their own meaning of the concepts of of human development and language learning, through observing their students, gathering evidence of learning, and making decisions based on that information. Finally, they maintain that without authentic caring, instruction may be relegated to books and machines. These research-supported position statements are summarized in Table 2.2.

TABLE 2.2 Pinnell and Galloway's Positions Concerning the Roles of Teachers

1. Teachers should recognize the students' contribution to the educational process.
2. Learning occurs when students need to know.
3. Learning is holistic in nature.
4. Teachers should recognize the power of the social context in all learning.
5. Teachers should develop their own understandings of human development and learning.
6. Caring teachers are at the heart of school success for students.

Source note: This table was constructed from an article by G. S. Pinnell and C. M. Galloway, "Human Development, Language, and Communication: Then and Now," in *Theory into Practice, 26* (Special Issue), 353–357, 1987. The table does not exist in the original publication.

Objective Five: *To Recognize the Role of Cultural Diversity in Perceived Differences Among Students*

Students enter school with culturally determined patterns or styles of interaction. Ogbu (1985) suggests at least two types of cultural/language differences. The first type, primary differences, existed before the group became a minority. The second group are those differences which develop after the minority group has become subordinate to the majority culture. Minorities, then, develop cultural mechanisms to protect their identity, maintain cultural boundaries, and project stylistic differences. Sometimes, these secondary differences are reflected in communication patterns which are different from the patterns of teacher-student interaction in a traditional classroom. The implications of this lack of congruence between the culture of the school and the cultural influences of family and community has been discussed by researchers such as Heath (1983), Macias (1987), Au (1980), and many others.

Heath's work in two working-class Appalachian communities provides well-documented illustrations of cultural influences on children's communication patterns. Her observations indicated distinct patterns of adult-child interactions in the two communities. In the Trackton community, adults typically interact with one another rather than address young children directly. Babies and young children in Trackton spend time around a number of adults. Consequently, the children learn to be very sensitive to speaker's nonverbal signals (posture and gesture). As they attempt to become conversationalists, they learn a variety of verbal and nonverbal strategies for breaking into adult conversations (e.g., asking a question, getting in front of the speaker's face, calling out the speaker's name, tugging at the speaker's arms or leg).

Heath observed a strong emphasis on interactions with adults and other siblings as Roadville children develop language. Caregivers practice language through the use of games and engage in conversations with children (in contrast to Trackton adults who socialize with one another rather than address speech to a very young child). As children grow older, differences in oral and literate traditions (e.g., traditions of story telling, uses of reading and writing) are evident between the communities.

When Trackton and Roadville children entered preschool, differences in communication patterns and other behaviors proved challenging to teachers. For example, the concept of play centers on which specific toys were used for allotted time periods appeared puzzling to Trackton children. When asked to "play," their improvisations and flexible use of toys did not match the teachers' notion of play in certain areas of the room with specific toys for specified periods of time. While

Roadville children were more accustomed to schedules for certain activities, some of their home play habits were not possible in school. When they "made cookies" at home, they typically used water, flour, and other real substances. In school, Roadville children were asked to imagine these substances and gradually dropped this play activity in favor of others. Teachers' attempts to maintain schedules and encourage play activities were met with student frustration.

Other differences between home and school culture and expectations related more specifically to communication patterns. A teacher's use of indirect questions such as "Is that where the truck belongs?" were difficult for students to interpret. When the teacher gathered a small group for story time, Trackton children interrupted and often spoke with other children rather than attend to the teacher. These differences in use of space and time (e.g., specific times for specific tasks) and interactional patterns (such as the use of indirect questions) sometimes yielded breakdowns in communication.

Teachers began to describe interactions and interviewed families with the intent of discovering how children learned and used language. The teachers also noted their interactional styles both at home and at school. Their perceptions of students and student behavior changed as teachers discovered the lack of congruity between home and school expectations for communication. Following their discoveries, teachers became more flexible about scheduling some activities and helped students develop a sense of time through explicit discussion of time boundaries for certain activities. In addition, teachers used more direct requests when giving specific directions, such as "Please put the toys away" rather than "Is that where those toys belong?" They designed instructional activities which related to children's concepts of print and story telling. The teachers' willingness to adapt to student needs, to build on home skills and ways of talking, proved highly successful.

Other teachers and researchers have observed the impact of a lack of congruity between school and cultural interactional styles (Au, 1980; Cazden, 1988; Macias, 1987; and Martin, 1987). Macias (1987) observed characteristics of reticence, social deference, and restrained speech in Papago preschoolers(members of an American Indian group in Arizona). Teacher behaviors such as calling on children and encouraging them to "speak up" in group activities were in direct conflict with students' cultural patterns of communication. As the teachers in the Heath study, the Papago teachers adapted instructional activities and modified their expectations for interaction based on Papago interactional patterns. They were tolerant of children listening and sitting quietly rather than actively participating. In addition, they structured the classroom so that the students could remain independent (valued in the Papago culture).

Au (1980) reported that reading lessons structured in a manner consistent with Hawaiian children's culture was more conducive to student learning. When the lesson was similar to a "talk story" which was a familiar speech event in nonschool settings, students actively participated in the lesson. Rather than maintain a highly directive role allocating turns and preventing interruptions, the teacher was tolerant of overlapping turns and joint performance, which are characteristics of the talk story. Again, the teachers' sensitivity to culturally determined patterns of communication facilitated student learning.

SUMMARY

An understanding of classroom communicative processes is critically important for teachers as they attempt to design and maintain environments which support learning. As students and teachers interact around instructional activities, a communicative context is formed which provides a frame through which students interpret the meaning of events and instruction. Teachers may support student learning through facilitating the development of communicative competence. For example, behavior problems resulting from breakdowns in communication and participation in instructional activities may be eliminated as students develop more effective communication strategies. It should be noted, however, that some problems result from teacher interactional styles which are not conducive to student learning. In contrast to a directive style which may inhibit opportunities for interaction and participation, a facilitative stance is suggested.

As discussed in Chapter One, the complexity of the classroom environment requires that teachers make numerous decisions. Donnellan's (1984) suggestion of the "criterion of least dangerous assumption," as well as Englemann et al.'s (1979) discussion of minimum knowledge assumption, provide some professional considerations related to decision making and planning for effective classroom management. More important, teachers recognize the role of human development and language learning in developing and managing classroom activities. In addition, teachers should be aware of the potential impact of cultural influences on student learning. Discontinuities between home/community and school expectations for participation and communicative interaction should be addressed.

REVIEW QUESTIONS

1. A key point of the chapter involves the relationship of communication to behavior. Describe how counterproductive teacher behaviors may contribute to student behavior problems.

2. The definition of communicative competence mentioned in this chapter refers to an individual's cultural group. Why should teachers be concerned with cultural patterns of communication and interaction?

3. How does teacher stance affect student-teacher interaction? Relate these ideas to your interactions with teachers of classes in which you are currently enrolled.

4. Contrast directive and facilitative interactional styles. How might a directive interactional style limit opportunities for student participation? Describe the impact of a facilitative style of interaction on student learning and interpersonal behavior.

5. Define the "criterion of least dangerous assumption." Describe how the application of this criterion might influence teacher decisions about management.

APPLICATION ACTIVITY

Classrooms are rich environments consisting of multiple layers of communicative interactions. Imagine the dismay felt by an instructor upon reading the following entry in a preservice teacher's journal: "Nothing happened in class today." For this preservice teacher, it is likely that too much activity was going on in the classroom for him to make sense of it. In this application activity, you will use the following questions to discover interactional patterns in a classroom of your choice.

Select a school classroom or college class which you can observe as unobtrusively as possible. (It might take you several visits to establish rapport with the teacher or instructor.) Inform the teacher that you are interested in observing classroom interactional patterns and that you will probably take notes on the interactions. Assure the teacher that your observational notes will maintain anonymity of the people in the classroom.

The purpose of this activity is to determine teacher stance through observation of specific communicative interactions between students and the teacher. Observe two classroom activities: one involving instruction in an academic area and another involving an activity such as recess, art, or morning sharing time.

Comment on the following questions:

❖ Communication in classrooms is both implicit and explicit. Determine whether the teacher uses certain messages, phrases, or questions across the two activities you observe. How do the students' responses to similar messages differ across the two contexts?

❖ How do students gain the opportunity to participate in the interaction? Does the teacher explicitly state rules for participation? Is there one student or a group of students whose comments or interactions do not conform to the teacher's rules for participation? If so, how did the teacher deal with the breakdown of communicative interaction?

❖ How would you describe the teacher's stance? On what basis did you make your decision? What sources of information did you gather to help you make this determination? How does the teacher's stance affect student opportunities for participation and other classroom interactions?

REFERENCES

AU, H. K. (1980). Participation structures in a reading lesson with Hawaiian children: Analysis of a culturally appropriate instructional event. *Anthropology and Education Quarterly, 11,* 91–115.

BARNES, D. (1982). *From communication to curriculum.* Middlesex, England: Penguin.

CARR, E. G., & DURAND, V. M. (1985). The social-communicative basis of severe behavior problems in children. In S. Reiss & R. R. Boutzin (Eds.), *Theoretical issues in behavior therapy* (pp. 219–254). New York: Academic Press.

CAZDEN, C. B. (1988). *Classroom discourse.* Portsmouth, NH: Heinemann.

DONNELLAN, A. M. (1984). The criterion of the least dangerous assumption. *Behavioral Disorders, 9,* 141–149.

DOYLE, W. (1986). Classroom organization and management. In M. C. Wittrock (Ed.), *Handbook of research on teaching* (3rd ed., pp. 392–431). New York: Macmillan.

ENGLEMANN, S., GRANZIN, A., & SEVERSON, H. (1979). Diagnosing instruction. *Journal of Special Education, 13*(4), 365–369.

EVERTSON, C. M. (1987). Creating conditions for learning: From research to practice. *Theory into Practice, 26* (Special Issue), 44–50.

HEATH, S. B. (1983). *Ways with words.* New York: Cambridge University Press.

MACIAS, J. (1987). The hidden curriculum of Papago teachers: American Indian strategies for mitigating cultural discontinuity in early school. In G. Spindler & L. Spindler (Eds.), *Interpretive ethnography of education: At home and abroad* (pp. 363–380). Hillsdale, NJ: Lawrence Erlbaum.

MARTIN, G. (1987). A letter to Bread Loaf. In D. Goswami & P. R. Stillman (Eds.), *Reclaiming the classroom: Teacher research as an agency for change* (pp. 165–169). Upper Montclair, NJ: Boynton/Cook.

McGEE, J. J., MENOLASCINO, F. J., HOBBS, D. C., & MENOUSEK, P. E. (1987). *Gentle teaching.* New York: Human Science Press.

MIRENDA, P., & DONNELLAN, A. (1986). Effects of adult interaction style versus conversational behavior in students with severe communication problems. *Language, Speech, and Hearing Services in the Schools, 17,* 126–141.

MOUR, S. (1977). Teacher behaviors and ecological balance. *Behavioral Disorders, 3,* 55–58.

OGBU, J. U. (1985). Research current: Cultural-ecological influences on minority school learning. *Language Arts, 62*(8), 860–869.

PINNELL, G. S., & GALLOWAY, C. M. (1987). Human development, language, and communication: Then and now. *Theory into Practice, 26* (Special Issue), 353–357.

PURO, P., & BLOOME, D. (1987). Understanding classroom communication. *Theory into Practice, 26* (Special Issue), 26–31.

ROGERS, D. L., WALLER, C. B., & PERRIN, M. S. (1987). Learning more about what makes a good teacher good through collaborative research in the classroom. *Young Children, 34*, 34–39.

ROHRKEMPER, M. M. (1984). The influence of teacher socialization style on students' social cognition and reported interpersonal classroom behavior. *Elementary School Journal, 85*(2), 245–275.

SHULTZ, J. J., FLORIO, S., & ERICKSON, F. (1982). Where's the floor? Aspects of the cultural organization of social relationships in communication at home and in the school. In P. Gilmore & A. A. Glatthorn (Eds.), *Children in and out of school: Ethnography and education* (pp. 88–123). Washington, DC: Center for Applied Linguistics.

STORY, C. M. (1985). Facilitator of learning: A micro-ethnographic study of the teacher of the gifted. *Gifted Child Quarterly, 29*(4), 155–158.

YINGER, R. J. (1987). *The conversation of practice.* Paper presented at the Reflective Inquiry Conference, College of Education, University of Houston, Houston, TX.

CHAPTER THREE

Developing an Agenda for Managing Classrooms

SITUATIONS

Setting: High school civics class; teacher is collecting assignments.

Ms. M: That's the bell. Let's get ready to work [pauses, waits for students to settle]. Thanks. Your assignment was to interview two adults about the upcoming primary election. Make sure you have your notes out so you can share the comments accurately. [Waits for students to take notes out of notebooks. Stuart's desk remains clear]. Stuart, where are your notes?

Stuart: I don't have any.

Ms. M: You didn't take any notes when you did your interviews?

Stuart: No, I didn't do any interviews.

Ms. M: And why not?

Stuart: I don't know two adults.

Ms. M: [Class laughs] Stuart, this is the basis of our work and you're going to have to take another zero.

Stuart: Not fair. It was a stupid assignment. I don't know who gives a _____ about this _____ anyway.

Ms. M: That comment will get you a ticket to the principal's office.

Stuart: Big deal. I got a "zero" for today anyway. I'd rather sit there than here.

*   *   *

Setting: Junior high school mathematics class; teacher is working examples on the board with total group.

Mr. Riley: Okay, folks. Let's look at this one. Again, we need to isolate our unknown. Any ideas?

Nolan: Subtract 6 from each side.

Mr. Riley: Nolan, I was hoping for "hands"—we need to spread out who answers in here. Okay, so we subtract 6 from each side [turns to write on the board]. Now what?

Nolan: Divide by 2.

Mr. Riley: Nolan, c'mon here. Anybody else?

Nolan: [Under his breath] Sorry.

Mr. Riley: Elaine?

Elaine: Apply identity property and divide each side of the equation by 2.

Mr. Riley: That's a fine answer. So we divide each side by 2 [turns to write on the board].

Nolan: $3y$.

Mr. Riley: [Exasperated] Nolan, we can all see it's $3y$. We really don't need you're continual assistance to do boardwork.

Nolan: Sorry.

*   *   *

Setting: Elementary classroom. Students are completing individual math worksheets following group instruction.

Ms. T.:   Now that we've finished doing these examples, I'm going to distribute the worksheets. But, first, let's go through the process one more time. Lisa, what's the first thing to do when you begin to divide?

Lisa: See if the divisor goes into the first digit of the dividend.

Ms. T.: Great. Then? Michael.

Michael: Put how many times it goes into either the first number or the first two numbers, and put it over the top of the right number.

Ms. T.: And then? Elizabeth?

Elizabeth: Multiply, then subtract.

Ms. T.: Joe?

Joe: Bring down the next number and see how many times the divisor goes into that. Write the number on top, multiply and subtract again, and its done.

Ms. T.: I think we're ready to work. Earl, you've been looking out the window the entire time. Are you going to be able to do these?

Earl: What?

Ms. T.: You have to try to pay attention [passes papers, goes to Earl's desk]. You've been daydreaming this entire lesson. I'm going to stand here and watch you do one of these problems.

Earl: [Works silently, completes the problem accurately.]

Ms. T.: I'm surprised, but nice work. You have to try to pay attention. If you can do this, you should participate.

*   *   *

Each of these situations supports the contention that teaching is an achieved role that requires the complementary performance of at least one other person (Cazden, Cox, Dickinson, Steinberg, and Stone, 1979). In each situation, the teacher is being challenged by a student's participation in the activities. The student's manner of participation varies from that of his or her peers. In this chapter, developing an agenda for your management of the classroom, to address situations such as those described, is discussed. The first three objectives in this chapter provide the reader with more information about our stance as teachers and researchers. Our intent throughout the book is to provide support for the development of your stance as a facilitative teacher. The specific form of support is presented in the last objective: a framework for developing an agenda for classroom management. Although this framework draws from the emerging behavioral approach of studying the context, our goal is not to "control" behavior. Through the four-phase framework, ways to manage and structure the classroom to encourage a "complementary performance" are developed.

SELF-EVALUATION

Please indicate whether you agree or disagree to each of the items below.

1. Teaching is the imparting of information to learners through academic activities.
2. Students learn rules for classroom behavior and interaction primarily through explicit statements by the classroom teacher.
3. Inappropriate classroom behaviors include talking during independent work time, speaking without being "recognized" by the teacher, and not paying attention to the instructional activity.
4. An effective teacher carefully designs interventions for eliminating inappropriate behaviors.
5. To generate a picture of an instructional problem or management issues, it is important to obtain the student's perception of that problem.
6. Sometimes behavior management issues are related to the nature of the instructional material or activity.
7. Management issues are raised most often when a mismatch exists between the teacher's interactional style and student's level of communicative competence.

KEY WORDS

participation structures

conventional

agenda

OBJECTIVES

After completing this chapter, you will be able to:

1. Describe participation structures and their role in classroom management.
2. Contrast "conventional" and "appropriate" views of behavior.
3. Describe proactive versus intervention-based classroom management.
4. Describe a framework for developing an agenda for classroom management.

Objective One: *To Describe Participation Structures and Their Role in Classroom Management*

Cazden and associates (1979) contend that teaching is more than telling, more than "making students learn." Teaching requires the negotiation of interpersonal relationships. Participation of students in classroom activities is, in itself, a part of this negotiation of interpersonal relationships. In Chapter Two, we presented the notion of facilitative "stance" and described the potential impact this stance might have on students' interpersonal behavior. Although stance provides a critically important frame or guide for teachers as they attempt to create "inviting" learning environments, a closer look at the complex nature of classroom environments is necessary.

Doyle (1980), for example, describes several features of classrooms which contribute to their complexity. He suggests that classrooms are *multidimensional*, with a large quantity of events and tasks occurring. In addition, a single event may have multiple consequences. Classrooms are *simultaneous* in that many things occur at once. *Immediate* action is usually required by both teacher and student, and classrooms are *unpredictable*, with events frequently unwinding in unexpected ways. Classrooms are also *public*, in that events are witnessed by large numbers of persons. Finally, classrooms generate a *history*, gradually accumulating a set of experiences, routines, and practices that serve as a foundation for activities.

Another means for examining the complexity of the classroom is to consider two specific features of learning environments: academic task structures and social participation structures. Erickson (1982) first described these features in the context of teachers and students engaged in "doing a lesson together." Academic task structures are those constraints on the lesson related to the nature of the academic task itself. For example, if the academic task involves instruction in solving math problems, there are certain steps that teachers and students will follow that are dictated by the problem itself. A discussion of hardships faced by pioneers on the Oregon Trail also includes a set of "moves" or steps teachers and students will follow to accomplish this task. The social participation structures relate more specifically to the social context and interactional processes involved in teaching and learning. Before presenting more details and examples of social participation structures, a brief discussion of social context is necessary. In a later section, the role of academic task structures on classroom management will be discussed (Section Three, "Teacher-Focused Activities").

The social context of classrooms is constructed through the face-to-face interactions of students and teachers. Teachers and students continue to build on each other's communicative behavior as they work together to meet the curricular goals and carry out everyday classroom activities (Bloome and Knott, 1985). The classroom, then, is as much a social occasion as a learning setting (Bremme and Erickson, 1977). As a social occasion, it requires students to determine the shifting social context from moment to moment. This is a complex task. Students must interpret the social meaning of others' behaviors in view of the social situation in progress. In response, students must identify and produce, from their repertoire of behaviors, actions which are considered appropriate for the social situation in progress. In order to be accurate in this interpretation, the student must attend not only to verbal but nonverbal cues in the classroom.

The social context of the classroom is complicated by the communicative and behavioral demands placed on students. These demands, the participation structures, include speaking, listening, initiating and maintaining an interaction, and leading and following discussions. Participation structures are the patterns of conversational turns and the allocation of interaction rights and obligations. These interaction rights and obligations include knowing who are the primary attenders, secondary attenders, and the speaker. In following participation structures, students recognize the rights and obligations of interacting in the activity. This interaction continually requires readjustment and redistribution of differing actions. Students who do not adjust, or who fail to recognize the rights and obligations of participating may be described as behavior problems or as demonstrating inappropriate behavior (Erickson, 1982; Erickson and Shultz, 1981; Shultz, Florio, and Erickson, 1982). In the mathematics example at the beginning of the chapter, Nolan continually violated the participation structures of the classroom, saying the answers out loud, rather than waiting to be recognized by the teacher.

Objective Two: *To Contrast Conventional and Appropriate Views of Behavior*

The literature on classroom management is teeming with suggestions for dealing with behaviors which are "inappropriate." Each of the students in the situations at the beginning of the chapter, for example, may be viewed as behaving inappropriately in the classroom. As facilitators, rather than as directive teachers, we suggest that rather than decreasing inappropriate behaviors, teachers strive to help students develop behaviors which are more "conventional," that is, behaviors which follow the participation structures in the classroom. By conventional, we mean "the degree to which the meaning of signals is shared or understood by the social community" (Prizant and Wetherby, 1987, p. 474). This idea of "convention," related to Shultz and associates' (Shultz, Florio, and Erickson, 1982) definition of communicative competence, denotes being able to interact with others in ways that are both socially appropriate and strategically effective.

Demanding "appropriate" behavior is a value judgment; discrepancies in teacher and student values may in themselves increase undesirable behaviors. For example, a kindergarten teacher may determine that students should remain in seats, at their desks, working quietly, for a 45 minute period. This "quiet working" may be deemed appropriate classroom behavior. However, in working with twenty 5-year-olds, you become aware that "quiet working" is not really a conventional behavior. Young children move, fidget, chat to themselves and others, and rarely work in complete silence without moving. The conventional behavior would be to develop work skills within the developmental continuum of behaviors for 5-year-olds. It would be conventional for a kindergarten student to make noises or to verbalize about a picture being colored. However, it would be less conventional for a student to make noises when the teacher is attempting to converse with the student. Through targeting "conventional" behavior, we are striving to help students perform to their potential, while avoiding the imposition of our culturally induced rules or constrictions. We are assisting them in participating in socially appropriate and strategically effective ways.

Objective Three: *To Describe Proactive versus Intervention-Based Behavior Management*

Doyle (1986) suggests that the need to intervene in a classroom is a sign that the mechanisms the teacher is using to establish and sustain order are not working. He contends that the intervention process is complex and risky. Management, Doyle suggests, is fundamentally a process of solving the problems of order in the classroom rather than the problem of nonconventional student behavior. Doyle suggests the following considerations which represent a "reasonably comprehensive framework for integrating knowledge about processes of classroom organization and management" (p. 423):

1. The teacher's task in classroom management is to establish and maintain a work system rather than spotting and intervening with student behavior.
2. Order in classrooms is based on a harmony of action with structure and purpose. Classroom management is embedded in the strength and durability of the program of action in the classroom.
3. Students contribute to the quality of order in a classroom, and all interactions are jointly enacted.
4. Classroom management is defined by both social and academic participation.

5. Order in classrooms is context specific; teachers must continually monitor and protect the programs of action.
6. Effective management includes teachers seeking to understand and interpret classroom interactions. Comprehension and interpretation are skills necessary for teachers to recognize when to act and how to improvise in view of the shifting social context in the classroom.

In view of these themes, effective classroom management implies that teachers have a an underlying method of operation which is represented throughout all verbal and nonverbal communication. The teacher's stance should communicate an underlying agenda for classroom management. For effective managers, each interaction is understandable in view of the teacher's stance (Bauer, Lynch, and Murphy, 1988; Edelsky, Draper, and Smith, 1983).

Leinhardt and Greeno (1986) hypothesize that classroom activities are based on operational plans which they refer to as "agenda." These agenda include activity structures, routine, and all the interactional elements which permit the continuous interactions which occur in classrooms.

One example of the effectiveness of an overriding agenda in classroom management is described by Bauer, Lynch, and Murphy (1988). In describing her stance, the teacher in this study stated, "The best thing I can do for my students is to help them come to the sense themselves that 'No one can live my life for me, everything I do I pay consequences for and I learn from it.'...I know my responsibility with my students is to help them sense their strengths; to help them realize that nobody can change them but themselves." In her interactions in the classroom, the teacher demonstrated student ownership of control of personal behavior and participation in problem solving. The teacher spoke about students making decisions, about the consequences of their choices, and their self-control. The teacher emphasized ownership in student planning; students made their own activity choices for a play break, but were asked what decisions they would make about partners and places to play which would not generate a problem. In a study of interactions in a classroom utilizing a whole language approach (reading and writing instruction which emphasizes the communicative nature of text, in contrast to focused skills practice such as phonics and spelling instruction), the teacher's goals and operating statements were consistent with her actions and her reinforcement of student actions in the classroom (Edelsky, Draper, and Smith, 1983). These examples provide illustrations of the power of an overriding agenda for classroom management that is explicitly conveyed to the students through the teachers' verbal and nonverbal communication.

A teacher's agenda for classroom management emanates from his or her stance. However, the development and implementation of this stance and rationale in view of an individual class or student is a complex process. Earlier in the chapter, information related to our stance was presented (i.e., the need to consider the social context of the classroom, "unconventional" versus "inappropriate" views of behavior; and presentation of a rationale for a proactive stance toward management questions). In the remainder of the chapter, a framework for developing a management agenda, based on a teacher's stance and operational rationale, is discussed.

Objective Four: *To Describe a Framework for Developing an Agenda for Classroom Management*

In our work in classrooms, we have learned to recognize that even the most effective teachers are at times "stumped" by students who demonstrate behaviors which are less conventional than those of their peers. In designing a classroom management agenda regarding these students, we suggest a four-phase framework. The four phases of this framework are presented in Table 3.1.

Describe the Behavioral Issue or Instructional Question. Strahan (1983) suggests that teachers perform many of the activities of ethnographic research in their classrooms. McDermott (1982) describes ethnography as a rigorous attempt to account for people's behavior in terms of their relations with those around them in a variety of situations. He suggests that teachers make observations, generate theories, and develop predictions. McDermott (1982) supports this contention, suggesting that good ethnography is the first principle of good pedagogy, but also suggests that teachers often proceed intuitively rather than rationally. In this first phase of the framework, the teacher makes a "rigorous attempt" to develop a description of the behavior. The apparent problem, such as failing to complete assignments, not attending, or talking out, may not actually be the issue upon which more positive interactions may be based. For example, the student who does not complete assignments may be overwhelmed by their size, and may need assistance in breaking work

TABLE 3.1 A Framework for Behavior Management Plans

> I. Describe the behavioral issue or instructional question.
> II. Analyze the behavioral issue or instructional question.
> III. Generate hypotheses and define an agenda to develop more conventional behaviors.
> IV. Evaluate and modify the agenda.

into more doable units. The student who is "not attending" may be occupied with other issues, for example, personal concerns or family difficulties. The student who "talks out" may be unable to stem his or her enthusiasm. Without an accurate description of the issue, facilitating more positive behaviors is difficult.

Lane (1986) concurs with the need to describe behaviors accurately before developing a management agenda. He maintains that no teacher action can be predetermined in advance of an analysis of the situation and the construction of a formulation which explains why the behaviors occur in a given context. Any management activities, he maintains, must be based on the formulation.

In describing behavioral issues and instructional questions, perceptions of all individuals involved should be attained. A strategy for *obtaining your perception of the issue* is to sit down and write (1) why the issue or question has come to your attention; (2) if the question or issue is disruptive to the learning environment of the classroom, or whether it simply makes you ill at ease; (3) why you think the student is interacting in that manner; and (4) what is the actual question or issue.

Although this activity may clarify your thoughts about the issue or question, it responds to only a portion of the issue. Perceptions of the student should also be obtained. Confrontation, however, may produce a defensive response which will provide you with little information. A nondirective interview may be the most successful in gaining the student's perceptions of the behavior. Through this interview, the teacher mirrors the student's thoughts and comments through reflective comments. Rogers (1971) suggests four qualities to demonstrate during the nondirective interviews. The teacher should express warmth and responsiveness, with genuine acceptance for the student. The student should be free to express himself or herself without the teacher judging or placing values on comments. The student, however, is not free to be aggressive or impulsive during the discussion. Finally, the teacher should assure that the interview is free of coercion or pressure.

After ascertaining the student's perception of the issue, the teacher should *review all possible information about the issue.* Parents, former teachers, and supervisors may be queried about the presence or state of the issue or question in their interactions with the student. An external observation by a peer teacher may be helpful in getting additional, objective information about the issue or problem. For example, in the junior high school situation which opens this chapter, a peer teacher may be able to remind you that Nolan is extremely enthusiastic about math and may be "talking out" due to that enthusiasm.

At this point, *further information about the student should be identified.* The student's age, achievement, social development, school placement, and health and medical status should be reviewed. In the elementary school situation, for example, Earl may have an ear infection, making his attending to a highly verbal lesson auditorily difficult. Or a change in his current life pattern, such as parent separation or divorce, may make issues such as long division seem less than pertinent.

Finally, *your interaction with the student should be described.* How do you currently react when the issue or question becomes apparent? What is your current perception of this reaction? Are you satisfied, frustrated, angry (with yourself or the student), or threatened? In addition, the student's perceptions of your current reaction should be ascertained. In the senior high school situation, for example, the teacher probably feels powerless and frustrated. The teacher initially had no intention of forcing Stuart from her class; the unfolding of the situation in that way may feel defeating for the teacher.

Through these efforts, you should have a clear description of the issue or question. The activities involved in these efforts are summarized in Table 3.2. After completing these activities, you are ready to organize your information and begin to analyze the issue or question.

Analyze the Issue or Question. After completing the activities, you should have a clearer description of the issue or question. At this point, you are ready to begin to analyze the issue or question. To begin this analysis, a *description of the development of the issue or question should be generated.* The onset and duration of the problem should be described, as well as any patterns of increases or decreases

TABLE 3.2 Activities for Describing Issues or Questions

> A. Attain perceptions of the issue or question
> - ❖ Perceptions of the teacher
> - ❖ Perceptions of the student
>
> B. Review information from other sources
> - ❖ Parents
> - ❖ Former teachers
> - ❖ Supervisors
> - ❖ Observations by peer teachers
>
> C. Identify information about the student
> - ❖ Student data (age, grade levels, family situation)
> - ❖ Current classes
> - ❖ Medical and health status
>
> D. Describe your current interaction pattern
> - ❖ Your perception of your reactions
> - ❖ Student's perception of your reaction

in the intensity of the issue or question. In addition, any past attempts at working with the problem or issue should be described. For example, in the high school situation, the issue is very different if the student has a history of failing to complete assignments rather than if the problem has just begun and is specific to civics class.

After generating this history, *a clear present blow-by-blow description of the issue or problem should be generated.* The usual format for this observation is the "antecedent-behavior-consequence" or "ABC" chart. Each behavior, the event which occurred immediately before it, and the consequences which followed are listed in the three-column format. The consequences of a behavior may serve as the antecedent for the following behavior. An "ABC" for the high school situation described at the beginning of the chapter is presented in Table 3.3.

After generating an "ABC" chart, you are ready to begin to *analyze the context* which surrounds the behavior. Four sets of variables should be considered. The first set includes teacher variables, such as expectations and perceptions, communication patterns, and philosophy of teaching and learning. The second set of variables, student variables, also includes expectations, perceptions, and communication patterns, as well as changes in life patterns, strengths and weaknesses, and the student's developmental level. Task variables,

TABLE 3.3 Antecedent-Behavior-Consequence Chart

ANTECEDENT	BEHAVIOR	CONSEQUENCE
Teacher asks about assignment.	Student replies he does not have it.	Teacher asks again for clarification.
Teacher asks for clarification.	Student clarifies.	Teacher asks why.
Teacher asks why.	Student replies, "I don't know any adults."	Class laughs.
Teacher tells student he will "take a zero."	Student replies, "It isn't fair."	Teacher sends student to office.
Teacher sends student to office.	Student states he'd rather go to office.	Student leaves.

the third area, include the nature of the instructional materials, the reinforcement and preference value of the materials, the difficulty level of the assignments, the interest level of the activity, and the variety of materials available. Finally, the setting variables should be addressed. These include peers, persons present when the behavior occurs, personnel available to assist with the issue or question, the environment, instructional grouping, and opportunities. A self-evaluation questionnaire addressing these issues is presented in Table 3.4. Because an analysis of the context is critical to the successful application of the framework, what follows is a detailed description of the contextual variables to be examined. This analysis may be difficult to complete alone, and using a consultant, peer teacher, or supervisor may be a great help.

TEACHER VARIABLES

Philosophy and purpose. Fenstermacher (1986) suggests that teaching is a moral, purposeful activity. A teacher's performance, he suggests, emerges from decisions and judgments which are grounded in assumptions about teaching, learning, and classrooms. He suggests that teachers are not mechanistic implementors of teaching techniques. Ayers (1986) describes the impact of this role, in that the teacher's role is to empower students, assisting them to take active control of their learning

In view of the role which Ayers describes, the teacher's purpose for her activities is important. A teacher whose purpose is to maintain a quiet, controlled, predictable classroom is quite different from a teacher whose purpose is to develop independent, spontaneous students. Teachers who express the need to "get through the book" differ from teachers who strive for student mastery.

With regard to the purpose of teaching, effective teachers recognize the learner's contribution to learning. Pinnell and Galloway (1987) suggest that an effective teacher recognizes the social context of the classroom. In addition, the learner's role in instruction should be viewed through an understanding of human development and the ways in which they learn language.

Communicative competence. Classroom communication is, as Erickson (1982) suggests, "radically cooperative." In classroom activities, he contends, orientation to the task at hand is completed predominantly through talk. A teacher's clarity in providing a context to the activities is necessary not only for effective activities, but for activities which are intelligible to students.

In their study of teacher characteristics, Emmer, Evertson, and Anderson (1980) demonstrate that management characteristics of teachers are at least moderately, and in some way highly predictable

TABLE 3.4 Self-Evaluation of Teacher, Student, Task, and Context Variables

---

Teacher Variables

Do my expectations for this student impact on our interactions?

Are my perceptions of this behavior impacting on our interactions?

Are my communication patterns clear for this student?

Are there cultural issues which impact on our interactions?

Does this student present a challenge to my philosophy of teaching and learning?

Student Variables

Does this student have expectations which are inconsistent with mine?

Are the student's perceptions of the issue or question impacting on our interactions?

Are the student's communication patterns clear to me?

Has the student recently experienced a change in life pattern (recent move, loss of family member, parent separation or divorce)?

Are there cultural issues which impact on the student's interactions with peers and teachers?

What are the student's strengths? How can they be used to address the issue or question?

What are the student's weaknesses? How can they be mitigated?

What is the student's developmental level? Is the issue or question perhaps a question of maturity or lack of learning?

Task Variables

What materials are being used when the issue or question arises?

How reinforcing are the materials or activities? Does the student prefer these materials or activities?

How difficult are the activities or materials for the student?

How interested is the student in the content?

Are a variety of materials or activities available?

Setting Variables

Do peers contribute to the issue or question?

Who is usually present when the issue or question arises?

Who is available to provide support to the student regarding the issue or question?

Are their any environmental pollutants? Is the room noisy? warm? cold? bright? dark? Where is the classroom in relation to outdoor activity?

How does the student interact during group activities? individual activities?

What opportunities does the student experience for positive teacher or peer interaction?

from the behavior of the first week. Better managers, they found, spend a considerable amount of time during the first week of school clearly communicating the rules, routines, and consequences of the classroom.

Successful teachers are effective managers in that they communicate the importance of classroom activities. McDermott (1982) suggests that teaching is a coercive activity. Teaching requires the cooperative performance of at least one other individual. Teachers vary, however, in their communication of this coercion. Brooks (1985) suggests teacher organization is central to the clear communication of the purpose and importance of activities. Burns and Anderson (1987), in their discussion of classroom activities, suggest that the initial sequence of lesson segments was the communication of the purpose of the activity.

Individual frames of reference. Green and Weade (1987) suggest that individual frames of reference greatly impact on the teacher's interaction with students. They suggest that each individual brings a personal frame of reference to an activity, composed of past experiences, beliefs and expectations about the activity, and personal strengths and weaknesses to each activity. This frame, they maintain, serves as a "lens" through which each individual views the activity. In addition to this personal frame of reference, Green and Weade suggest that each activity has a social frame. The social frame is the pattern of expectations held by individuals as to "how to be a student" or "how to be a teacher" in the activity. Miscommunication and less effective interaction occurs when there is a mismatch between the teacher and student's personal and social frames of reference.

STUDENT VARIABLES

Communicative competence. In classrooms, students are expected to be able to read both the teacher's explicit and implicit messages (Erickson, 1982). Creaghead and Tattershall (1985) suggest that there are three underlying competencies related to communicative competence and productive performance in school. First, they suggest that students should be able to understand classroom routines and the specific formats of school conversations and written material. In addition, students should be able to follow and give oral and written directions. Finally, students should be able to comprehend and use nonliteral language. These skills are necessary for school success, and students who are unable to perform them effectively challenge their teachers.

Developmental level. Pinnell and Galloway (1987) suggest that teachers should have an understanding of human development to work successfully with students. They suggest that learning is a complex process, and teachers need to deepen their understanding of development and the contextual factors that effect it.

Cultural differences among students. Cazden (1988) contends that all human behavior is culturally based. Nonmajority culture students may demonstrate personal and social frames which do not match that of a majority culture teacher. Hymes (1981) suggests that the most stereotyped cultural differences are those usually addressed by schools. He cautions that more subtle differences, in view of everyday etiquette, interaction, values, and norms of communication may be "slighted" in teachers' attempts to address cultural differences.

In working with students from different cultures, Au (1980) suggests developing a social context which is comfortable for the children and comfortable for teacher. The context should also promote better acquisition of basic skills. Au suggests that through the constant interweaving of text-derived information and personal experience, a more comfortable social context evolves. For example, relating reading materials to personal experience can assist students in comprehending the stories which they read.

TASK AND SETTING VARIABLES. Students and teachers in classrooms interact around tasks and products (Marx and Walsh, 1988). Curriculum demands, and time and materials (Green and Weade, 1987) impact on student-teacher interactions.

Number of participants. Cazden (1988) suggests that teacher-student interaction occurs individually as well in groups. Although the teacher has the right to speak to any student at any time, students are more limited in their right to access the teacher. Merritt (1982) suggests that simply changing the number of participants does not change the nature of teacher and student interaction. Edwards and Furlong (1978), in their study of an individualized social studies program, also found that simply increasing student's control over the pacing of their work did not change the teacher's control over the activity.

Teacher Control of Knowledge. Barnes (1982) suggests that teachers control the knowledge to be transmitted or learned in the task through spoken interchange or written activities. Teachers constrict the ways in which students may participate in lessons, and what is a valid or an invalid contribution. Teachers may not allow exploratory talk, redirecting students to the task being considered. Personal knowledge and contributions may be excluded from discussions; the value of student contributions to the discussion may not even be recognized by the teacher.

In terms of "control by worksheet," Barnes supports Edwards and Furlong's (1978) findings concerning individualized work. He maintains that the only individual characteristic addressed is speed. The written worksheet is perhaps even less responsive to students as individuals than in face-to-face interaction. As learning activities, Barnes suggests that worksheets isolate learners at their tasks and keep control firmly in the hands of the teacher.

The next activity in analyzing the behavior is *determining the communicative function of the issue or question.* "Behaviors" represent communicative attempts and, as such, may be ways of making requests, negations, declarations or comments, or noninteractive communication. Ascertaining "what the student is saying" as well as what he or she is "doing" is necessary to develop a strategy for facilitating more conventional behaviors. For example, the possible communicative functions of behaviors are presented in Table 3.5.

Further insights can be gained by *studying the nature of the behavior and generating hypotheses.* Dreikurs and Cassel suggest that children act in a certain manner for one of four reasons: (1) to gain attention, (2) to control, (3) because they have not yet learned an alternative, or (4) because of immaturity or lack of readiness (Dreikurs and Cassel, 1972). Based on Dreikurs's theory, one can assess a student's "problem" by the way you are made to feel. If your reaction to the student's behavior is annoyance, the nature of the behavior is probably attention getting. If you feel threatened, the issue is probably one of control. Feeling the need to teach may signify that a student has not yet learned an alternative behavior, and a feeling of helplessness suggests immaturity. The nature of Stuart's behavior in the high school example may be one of control: the teacher feels threatened in her role as teacher, manager of the classroom.

After you have generated a plausible hypothesis concerning the behavior, the *hypothesis should be validated with the student and fellow teachers.* A disconfirmatory approach may be taken to reduce the extent to which unintentional bias influences the decision regarding the validity of the hypothesis. After validating the hypothesis, it is necessary to determine the extent of the disruption caused by the issue. Successful teachers "choose their battles." If a behavior rarely disrupts activities, other students, or the student's learning, then developing a plan for the behavior may be inappropriate.

TABLE 3.5 Communicative Functions of Behavior

REQUESTS FOR	NEGATIONS	DECLARATIONS/COMMENTS
Attention	Protests	About events
Social interaction	Refusals	About objects
Play	Cessation	Affirmation
Affection		Greeting
Permission		Humor
Assistance		About feelings
Additional information or clarification		
Objects		

Source note: This table was constructed from an article by A. M. Donnellan, P. L. Mirenda, R. A. Mesaros, and L. L. Fassbender, "Analyzing the Communicative Functions of Aberrant Behavior," in *Journal of the Association for Persons with Severe Handicaps, 9,* 201–212, 1984. The table does not exist in the original publication.

The detailed suggestions for analyzing a behavior are summarized in Table 3.6.

TABLE 3.6 Activities Related to Analyzing Issues and Concerns

A. Depict the development of the referral issue
  ❖ Discuss onset and duration
  ❖ Describe any patterns of increases or decreases in intensity
  ❖ Describe any former interventions
B. Observe behavior
  ❖ Antecedents, behaviors, consequences
C. Analyze the context
  ❖ Mediator variables
      Expectations and perceptions
      Communication patterns
      Philosophy of teaching and learning
  ❖ Student variables
      Expectations and perceptions
      Communication patterns
      Changes in life patterns
      Strengths and weaknesses
      Developmental level
  ❖ Task variables
      Nature of materials
      Reinforcement and preference value
      Difficulty level
      Interest level
      Developmental level
  ❖ Setting variables
      Peers
      Persons present
      Mediators available
      Grouping
      Opportunities for interaction
D. Analyze the communicative function
  ❖ Requests
  ❖ Negations
  ❖ Declarations/comments
  ❖ Noninteractive
E. Generate hypotheses about the nature of the behavior
  ❖ Attention getting
  ❖ Control
  ❖ Lack of learning
  ❖ Immaturity
F. Validate hypotheses
  ❖ Validate with mediator
  ❖ Validate with student
  ❖ What is the extent of disruption caused by the issue?

Generate Hypotheses and an Agenda for Facilitating the Development of More Conventional Behaviors. After analyzing the behavior, hypotheses and an agenda for facilitating the development of more conventional behaviors should be developed. A wide range of alternatives are available (they encompass the third section of this book), but generically they may include programming in a positive way to increase a conventional equivalent. In addition, as a teacher, you may manage your own behavior, the task or activity, and the setting in which you interact with the student. You may also alter the events that occur immediately before and after the issue occurs. Another alternative is to "parallel talk," providing the student with interpretation and reconstruction of the issue. For example, in the junior high school example, Mr. Riley may say to Nolan, "I understand that you're excited about math and that you can work this problem easily. But for others to participate, you have to manage that excitement."

After selecting an agenda, you need to formulate hypotheses about the impact of the action (or inaction). Consider the side effects of implementing and not implementing the agenda. Try to consider the potential effects of each of the alternatives you describe. Finally, develop a plan for implementation. This plan should include target dates and the way in which you would evaluate the plan. The activities included in this step are summarized in Table 3.7.

TABLE 3.7 Activities in Generating Hypotheses/Strategies for Intervention

---

A. Generate hypotheses for intervention
- ❖ Positive programming for conventional equivalent
- ❖ Managing mediator variables
- ❖ Managing task variables
- ❖ Managing setting variables
- ❖ Managing antecedents and consequences
- ❖ Interpretation and reconstruction for student

B. Formulate hypotheses about the impact of the intervention
- ❖ Potential effects of positive programming for conventional equivalent
- ❖ Potential effects of managing mediator variables
- ❖ Potential effects of managing task variables
- ❖ Potential effects of managing setting variables
- ❖ Potential effects of managing antecedents and consequences
- ❖ Potential effects of interpretation and reconstruction for student

C. Develop a plan for implementation (target dates, method of evaluation)

Evaluate and Modify the Agenda. Evaluation is necessary to arrange the most effective learning opportunities for your students. Through evaluation, teachers are provided with an opportunity for feedback for further program development. In addition, reviewing progress can provide reinforcement for both teacher and student. Through evaluation, the possibility that you will pursue an ineffective agenda is reduced.

There are several options available to teachers in evaluating agendas. The most rapid, perhaps, is the use of a pretest/posttest format. In working with an instructional question, you would test the student's achievement level on the content or process before applying the framework mentioned in this chapter, using the framework, and then test again. In addition, behavior rating scales and self-rating scales may be applied in a pretest/posttest format.

When a pretest/posttest format is not being used, the student's level of performance before the implementation of the agenda/strategy must be documented in some way. This "prestrategy" documentation is usually referred to as a baseline. A baseline should be taken for three to five days or periods, or until a steady prestrategy level of the behavior is documented (Shea and Bauer, 1987). This documentation before implementing the agenda/strategy provides a means of comparison and a way of determining effectiveness of the strategy.

Another means of evaluating an agenda is to keep permanent products. For example, in evaluating a student's progress in handwriting, you would periodically keep copies of the student's work. In addition, you may record the percent correct a student achieves on a set body of information, such as multiplication facts, or periodically compare a student's performance to a set criterion.

Another option for working with students is to record the level of assistance needed to complete the work successfully. In using this technique, you record whether a student completed the activity or task, or followed the rule independently, with a verbal cue from the teacher, with a demonstration of the desired response, with physical prompting, or if the student failed to complete the activity or task or follow the rule successfully. A format for fast and easy recording of level of assistance information is recorded in Table 3.8.

In addition to permanent products, the frequency and duration of behavioral issues and instructional questions may be documented. Through using frequency charts, you can evaluate a student's progress in producing numbers of (1) correct items, (2) positive comments to others, (3) positive contributions to discussion, and (4) number of

TABLE 3.8   Recording Format for Level of Assistance Information

Student's name_____							
Objective _____							
Dates							
1.	3 2 1 0	3 2 1 0	3 2 1 0	3 2 1 0	3 2 1 0	3 2 1 0	3 2 1 0
2.	3 2 1 0	3 2 1 0	3 2 1 0	3 2 1 0	3 2 1 0	3 2 1 0	3 2 1 0

3—Student completes activity or follows rule independently
2—Student completes activity or follows rule with verbal reminder
1—Student completes activity or follows rule with demonstration or model
0—Student does not successfully complete activity or follow rule

Source note: This table was adapted from T. M. Shea and A. M. Bauer, *Teaching Children and Youth with Behavior Disorders,* (2nd edition, p. 127). Englewood Cliffs, NJ: Prentice Hall, Inc., 1987. Reprinted with permission of the authors and the publisher.

assignments completed, to name a few. In using duration charts, you can evaluate student progress in the amount of time (1) consistently working, (2) remaining in a discussion, or (3) playing without incident on the playground, for example. Sample frequency and duration charts are presented in Tables 3.9 and 3.10.

In evaluating an agenda, the information collected throughout the process must be used. Schloss, Halle, and Sindelar (1984) note several techniques which assist the teacher in using the information in making decisions about continuing, modifying, or discontinuing the strategy. In looking at the chart, you can first look at the mean, or average response. By comparing a student's average performance at baseline with average

TABLE 3.9. Frequency Chart

| Student's name_____ |
| Objective_____ |
| This chart represents the number of times this student _____ |
| _____during a_____minute period. |
| Recording occurs (time and setting)_____. |

15	15	15	15	15	15	15	15	15	15	15	15
14	14	14	14	14	14	14	14	14	14	14	14
13	13	13	13	13	13	13	13	13	13	13	13
12	12	12	12	12	12	12	12	12	12	12	12
11	11	11	11	11	11	11	11	11	11	11	11
10	10	10	10	10	10	10	10	10	10	10	10
9	9	9	9	9	9	9	9	9	9	9	9
8	8	8	8	8	8	8	8	8	8	8	8
7	7	7	7	7	7	7	7	7	7	7	7
6	6	6	6	6	6	6	6	6	6	6	6
5	5	5	5	5	5	5	5	5	5	5	5
4	4	4	4	4	4	4	4	4	4	4	4
3	3	3	3	3	3	3	3	3	3	3	3
2	2	2	2	2	2	2	2	2	2	2	2
1	1	1	1	1	1	1	1	1	1	1	1
0	0	0	0	0	0	0	0	0	0	0	0

^Dates

Source note: This table was adapted from T. M. Shea and A. M. Bauer, *Teaching Children and Youth with Behavior Disorders*, (2nd edition, p. 125). Englewood Cliffs, NJ: Prentice Hall, Inc., 1987. Reprinted with permission of the authors and the publisher.

performance during the application of the strategy, you can make a judgment about the extent of change. In addition, by looking at the data, you can determine the general level of the behavior and the trend of change. Another bit of information gleaned from charts is the "latency," or the amount of time which has elapsed between the baseline and the changes in performance which you desire.

After inspecting your information, you can decide whether to continue the agenda as it is written, modify it, or discontinue it. Haring, Liberty, and Guess (1980) have several suggestions for modifying strategies. They suggest changing reinforcers, materials, or the instruction (in terms of cues, language, and prompts used). In addition, checking the error pattern may provide additional insights into the behavior or question. Another issue may be readiness; the student may not have the prerequisite skills for the task, activity, or behavioral

TABLE 3.10. Duration Chart

Student's name_____
Objective_____

This chart represents the number of times this student _____

_____during a_____minute period.
Recording occurs (time and setting)_____.

20	20	20	20	20	20	20	20	20	20	20	20
19	19	19	19	19	19	19	19	19	19	19	19
18	18	18	18	18	18	18	18	18	18	18	18
17	17	17	17	17	17	17	17	17	17	17	17
16	16	16	16	16	16	16	16	16	16	16	16
15	15	15	15	15	15	15	15	15	15	15	15
14	14	14	14	14	14	14	14	14	14	14	14
13	13	13	13	13	13	13	13	13	13	13	13
12	12	12	12	12	12	12	12	12	12	12	12
11	11	11	11	11	11	11	11	11	11	11	11
10	10	10	10	10	10	10	10	10	10	10	10
9	9	9	9	9	9	9	9	9	9	9	9
8	8	8	8	8	8	8	8	8	8	8	8
7	7	7	7	7	7	7	7	7	7	7	7
6	6	6	6	6	6	6	6	6	6	6	6
5	5	5	5	5	5	5	5	5	5	5	5
4	4	4	4	4	4	4	4	4	4	4	4
3	3	3	3	3	3	3	3	3	3	3	3
2	2	2	2	2	2	2	2	2	2	2	2
1	1	1	1	1	1	1	1	1	1	1	1
0	0	0	0	0	0	0	0	0	0	0	0

^Dates

Source note: This table was adapted from T. M. Shea and A. M. Bauer, *Teaching Children and Youth with Behavior Disorders,* (2nd edition, p. 126). Englewood Cliffs, NJ: Prentice Hall, Inc., 1987. Reprinted with permission of the authors and the publisher.

demand. When confronted with progress which you consider inadequate, it may be necessary to simplify the task or attempt to increase its relevance. Finally, it may be appropriate to discontinue the agenda and attempt a more relevant or individually appropriate agenda.

SUMMARY

Thus far, we've talked about the classrooms as complex environments in which teachers, students, and subject matter interact. The teacher's management task is to establish and maintain an interesting and flexible learning environment. A facilitative stance is one means for dealing with the classroom complexity and possible challenges to student participation. Serving as a general "guide" to interactions, teacher stance provides a basis for establishing positive relationships with students. These relationships are particularly important given our view of teaching as an achieved role that requires the complementary performance of at least one other person.

Complex communicative and behavioral demands are placed on students as they participate in classroom interactions. These demands, or social participation structures, include speaking, listening, getting the floor and holding it, and leading and following discussions. Breakdowns in classroom interactions may occur when students do not recognize or adjust to the multiple shifts in the requirements for participation which may exist during a single instructional activity.

Two other issues related to stance were described in this chapter. First, a consideration of behaviors along a continuum of conventionality is useful as teachers facilitate student participation in learning activities. Demands for "appropriate behavior" are judgmental and may not take into account culturally diverse communication or interaction patterns. Second, a proactive stance toward behavior management is suggested. Rather than solving the problems of order in classrooms through intervention, teachers should develop an underlying agenda for classroom management and convey this agenda through all their actions.

A four-phase framework for designing an agenda for classroom management was presented. Beginning with a general description, teachers move to a more in-depth analysis of the issue. A key step in this analysis is a consideration of the impact of contextual variables such as teacher, student, task, and setting variables on the issue. Following this analysis process, hypotheses are generated and plans are developed, implemented, evaluated, and modified as needed. Developing an agenda for classroom management is not a simple process. However, an explicit agenda conveyed through all verbal and nonverbal communication is very powerful. The framework described in this chapter provides support for teachers as they design their agendas. Our intent is to help teachers develop agendas based on a proactive stance that views behavior along a continuum of conventionality and that is designed to assist students in participating in the learning process in strategically effective ways.

REVIEW QUESTIONS

1. Our contention is that teaching is an interactive process which requires teachers and students to work together to carry out classroom activities. Generate several examples of communicative and behavioral demands placed on students during a teaching activity.

2. The social context of the classroom may shift from moment to moment within an instructional activity. How is this social context constructed? What is meant by a social frame of an activity? How are these two ideas related?

3. Contrast a proactive stance toward behavior management with an intervention-based stance. Describe the impact of intervention-based behavior management on classroom interactions.

4. Describe the implications of viewing behavior in terms of a continuum of conventionality. How might this view affect a teacher's interactional style?

5. How does an overriding agenda for classroom management assist teachers in dealing with the complexity of the classroom? Think about effective and less than effective teachers you've observed recently. How did those teachers convey their classroom management agendas?

6. Why is it important to obtain student perceptions of behavioral issues? What other sources might you consult when generating an initial description of a behavioral issue?

7. An analysis of the context which surrounds the behavioral issue is the second step in the framework presented in the chapter. Suppose a teacher was observed to inhibit student contributions to discussion. What might this indicate about her communicative competence? her personal frame of reference?

APPLICATION ACTIVITY

A teacher's stance and overriding management agenda are conveyed through classroom interactions. In addition, the teacher's agenda is represented throughout all verbal and nonverbal communication.

In this activity, you will continue your observations in a classroom of your choice. (Note: This activity would be easiest to complete if you return to the class you observed for the last application activity.) The purpose of this activity is to determine a teacher's management agenda through observation and interviews. Observe during at least one period which appears less structured (such as transitions between activities, initial entrance into the class). Comment on the following questions:

❖ How is the teacher's management agenda conveyed to students? Is this agenda rigidly followed across all activities or does the teacher maintain flexibility in her classroom management style?

❖ Describe the social context of the classroom. What are the demands for participation? How are these demands conveyed? Do the demands change across activities? Are the demands for communication and behavior the same for all students?

❖ Conduct a brief interview with the classrocm teacher. If possible, tape the interview (with permission, of course) so that you can use it for analysis.

❖ What does this teacher say about her management style? Does the teacher look at challenges to participation in activities from an intervention-based stance or proactive view of behavior management? Did you observe any discrepancies between the teacher's description of management style and the teacher's actions?

REFERENCES

AU, H. K. (1980). Participation structures in a reading lesson with Hawaiian children: Analysis of a culturally appropriate instructional event. *Anthropology and Education Quarterly, 11*, 91–115.

AYERS, W. (1986). Thinking about teachers and the curriculum. *Harvard Educational Review, 56*, 49–51.

BARNES, D. (1982). *From communication to curriculum.* Upper Montclair, NJ: Boynton/Cook.

BAUER, A. M., LYNCH, E., & MURPHY, S. (1988). *A teacher's stance: Relational honesty in a classroom for students with behavioral disorders.* Unpublished manuscript, University of Cincinnati.

BLOOME, D. & KNOTT, G. (1985) Teacher-student discourse. In D. N. Ripich & F. M. Spinelli (Eds.), *School discourse problems* (pp. 53–76). San Diego, CA: College Hill Press.

BREMME, D. W., & ERICKSON, F. (1977). Relationships among verbal and nonverbal classroom behaviors. *Theory into Practice, 16*, 153–161.

BROOKS, D. M. (1985). The teacher's communicative competence: The first day of school. *Theory into Practice, 24*, 63–70.

BURNS, R. B., & ANDERSON, L. W. (1987). The activity structure of lesson segments. *Curriculum Inquiry, 17*, 31–53.

CAZDEN, C. B. (1988). *Classroom discourse.* Portsmouth, NH: Heinemann.

CAZDEN, C. M., COX, D., DICKINSON, Z., STEINBERG, & STONE, C. (1979). "You all gonna hafta listen" Peer teaching in a primary classroom. In W. A. Collins (Ed.), *Children's language and communication* (pp. 183–231). Hillsdale, NJ: Lawrence Erlbaum.

CREAGHEAD, N. A., & TATTERSHALL, S. S. (1985). Observation and assessment of classroom pragmatic skills. In C. S. Simon (Ed.), *Communication skills and classroom success* (pp. 105–131). San Diego, CA: College Hill Press.

DONNELLAN, A. M., MIRENDA, P. L., MESAROS, R. A., & FASSBENDER, L. L. (1984). Analyzing the communicative functions of aberrant behavior. *Journal of the Association for Persons with Severe Handicaps, 9*, 201–212.

DOYLE, W. (1980). *Classroom management.* West Lafayette, IN: Kappa Delta Pi.

———. (1986). Classroom organization and management. In M. C. Wittrock (Ed.), *Handbook of research on teaching* (3rd ed., pp. 392–432). New York: Macmillan.

DREIKURS, R., & CASSEL, P. (1972). *Discipline without tears.* New York: Hawthorn Books.

EDELSKY, C., DRAPER, K., & SMITH, K. (1983) "Hook 'em at the state of school" in a whole language classroom. *Anthropology and Education Quarterly, 14,* 257–281.

EDWARDS, A. D., & FURLONG, J. J. (1978). *The language of teaching: Meaning in classroom interaction.* London: Heinemann.

EMMER, E., EVERTSON, C., & ANDERSON, L. (1980). Effective classroom management at the beginning of the school year. *Elementary School Journal, 80*(5), 219–231.

ERICKSON, F. (1982). Classroom discourse as improvisation: Relationships between academic task structure and social participation structure in lessons. In L. C. Wilkinson (Ed.), *Communicating in classrooms* (pp. 153–181). New York: Academic Press.

ERICKSON, F. & SHULTZ, J. (1981). When is a context? Some issues and methods in the analysis of social competence. In J. L. Green & C. Wallat (Eds.), *Ethnography and language in educational settings* (pp. 147–160). Norwood, NJ: Ablex.

FENSTERMACHER, G. D. (1986). Philosophy of research on teaching: Three aspects. In M. C. Wittrock (Ed.), *Handbook of research on teaching* (3rd ed., pp. 37–49). New York: Macmillan.

GREEN, J., & WEADE, R. (1987). In search of meaning: A sociolinguistic perspective on lesson construction and reading. In D. Bloome (Ed.), *Literacy and schooling* (pp. 3–34). Norwood, NJ: Ablex.

HARING, N., LIBERTY, K. A. & GUESS, D. (1980). Rules for data-based strategy decisions in instructional programs: Current research and instructional implications. In W. Sailor, B. Wilcox, & L. Brown (Eds.), *Methods of instruction for severely handicapped students* (pp. 159–192). Baltimore: Brookes.

HYMES, D. (1981). Ethnographic monitoring. In H. T. Trueba, G. P. Guthrie, & K. P. Au (Eds.). *Culture and the bilingual classroom: Studies in classroom ethnography* (pp. 56–68). Rowley, MA: Newbury House.

LANE, D. A. (1986). Promoting positive behavior in the classroom. In D. P. Tattum (Ed.), *Management of disruptive pupil behavior in schools* (pp. 123–140). Chichester, England: John Wiley.

LEINHARDT, G., & GREENO, J. G. (1986). The cognitive skill of teaching. *Journal of Educational Psychology, 78*(2), 85–95.

MARX, R. W., & WALSH, J. (1988). Learning from academic tasks. *Elementary School Journal, 88,* 207–219.

MERRITT, M. (1982). Distributing and directing attention in primary classrooms. In L. C. Wilkinson (Ed.), *Communicating in the classroom* (pp. 223–244). New York: Academic Press.

MCDERMOTT, R. P. (1982). Social relations as contexts for learning in school. In E. Bredo & W. Feinberg (Eds.), *Knowledge and values in social and educational research* (pp. 252–270). Philadelphia: Temple University Press. (Originally published in *Harvard Educational Review, 47*(2), 198–213, 1977.)

PINNELL, G. S., & GALLOWAY, C. M. (1987). Human development, language, and communication: Then and now. *Theory into Practice, 26*, 353–357.

PRIZANT, B. M., & WETHERBY, A. M. (1987). Communicative intent: A framework for understanding social-communicative behavior in autism. *Journal of American Academy of Child and Adolescent Psychiatry, 26*, 472–479.

ROGERS, C. (1971). *Client centered therapy.* Boston: Houghton Mifflin.

SCHLOSS, P. J., HALLE, J. W., & SINDELAR, P. T. (1984). Guidelines for teacher's interpretations of student performance data. *Remedial and Special Education, 5*(4), 38–43.

SHEA, T. M., & BAUER, A. M. (1987). *Teaching children and youth with behavior disorders.* Englewood Cliffs, NJ: Prentice Hall.

SHULTZ, J. J., FLORIO, S., & ERICKSON, F. (1982). Where's the floor? Aspects of the cultural organization of social relationships in communication at home and in the school. In P. Gilmore & A. A. Glatthorn (Eds.), *Children in and out of school* (pp. 88–123). Washington, DC: Center for Applied Linguistics.

STRAHAN, D. B. (1983). The teacher and ethnography: Observational sources of information for educators. *Elementary School Journal, 83*, 195–203.

CHAPTER FOUR

Managing
the Physical Context

SITUATIONS

Setting: Kindergarten classroom, immediately following recess.

Teacher:	Children, everybody get in your seats and begin work on your folders. I'd like to see the red group at my table.
Marsha:	[Standing next to the teacher, tugging on her arm] Ms. M., did you see how far I kicked that ball? Lena and Marcus both got in before anybody caught it.
Teacher:	You seemed to be having a good time, didn't you. I always liked kickball too.
Marsha:	You did? I want to play kickball all the time.
Teacher:	That's nice. Now, Marsha, in your seat. Recess is over.
Marcus:	Ms. M., we gonna play kickball tomorrow or circle games?
Teacher:	Recess today is over. Tomorrow we'll talk about recess again.
Marsha:	I wanna play kickball. I'm good at kickball.

Luis: No you ain't; we're gonna beat you tomorrow.

Teacher: That's it. Recess is over. The next talk about recess will cost the whole class part of their free time.

*   *   *

Setting: Fifth grade self-contained classroom, immediately after lunch.

Teacher: Chairs should be in a circle to begin our afternoon meeting. As soon as we complete our meeting, you can break into your small groups and work on your projects [teacher moves her chair into place].

Marc: Lunch was too strange, Ms. L. We had tacos with salad on them then more salad.

Teacher: [Keeping eye contact on total group, Marc moves away and gets a chair to join the group.] Thanks for moving into group so quickly. I appreciate your help in getting the afternoon off to a good start.

*   *   *

Teachers communicate with their students both explicitly and implicitly. In the contrasting examples presented, the kindergarten teacher explicitly stated it was time to work, but by conversing with a student, implied that she would continue to discuss recess. The junior high school teacher, however, both verbally and nonverbally communicated that it was time to work.

Each student's learning in the classroom is defined by the interactional contexts in which students and teachers are involved. Puro and Bloome (1987) suggest that the communicative contexts are mitigated by the tasks and physical arrangements in the room. The interaction of students, teachers, tasks, and physical setting becomes the frame through which students interpret and redefine classroom learning. In this chapter, the variables contributing to the learning context in classrooms are explored. Issues in managing the physical context, through routines, schedules, grouping, allocating space, and selecting materials are presented.

In Chapter Five, we discuss the three basic foci of learning activities that occur in classrooms. Each of these patterns will be described in detail in Sections Three, Four, and Five. For each family of activities within each pattern, we will explore the rationale and research base, provide research based examples of the implementation of these activities, and describe ways in which you can prepare, evaluate, and incorporate these patterns into your classroom management agenda.

SELF-EVALUATION

Indicate whether you agree or disagree with each statement:

1. The school day is comprised by a series of activities.
2. Routines become established in classrooms with little direct instruction or rehearsal.
3. Rules and routines are synonymous.
4. Routines most commonly evolve through a shared exchange of cues.
5. Routines slowly emerge at a uniform rate throughout the school year.
6. Providing students with copies of rules is effective in classroom management.
7. The amount of time scheduled for an academic subject is equivalent to the time students spend engaged in that task.
8. Group instruction is more effective than is one-to-one instruction.
9. The physical environment of a classroom may limit classroom interaction and participation.

KEY WORDS

activity

scripts

routines

rules

allocated time

engaged time

cooperative learning

peer tutoring

OBJECTIVES

After completing this chapter, you will be able to:

1. Recognize the importance of communication and implementation of routines in structuring classroom events.
2. Develop an effective classroom schedule.
3. Plan instructional groups.
4. Describe considerations in designing physical classroom space.
5. Describe a process for selecting and evaluating materials.

Objective One: *To Recognize the Importance of Communication and Implementation of Routines in Structuring Classroom Events*

Throughout our research and observations in classrooms, we are continually amazed by teachers who effectively design and orchestrate classroom events. These events may materialize in several ways. In his study of classroom interaction, Yinger (1979) found that nearly all classroom action and interaction takes place within the boundaries of events he called "activities." The remaining time was involved in the preparation and transition between activities.

Doyle (1984) further defines an activity as "a bounded segment of classroom time, characterized by an identifiable focal content or concern, and by a pattern or program of action" (p. 259). He suggests that successful teaching is grounded in the management of classroom activities.

Although they have a single focal content and concern, it is helpful to consider activities as comprised of multiple segments. Burns and Anderson (1987) suggest that classroom activities are a sequence of segments. Each of these segments is comprised of a purpose, a format, and an activity. Burns and Anderson suggest that "scripts" (a series of experienced-based expectations about the ways in which the segments proceed) assist students in moving smoothly from segment to segment. These scripts are collaboratively developed and maintained by students and teachers.

In addition to scripts, teachers use routines to move activities along. Routines are shared and socially scripted patterns of behavior (Leinhardt, Weidman, and Hammond, 1987). They are established procedures whose purpose is to manage and coordinate specific sequences of behavior (Yinger, 1979). Routines act as a mechanism to establish and regulate instructional activities and, as such, increase the predictability of the teaching environment (Yinger, 1979). Teachers may use routines to communicate to students the context of the activity and the fact that behavioral expectations are changing. For example, Shultz and Florio (1979) describe "stop and freeze," a routine utilized by a kindergarten teacher, to bring closure to one segment of worktime. The teacher communicated "stop and freeze" through the consistent use of the phrase, a specific body posture, and taking a specific position in the room.

Although they may serve similar purposes of regulating behavior, routines are not rules. Leinhardt and associates (1987) differentiate rules and routines. They suggest that although some rules may serve as routines, most rules are statements of limits or are explicit or implicit constraints. Routines, however, are fluid and scripted segments of behavior that help move interaction toward a shared goal. Although rehearsal is necessary to establish routines, they most commonly simply evolve through a shared exchange of cues. For example, a morning routine usually emerges during the first several days of school. Children enter the classroom, put away their belongings, and begin the assignment on the chalkboard. After several days of school, the cues for the routine have faded to "You all know what you should be doing."

Rohrkemper (1985) found that the use of routines increased the similarity between student and teacher perceptions of classroom events. Approximately one-third of the routines used in classrooms were developed during the first two days of school (Leinhardt et al., 1987). The routines which are established earliest during the school year include response patterns such as raising hands, making choral responses, and teacher cycling through students for responses.

There are three basic kinds of routines. Leinhardt and associates relate these to a dance performance to emphasize the interdependence of the different kinds of routines. They suggest that first, there are *management routines*, which include "housekeeping" tasks (taking attendance, collecting lunch money), moving the class to different parts of the school building, and setting basic behavioral limits. These they describe as the "stage directions." The second set of routines are *support* routines. These routines define and specify the behaviors and actions needed for teachers and students to interact in classroom activities. Examples of these routines are procedures for distributing and collecting papers, breaking into groups, and preparing materials. Leinhardt and her colleagues equate these routines with the "steps to the dance." Finally, *exchange* routines serve as interactive behaviors which allow teacher-student interactions to occur. These routines communicate the communication structures that are preferred in the classroom and patterns of appropriate social contact. Leinhardt and associates suggest that these routines are the pas de deux, the point at which interaction comes together and "clicks."

The use of routines has several advantages (Leinhardt, Weidman, and Hammond, 1987; Levine and Mann, 1985; Yinger, 1979):

❖ Routines increase the shared context for an activity between teachers and students.
❖ The complexity of the classroom environment is reduced in that there is a predictable structure in place.
❖ Activities are streamlined providing more time for content, presentation, assessment, and evaluation.
❖ Activities need not be planned "from scratch."

The routines a teacher uses may vary as a function of the individual task. Different students may require different routines in order to support students with different frames of reference or abilities (Levine and Mann, 1985). Routines can be invaluable in helping students make sense of the classroom and navigating through activities and the segments of which they are comprised (Shultz and Florio, 1979).

As discussed earlier, rules vary from routines in that they are usually specific statements which constrain behavior. Rules are essential to structure classroom interaction. Evertson and Emmer (1982) found that more effective teachers were more likely to be explicit about rules (e.g., provide students with copies). These rules were translated into specific procedures to manage behaviors. The effective teachers monitored rule compliance extensively and consistently invoked prestated consequences quickly.

Brooks (1985) provided a description of effective "first day" rule explanation to a class of middle school students. Organization was central to the teacher's presentation of rules and procedures. The specific recommendations derived from the study are presented in Table 4.1.

Objective Two: *To Develop an Effective Classroom Schedule*

The amount of freedom allotted teachers in developing instructional schedules varies with the school and level of class. Teachers in the elementary grades are usually afforded more freedom, with limited designated times to which they must comply (e.g., lunch, recess,

TABLE 4.1 Suggestions for Initial Presentation of Rules

1. Provide each student with a copy of the classroom rules and emphasize the importance of keeping them. Consider having students all keep their copy in a uniform place (stapled in the front of notebook, taped to inside of desk, etc.).
2. Review the rules as they occur on the student's copy.
3. Check student understanding of the rules frequently.
4. Follow a specific format for reviewing each rule. For example:
   a. State the rule.
   b. Provide a rationale for the rule.
   c. Provide an example of appropriate behavior.
   d. Describe consequences for failing to follow the rule.
5. Match your nonverbal presentation to your verbal content. Move the pace along quickly in a businesslike manner. Smile a great deal during the introduction and rarely smile during discussion of consequences.

Source note: This table was constructed from an article by D. M. Brooks, "The Teacher's Communicative Competence: The First Day of School," *Theory into Practice, 24,* 63–70, 1985. The table does not exist in the original publication.

physical education, music, art). Secondary teachers are limited to developing schedules within the framework of an instructional period, which may vary from 40 to 65 minutes. In either case, schedules provide a frame for organizing classroom activities and managing instruction.

Englert (1984) suggests that in developing effective schedules, teachers should review two concepts: allocated time and engaged time. Allocated time, she suggests, is the amount of time scheduled for an academic subject. This allocated time can be measured simply by examining teacher's schedule books. Engaged time is the amount of time the student is involved in work of at least moderate difficulty. In the first example, the kindergarten teacher may have from 10:15 A.M. to 10:45 A.M. allocated to seat work. However, by the time the students are in their seats and working, it may be 10:25 A.M. Engaged time has only the potential of being 20 rather than 30 minutes long. Englert suggests that through increasing direct instruction, monitoring seatwork, and demanding a high accuracy on seatwork, engaged time may increase. Rather than considering allocated time, Kavale and Forness (1986) suggest that academic learning time, the engaged time which occurs in classrooms, is what matters to students. This learning time is a function of classroom instructional processes in the environment.

Increasing Instructional Time. Rosenshine (1980) suggests that time available for instruction increases when teachers (1) follow schedules, (2) begin and end activities on time, (3) facilitate transitions from activity to activity, and (4) assign scheduled activities first priority rather than engaging in spontaneous alternative activities. In initiating activities, Brophy, Rohrkemper, Rashid, and Goldberger (1983) found that task engagement was higher when teachers initiated activities directly rather than when they made statements of beliefs, attitudes, or expectations about the task or student engagement.

Engelmann (1982) maintains that effective transitions are essential in increasing instructional time. He suggests that by modeling appropriate transition behaviors, moving between activities will become more efficient. In addition, providing a signal at the beginning and end of activities assists students. Good (1983) suggests establishing "work rules" to deal with students who finish early, are unable to continue their work, or need additional help. Work rules are communicated to students by teaching and rehearsing new lesson procedures before their implementation. For example, students can be taught how to use new equipment before it is actually applied in instructional purposes. By using rules and rehearsals, students become aware of what is expected of them and intrusions into teaching time are decreased.

Englert (1984) maintains that allocated time should not be increased arbitrarily without giving consideration to task engagement time. Task engagement should be measured during both direct instruction, that is, during teacher-directed lessons, and during seatwork. Seatwork can be evaluated by circulating among students.

Scheduling to Meet Students' Needs. Recent research has described the relationship among learning style, time preference, assigned instructional achievement time, and achievement. Dunn, Dunn, Primavera, Sinatra, and Virostko (1987) found that over 98 percent of the students achieved higher scores when taught at the best time for them and did poorly when taught at the "nonpreferred time." They suggest scheduling in consideration of preferred time to the greatest extent possible. Testing should also be scheduled for the student's most productive time. Students with similar "chronobiological" inclinations should be grouped.

Teachers in the elementary grades should make adjustments to their classroom schedules as students develop throughout the school year (Shea and Bauer, 1987). Modifications in schedules should occur when changes in the amount of time students can work independently or maintain interest in a learning activity become apparent. Teachers who maintain the same schedule from September to June are not addressing the changing needs of their students.

In summary, Doyle (1984) found that successful teachers are successful time managers. Successful teachers construct lessons that fit the externally spaced schedule of the school day. Activities which they facilitate have a clear program of action and are explicitly marked. Effective teachers demonstrate situational awareness by attending to details and commenting on events taking place in the room. They actively usher activities along, pushing students through the curriculum.

Objective Three: *To Plan Instructional Groups*

Whenever two or more persons are interacting in the classroom, a group is formed. Bloome and Knott (1985) describe three layers of social interaction which occur among groups in classrooms: teacher-class interaction, teacher-student interaction, and student-student interaction. All three layers of interaction should be considered when planning and monitoring instructional groups to achieve maximal levels of student participation.

Teacher-Class Interaction. Teacher-class social interaction is based on both explicit and implicit communication, yet is primarily conducted through talk (Erickson, 1982). Green and Smith (1983) suggest that teachers must effectively communicate a wide range of pieces to make up a working whole using both verbal and nonverbal cues. They suggest that teachers must communicate to the class the academic task involved and the participation rules related to the activity. The teacher, in addition, must manage the group as well as monitor and interpret student messages in several channels, to monitor the frame clashes described in Chapter Three. Whenever a teacher delivers academic content, he or she also provides information about how to participate, what behavior is appropriate, and when to talk.

Student-Teacher Interactions. Student-teacher interaction provides the context for all classroom learning. McDermott (1982) suggests that the trusting relationship between teachers and children underlies all the organizational work necessary for learning tasks to be presented and worked on by children. Trust, then, is achieved and managed through interaction.

Nonverbal behavior also plays an essential role in student-teacher interaction. Brooks and Woolfolk (1987) found that students' nonverbal behavior provides one basis on which teachers form opinions about pupils' dispositions, abilities, and characteristics. Students must also carefully attend to teachers' and other students' nonverbal behavior. They must actively monitor both direct and covert messages to determine what is occurring. In addition, they must deal with the discrepancy between expected and actual events.

Student-Student Interactions. When planning instructional groups, factors such as students' communicative competence must be considered. Cooper, Marquis, and Ayers-Lopez (1982) found that children who learn are those who ask, and children who give information are likely to be the ones who receive it. More competent children are approached by their peers not only to be asked questions, but also to be informed of new learning. Students can learn from their peers, particularly if they are allowed to develop areas of individual "expert power" or power that is attained from their perceived competence rather than through domination or coercion of others in the group. Teachers can then assist children in demonstrating their new competence to others.

Maximizing Learning Through Grouping. In addition to the layers of social interaction mentioned, other factors must be considered when planning instructional groups to ensure maximum student learning and facilitate effective management. One question relates to the issue of group versus individual instruction. Teachers may assume that to individualize instruction, they should minimize their use of groups. Polloway, Cronin, and Patton (1986) point out the distinction between individualization and one-to-one instruction. Individualization refers to organizing instruction to meet the needs of the individual child; one-to-one instruction refers to a means for delivering instruction. Although individualization occurs when instruction matches student need, it does not imply that the instruction was delivered in a one-to-one format. In their review, Polloway and his colleagues found that little research supported the use of one-to-one instruction. Group instruction was found to increase the use of teacher time, and was more efficient in student management. Instructional time and peer-to-peer interaction increased. In addition, students increased their observational learning, overlearning, and contact time with the teacher.

Brown, Holvoet, Guess, and Mulligan (1980) suggest that in grouping students, the structure, content, and individualization for students should be considered. In terms of the structure of groups, the teacher should determine if there will be interaction among students. Students may be grouped without systematic interaction among their activities or with planned interaction among the students. In terms of content, students may work on the same project or in sequential or interrelated projects. In terms of individualization, the ways in which students communicate during the interaction and materials may vary according to individual student needs.

Benefits from group interaction may be enhanced through careful monitoring of the interactional process. Newman (1982) suggests that teachers should recognize naturally formed groups (such as those formed during recess or free time), recognize emerging leaders and provide them with direction or support to maintain group leadership, group students carefully with attention to heterogeneity, and maintain flexibility in groupings to prevent entrenched cliques or rivalries.

Cooperative learning, or grouping of students to achieve a shared academic goal, provides an interesting form of instruction for students. This form of instruction will be discussed in detail in Chapter Eight. Schniedewind and Salend (1987) describe tips for teachers as they organize groups and monitor group interaction. They suggest that teachers should establish clear guidelines for the group work, select groups carefully, arrange the classroom to facilitate group interaction, and assist students as they develop communicative skills (e.g., making statements or asking questions that facilitate group interaction versus statements which hinder the group process such as "putdowns"). Smith (1987) contends that if students are not taught how to cooperate, it is likely that the interactions will be unproductive.

Peer tutoring is an additional option for grouping students. Advantages of peer tutoring include increased teaching, increased coverage of content, and increased self-concept. In terms of selecting tutors, Project STRETCH (1980) suggests using students who want to be a part of the relations. In addition, they should be of comparable size and age and same sex as the student who will be tutored. Tutors should be able to communicate the work involved and provide good models. Tutors should also be enthusiastic and voluntary; stars should be avoided.

Before initiating any peer tutoring situation, tutors should be trained in terms of the goals of the project, their listening skills, and their ability to work with a peer. The logistical problems of scheduling and finding space for the experience should be worked through. Teachers should communicate the requirements of the activity to both the tutor and the student being tutored, and provide supervision, and monitor materials and progress.

Group Management Problems. Johnson and Bany (1970) describe group management problems which may occur in classrooms. They suggest that group interactions in classrooms may be seriously affected by

1. A lack of classroom group unity, characterized by conflicts between individuals and subgroups.
2. Failure to adhere to behavioral standards and work procedures.
3. Negative reactions to individual students.
4. Class approval of misbehavior.
5. Frequent distraction or work stoppage.
6. Acts of protest or resistance.
7. Inability to adjust to change.

To manage group management problems, Johnson and Bany suggest fostering group unity and cooperation, allowing students opportunities to interact and communicate. Teachers should establish standards of appropriate behavior. Implementing problem-solving activities can assist students in working through group management problems. Finally, encouraging appropriate group goals, norms, and behaviors may be of assistance.

In summary, a number of factors must be considered when planning instructional groups. Zentall (1983) suggests that increased numbers of students in classrooms may reduce a child's access to the teacher and materials as well as reduce opportunities to respond actively to tasks. One means for providing greater access is through careful planning and use of instructional groups. Attention must be given to the multiple layers of social interactions involved in group processes. The question of individual versus group instruction must be addressed. Teachers should consider the structure and nature of groups, purposes for forming groups (e.g., cooperative learning activities, peer tutoring), and potential for management problems (e.g., a potential for disharmony) as they plan instructional groups to maximize learning outcomes.

Objective Four: *To Describe Considerations in Designing Physical Classroom Space*

Classroom Furniture. Desk arrangement has been related to student behavior. Rosenfield, Lambert, and Black (1985) found that students seated in circles engaged in significantly more on-task behaviors than those in rows. Students whose desks were arranged in clusters engaged in more on-task behaviors than did those in rows, but less than those in circles.

Weinstein (1979) in her review of physical features of classroom environment found that spatial organization has some effect on attitudes and conduct. The strongest variable which emerged was to separate and designate clearly areas serving different purposes and designing traffic patterns carefully. She reports that increased density was related to increased dissatisfaction, aggression, and decreased attention. The greater the amount of student choice and mobility, the greater the need for overt management by teachers. Sample floor plans of classrooms which have been utilized by strong, facilitative teachers are presented in Figures 4.1 and 4.2.

Classroom Acoustics. Smyth (1979) describes the need to consider the acoustics of a classroom when designing physical classroom space. He maintains that some classroom settings, such as tiled floors and high ceilings, may result in an echoing effect, which may make it difficult for some students to attend to and comprehend lessons. Nelson (1985) suggests using carpet squares or a similar materials applied to portable room dividers or classroom walls to absorb some of the sound.

Objective Five: *To Describe a Process for Selecting and Evaluating Materials*

Shavelson and Stern (1981) suggest that the basis of teacher planning is the creation of instructional tasks. They maintain that the selection of materials and the subsequent activity flow establishes the problem frame or boundaries within which decision making is carried on. Hill, Yinger, and Robins (1983) provide support for this contention in their study of teacher planning. They found that

FIGURE 4.1 Classroom Floor Plan

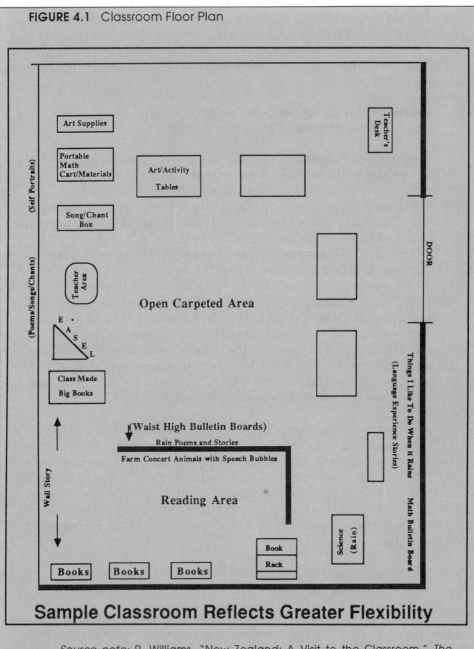

Sample Classroom Reflects Greater Flexibility

Source note: R. Williams, "New Zealand: A Visit to the Classroom," *The Whole Idea*, *1*(1), pg. 4. Reprinted with permission from The Wright Group, San Diego, CA. The newsletter is available from The Wright Group, 10949 Technology Place, San Diego, CA 92127.

FIGURE 4.2 Classroom Floor Plan

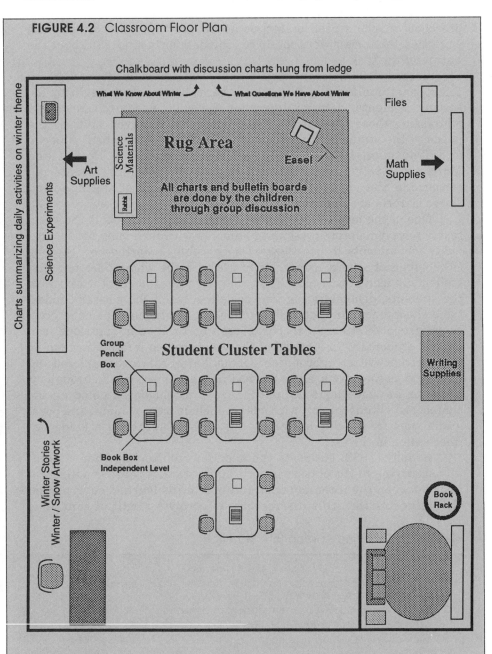

Source note: R. Williams, "A Visit to the Classroom: Canada," *The Whole Idea, 1*(2), pg. 6. Reprinted with permission from The Wright Group, San Diego, CA. The newsletter is available from The Wright Group, 10949 Technology Place, San Diego, CA 92127.

preschool teachers used materials as the starting point of planning activities. Materials were set up to provide cues to students about the nature of the task.

Brophy (1982) found that teachers are heavily dependent on commercial publishers. He found it rare that teachers begin by assessing students, determining what the child needs to learn, and addressing those objectives. Materials must, however, address the needs of the students with whom they will be used (Cohen, Alberto, and Troutman, 1979; Howell and Morehead, 1987). Howell and Morehead (1987) suggest several criteria for selecting a material, concerning the objectives, context, and emphasis of the material. These criteria are described in Table 4.2.

One of the most frequently used materials in schools is the basal text. However, simply presenting students with texts may not be adequate for students to use the text successfully. Maring and Furlong (1985) suggest several strategies to use with the whole class to assist students in using textbooks. First, they suggest exploring the text with the students, demonstrating and modeling use of the glossary, index, table of contents, and appendices. Reading to students, pausing occasionally to ask students to paraphrase or to answer questions, can provide students with a model of the way in which information can be derived from written information. Unfamiliar words can be explored and redefined as they are used in the text as a group activity. Throughout activities in which texts are used, key words should be noted on the chalkboard. Study guides, with cues to include page, column, and paragraph cues for specific questions can assist students in seeking out information in the text.

Brophy (1982) supports the need for monitoring what is actually occurring in the classroom. He suggests that there is a discrepancy between the intended curriculum and the learned curriculum. He maintains that this discrepancy is rarely a result of conscious

TABLE 4.2 Selecting Appropriate Materials

1. Do the materials address the correct objective?
2. Does the student have the necessary background information to derive meaning from the material?
3. Are accuracy, fluency, generalization, and maintenance addressed?
4. Is the material interesting?
5. Is the delivery method appropriate?

Source note: This table was constructed from material by K. Howell and M. K. Morehead, *Curriculum-based Evaluation in Special and Remedial Education.* Columbus, OH: Charles E. Merrill, 1987. The table does not exist in the original publication.

teacher decision. Rather, he suggests that materials may be distorted by students. The material "covered" may differ from material taught to mastery. Brophy contends that "teacher failure to explain the purpose of activities adequately often produces discrepancies between the meaning of those activities as seen by the teacher and students" (p. 10).

Finally, Weade (1987) presents a view of curriculum and instruction which is consistent with our view of classrooms as communicative environments in which teacher, students, and subject matter interact. Weade (1987) views curriculum and instruction as a dynamic, collaborative process through which students gain access to both social and academic content of lessons. She contends that differentiating curriculum and instruction may be an academic attempt. Rather, she maintains that students and teachers work together to construct the everyday events of classroom life and what occurs as a result of these evolving events. Teachers, then, she suggests, should continually monitor what is occurring and how it is being accomplished to determine their current rights and obligations for participating as well as what should occur next.

SUMMARY

In the first section of the book, ideas related to the communicative nature of the classroom were discussed. A framework for developing an agenda for classroom management was presented. Although the framework is most easily applied to challenges to student participation in classroom activities, the questions raised and the analysis procedures are applicable to other management issues (refer to Table 3.4 on teacher, student, task, and context variables).

The focus of this chapter was to provide teachers with information about structuring their classroom activities to preempt challenges or problems. Our contention is that effective management is facilitated through (1) clear communication and consistent implementation of routines, (2) explicit statement of rules, (3) establishing and maintaining schedules, (4) attending to the communicative interactions involved in instructional grouping, (5) designing physical space which promotes classroom interaction, and (6) selecting materials which match student need and support instructional activities.

REVIEW QUESTIONS

1. Define routines. How are routines established? Describe the distinctions between rules and routines.

2. What is the difference between allocated time and engaged time? What can teachers do to increase students' engaged time?
3. Describe the benefits of careful planning of instructional groups. What should teachers consider as they design groups and monitor group interaction?
4. How can the classroom physical environment inhibit student interaction?
5. Sometimes teachers allow a curriculum or set of materials "drive" the instructional process. What steps can teachers take to prevent this from occurring? *Or* does the careful use of instructional materials provide teachers with a means for organizing instruction? Try to present both sides of this argument.

APPLICATION ACTIVITY

Yinger (1979) observed that routines serve to establish and regulate instructional activities as well as help teachers and students cope with classroom complexity by increasing the predictability of instruction. In this activity, you will attempt to discern the routines used by a classroom teacher through observations and interviews.

This activity may be completed in several ways. It might be most beneficial to observe a classroom over at least a three-day period during a certain part of the school day (e.g., mornings before school starts until lunchtime). In this manner, you will be able to observe consistency in routines over time. Another way to complete this activity is to observe a classroom teacher for an entire day. This type of observation would yield information regarding consistency in routines across tasks.

Unfortunately, it is unlikely that you will be able to observe a teacher as he or she first establishes specific routines. However, you might observe some modifications to certain routine as the teacher makes adjustments based on the students' participation or instructional needs. As you complete this activity, be sure to address the following issues:

❖ Describe various kinds of routines: management routines, support routines, and exchange routines. During what types of activities are management routines most evident?

❖ How does the teacher communicate routines? Does he or she use a specific phrase, a certain posture, or position in the classroom (as in the "stop and freeze" routine)?

❖ How are changes in routines communicated to students? What evidence of flexibility did you observe? How do students react to changes in routines?

As always, include specific examples in your response to support your statements. Summarize your response by describing your impression of the teacher's consistency and flexibility in his or her use of routines. What are your thoughts about the teacher as an effective manager of classroom interaction?

REFERENCES

BLOOME, D., & KNOTT, G. (1985). Teacher-student discourse. In D. N. Ripich & F. M. Spinelli (Eds.), *School discourse problems* (pp. 53–76). San Diego, CA: College Hill Press.

BROOKS, D. M. (1985). The teacher's communicative competence: The first day of school. *Theory into Practice, 24*, 63–70.

BROOKS, D. M., & WOOLFOLK, A. E. (1987). The effects of students' nonverbal behavior on teachers. *Elementary School Journal, 88*, 52–63.

BROPHY, J. (1982). How teachers influence what is taught and learned in classrooms. *Elementary School Journal, 83*, 1–13.

BROPHY, J., ROHRKEMPER, M., RASHID, H., & GOLDBERGER, M. (1983). Relationships between teachers' presentations of classroom tasks and students' engagement in those tasks. *Journal of Educational Psychology, 75*, 522–544.

BROWN, F., HOLVOET, J., GUESS, D., & MULLIGAN, M. (1980). The Individualized Curriculum Sequencing Model (III): Small group instruction. *Journal of the Association for the Severely Handicapped, 5*, 352–367.

BURNS, R. B., & ANDERSON, L. W. (1987). The activity structure of lesson segments. *Curriculum Inquiry, 17*, 31–53.

COHEN, B. S., ALBERTO, P. A., & TROUTMAN, A. (1979). Selecting and developing educational materials: An inquiry model. *Teaching Exceptional Children, 12*(1), 7–11.

COOPER, C. R., MARQUIS, A., & AYERS-LOPEZ, S. (1982). Peer learning in the classroom: Tracing developmental patterns and consequences of children's spontaneous interactions. In L. C. Wilkinson (Ed.), *Communicating in the classroom* (pp. 69–83). New York: Academic Press.

DOYLE, W. (1984). How order is achieved in classrooms: An interim report. *Journal of Curriculum Studies, 16*, 259–277.

DUNN, R., DUNN, K., PRIMAVERA, L., SINATRA, R. & VIROSTKO, J. (1987). A timely solution: Effects of chronobiology on achievement and behavior. *The Clearing House, 61*, 508.

ENGLEMANN, S. (1982). Dear Ziggy. *Direct Instruction News, 1*(3), 9.

ENGLERT, C. S. (1984). Measuring teacher effectiveness from the teacher's point of view. *Focus on Exceptional Children, 17*(2), 1–14.

ERICKSON, F. (1982). Classroom discourse as improvisation: relationships between academic task structure and social participation structure in lessons. In L. C. Wilkinson (Ed.), *Communicating in classrooms* (pp. 153–181). New York: Academic Press.

EVERTSON, C. M., & EMMER, E. T. (1982). Effective management at the beginning of the year in junior high classes. *Journal of Educational Psychology, 74*(4), 485–498.

GOOD, T. L. (1983). Classroom research: A decade of progress. *Educational Psychologist, 18*(3), 127–144.

GREEN, J. L., & SMITH, D. (1983). Teaching and learning: A linguistic perspective. *Elementary School Journal, 83*, 353–391.

HILL, J., YINGER, R. & ROBINS, D. (1983). Instructional planning in a laboratory pre-school. *Elementary School Journal, 83*, 182–193.

HOWELL, K., & MOREHEAD, M. K. (1987). *Curriculum-based evaluation in special and remedial education.* Columbus, OH: Charles E. Merrill.

JOHNSON, L. V. E., & BANY, M. A. (1970). *Classroom management: Theory and skill training.* New York: Macmillan.

KAVALE, K. A., & FORNESS, S. R. (1986). School learning, time, and learning disabilities. *Journal of Learning Disabilities, 19*, 130–138.

LEINHARDT, G., WEIDMAN, C., & HAMMOND, K. M. (1987). Introduction and integration of classroom routines by expert teachers. *Curriculum Inquiry, 17*(2), 135–176.

LEVINE, H. G., & MANN, K. (1985). The nature and functions of teacher talk in a classroom for mentally retarded learners. *Elementary School Journal, 86*, 185–198.

MARING, G. H., & FURLONG, G. C. (1985). Seven "whole class" strategies to help mainstreaming young people, read better in content area classes. *Journal of Reading, 28*, 694–700.

MCDERMOTT, R. P. (1982). Social relations as contexts for learning in school. In E. Bredo & W. Feinberg (Eds.), *Knowledge and values in social and educational research* (pp. 252–270). Philadelphia: Temple University Press. (Originally published in *Harvard Educational Review, 47*(2), 198–213, 1977.)

NELSON, N. W. (1985). Teacher talk and child listening—Fostering a better match. In C. S. Simon (Ed.), *Communication skills and classroom success* (pp. 65–104). San Diego, CA: College Hill Press.

NEWMAN, R. G. (1982). A primer on subgroups. *The Pointer, 26*(3), 8–12.

POLLOWAY, E. A., CRONIN, M. E., & PATTON, J. R. (1986). The efficacy of group versus one-to-one instruction: A review. *Remedial and Special Education, 7*(1), 22–30.

Project STRETCH, (1980). *Grouping and special students.* Northbrook, IL: Hubbard.

PURO, P., & BLOOME, D. (1987). Understanding classroom communication. *Theory into Practice, 26* (Special Issue), 26–31.

ROHRKEMPER, M. (1985). Individual differences in students' perceptions of routine classroom events. *Journal of Educational Psychology, 77*, 29–44.

ROSENFIELD, P., LAMBERT, N. M., & BLACK, A. (1985). Desk arrangement effects on pupil classroom behavior. *Journal of Educational Psychology, 77*, 101–108.

ROSENSHINE, B. V. (1980). How time is spent in elementary classrooms. In C. Denham & A. Liberman (Eds.), *Time to learn* (pp. 107–126). Washington, DC: National Institute of Education.

SCHNIEDEWIND, N., & SALEND, S. J. (1987). Cooperative learning works. *Teaching Exceptional Children, 19*(2), 22–25.

SHAVELSON, R. J., & STERN, P. (1981). Research on teachers' pedagogical thoughts, judgments, decisions, and behavior. *Review of Educational Research, 51*, 455–498.

SHEA, T. M., & BAUER, A. M. (1987). *Teaching children and youth with behavior disorders*. Englewood Cliffs, NJ: Prentice Hall.

SHULTZ, J., & FLORIO, S. (1979). Stop and freeze: The negotiation of social and physical space in a kindergarten/first grade classroom. *Anthropology and Education Quarterly, 10*, 166–181.

SMITH, R. A. (1987). A teacher's views on cooperative learning. *Phi Delta Kappan, 68*, 663–666.

SMYTH, V. (1979). Speech reception in the presence of classroom noise. *Language, Speech, and Hearing Services in Schools, 10*, 221–230.

WEADE, R. (1987). Curriculum 'n' instruction: The construction of meaning. *Theory into Practice, 26*, 15–25.

WEINSTEIN, C. S. (1979). The physical environment of the school: A review of the research. *Review of Educational Research, 49*(4), 557–619.

WILLIAMS, R. (1988a). New Zealand: A visit to the classroom. *The Whole Idea, 1*(1), 4–5.

———. (1988b). A visit to the classroom: Canada. *The Whole Idea, 1*(2), 6–7.

YINGER, R. (1979). Routines in teacher planning. *Theory into Practice, 18*, 163–169.

ZENTALL, S. S. (1983). Learning environments: A review of physical and temporal factors. *Exceptional Education Quarterly, 4*(2), 90–115.

CHAPTER FIVE

Managing Classroom Events Through Patterns of Interaction

SITUATIONS

Setting: Fourth grade social studies class.

Teacher: Folks, if I could please have your attention [holds up one hand, and keeps it up until all students have made eye contact]. It's time to begin to wrap up your groups. You have five minutes, then we're back as a whole committee. [Students gather together papers, pencils, begin to move chairs into a single group.] Thank you for getting together so quickly. Reports of chairpersons? Roberto, start us off.

Roberto: We finished working on our report on religion, and Joel is going to be responsible for writing it up. We were going to start our report on food, but still need to figure out if we're going to talk about breakfast, lunch, and dinner, or do it with food groups.

Teacher: I think those are both great ways to organize your report. Listing "pros" and "cons" seems to be your step for tomorrow. Rachel, how about your group?

*   *   *

Setting: Senior high school biology class.

Teacher: Since this is the first day of lab, I want to go over some the procedures that we'll be following. To help you remember, I'm going to give you each a sheet that describes lab procedures. I'm passing the stapler around so that you can staple it into the front of your lab manuals like so [teacher holds up a copy of the manual with procedure sheet staple in appropriate place, and then begins to circulate the stapler].

Teacher: [Reading] The first procedure is to remove from the shelf only the equipment and materials needed to complete the activity. After a piece or equipment or material is no longer needed, please return it to the shelf. [Looking up at students] Why would it be so important to do this? [Responding to a raised hand] Michael?

Michael: So stuff doesn't get in the way?

Teacher: That's part of the reason. Anybody else? Susan?

Susan: There are a lot of people in this class and maybe not that much equipment?

Teacher: That's really observant. It wouldn't be efficient to have little jars of substances needed for the investigations for each lab pair. So, people need to take larger jars to their places, use what they need, and replace the larger jars. Michael is also right, in that a cluttered lab table makes it much easier to break things, knock things over, and make messes none of us wants to clean up. So, remember, only remove from the shelf the equipment and materials needed to complete the activity. After a piece or equipment or material is not longer needed, please return it to the shelf. [Pausing] Who's ready to read the next procedure?

In these examples, the teacher is using or teaching routines to facilitate classroom interaction. In the first situation, the routines of moving from small group to large group activities are in place so that students move efficiently, and the transition between parts of the activity are smooth. In the second situation, the teacher is rehearsing and teaching the routines for laboratory periods. In this chapter, using routines to structure classroom events will be discussed as part of the "preparatory" phase for instructional activities. Patterns that emerge in classroom events will also be discussed.

SELF-EVALUATION

Indicate whether you agree or disagree with each statement:

1. Students should be informed of the purpose of the activity before initiating the activity.
2. Routines are extremely useful during transitions between instructional activities.
3. Classroom activities may be focused around ideas presented by the teacher or student.
4. Patterns of interaction in classroom activities include the teacher, students, and some material or instructional problem to be addressed.
5. Through scaffolding, teachers can form student responses to their ends.
6. A smooth flow of classroom events is facilitated by clear markings of beginnings and endings of activities.
7. By reducing the amount of time a teacher waits for a student to respond, the teacher can present a greater amount of instructional material.
8. Disruptions in the natural flow of classroom events often occur because teachers give students warnings that transitions are going to occur.

KEY WORDS

preparation

closure

advance organizer

language of practice

practitioner

participants

place

scaffolding

dialogue

wait time

OBJECTIVES

After completing this chapter, you will be able to:

1. Describe the preparation, activity, and closure phases of classroom events.
2. Describe student-teacher interaction patterns which occur during the preparation phase.
3. Describe the three forms of student-teacher interaction patterns which occur during the activity phase.
4. Describe instructional strategies or techniques which may occur during any form of student-teacher interactional patterns evident in the activity phase.
5. Describe the interaction patterns which occur during the closure phase of classroom events.
6. Recognize the pattern-to-pattern flow which occurs during classroom events.

Objective One: *To Describe the Preparation, Activity, and Closure Phases of Classroom Events*

As discussed in Chapter Four, the school day is comprised of activities. The general structure of an activity includes a preparation phase (also referred to in the literature as "setup" or "getting ready"), the activity itself (also referred to as "lesson" or "focused time"), and closure (also referred to as "take down" or "windup") (Shultz and Florio, 1979; Yinger, 1979).

During the preparation phase, materials are distributed, students are directed to certain locations in the room, desks are rearranged, and other logistical needs for the lesson are met. During the lesson itself, the whole class, small group, or individual is involved in content-specific information. During the closure or transition phase, presenting new information ceases, assignments are made, and summarization or repetition takes place. This closure phase ends when the teacher dismisses the class, announces that the lesson is finished, or uses a signal (bell) to demonstrate that the activity is over. The relationship of these three phases and their components are depicted in Table 5.1. In the following objectives, the interaction patterns that occur during each of the three phases are described. Referring to the table throughout the following material may be helpful in developing a sense of the flow between the phases.

Objective Two: *To Describe Interaction Patterns That Occur During the Preparation Phase*

During the preparation phase, the teacher paves the way for the activity to take place. Kallison (1986) found that the use of explicit organization increases students' ability to participate successfully in activities. Rosenberg's (1986) research suggests that preceding the activity with a review of the rules tends to create greater academic focus and greater efficiency. In this preparation phase, Maclennan (1987) suggests that teachers increase student involvement in an activity to decrease the "stir factor" of opening a new activity.

Activities can be initiated explicitly through the use of advance organizers. Ausubel and Robinson (1969) defined an advance organizer as material that is presented "in advance of and at a higher level of generality, inclusiveness, and abstraction than the learning task itself" (p. 606) to increase knowledge about the clarity and organization of an activity. In her study of the use of advance organizers with listening comprehension tasks, Reis (1986) noted that comprehension improved when students were given organizers which included information relevant to the story as well as statements regarding the purpose of the task.

Lenz, Alley, and Schumaker (1987) suggest that teachers can build advance organizers into part of their presentation or train

TABLE 5.1 The Three Phases of Classroom Activities

Phase I: *Preparation*
  ❖ Teacher paves the way for the activity through the use of explicit statements and advance organizers.

Phase II: *Activity*
  ❖ Practitioner focused, participant focused, or place focused.
  ❖ Scaffolding.
  ❖ Dialogue.
  ❖ Wait time.

Phase III: *Closure*
  ❖ Review.
  ❖ Guided or independent practice.
  ❖ Summarizing to clarify relationships.

students to generate advance organizers internally by encouraging students to ask themselves questions and select information to prepare them for the activity. Whether they are externally generated by the teacher or internally generated by the student, advance organizers precede the activity itself and may incorporate several different components. The range of possible components of an advanced organizer (to be used either singly or in combination) is presented in Table 5.2.

In their review, Lenz, Alley, and Schumaker found advance organizers to be experimentally validated teaching tools. However, they also found that teachers rarely employ them.

In the first phase of an activity, then, teachers set the stage for the actual activity to be pursued. Effective interaction patterns for this phase include explicitness and the use of advance organizers.

Objective Three: *To Describe the Three Forms of Interaction Patterns That Occur During the Activity Phase*

The activity phase is the "action" phase of each classroom event. In describing the activity phase, we are choosing to describe a "language of practice" developed from our work in classrooms with teacher collaborators in research. The language of practice refers to the models of thinking and acting employed by practitioners to accomplish the tasks at hand effectively (Yinger, 1987). In this way, our discussion is grounded in the actions which teachers perform rather than the language for their performances.

There are three basic components of the activity phase: the practitioner (whoever is assuming the role of the teacher at the time), participants (whoever is assuming the role of the learner), and the

TABLE 5.2 Components of Advance Organizers

> ❖ Inform the learner of the purpose of the advance organizer itself.
> ❖ Clarify the physical limits of the teacher's actions.
> ❖ Clarify the physical limits of the students' action.
> ❖ Identify the topic of the activity.
> ❖ Provide students with background information.
> ❖ State the concepts to be learned through the activity.
> ❖ Motivate students through a rationale for the activity.
> ❖ Introduce or review new terms or words.
> ❖ Provide an organizational framework for the activity.
> ❖ State desired outcomes of the activity.

Source note: This table was constructed from an article by B. K. Lenz, G. R. Alley, and J. B. Schumaker, "Activating the Inactive Learner: Advance Organizers in the Secondary Content Classroom," *Learning Disability Quarterly, 10,* 53–67, 1987. The table does not exist in the original publication.

place (the data, task, problem, material, or social issue which is to be dealt with). In our work to describe the "patterns of practice" which teachers use in their classrooms (Truax, Bauer, and Sapona, 1988), we found that these three components interacted within three basic patterns. Patterns were differentiated by their emphasis. Each pattern includes all three components, yet the point of primary focus for each pattern differs. The activity phase may take its form or focus through some action by the practitioner, an action by the participant, or by the presence of the place (i.e., some task, problem, or material). We called these three kinds of patterns practitioner focused, participant focused, and place focused. These jointly constructed patterns of interaction which comprise the activity phase are depicted in Figure 5.1.

Practitioner-Focused Patterns. These patterns represent activities such as traditional expository teaching. The lead practitioner presents the place or problem through any of a variety of techniques. (Note that the lead practitioner may be the teacher or a student assuming the teacher role.) This pattern may include activities such as lecture, multimedia presentation, or demonstration. For example, in teaching algebra, the practitioner may lecture on the steps necessary to solve a problem. The nature of the interaction may be the lead practitioner reconstructing the place or problem through questions. That is, the practitioner may model the problem-solving process (making errors, talking through strategies for handling errors) as he or she works through a problem that has not previously been solved. Some of the patterns which may occur within this basic pattern are included in the representation of the interaction in Figure 5.2. Activities employing these patterns are described in Chapters Six and Seven.

Place-Focused Patterns. These patterns represent activities such as inquiry learning (Suchman, 1964) and inductive thinking activities (Taba, Durkin, Fraenkel, and McNaughton, 1971). The activity is framed or focused by the participant's confrontation with

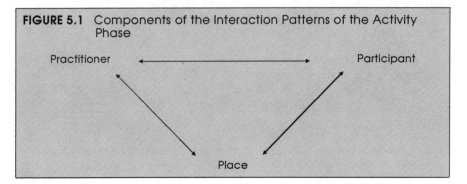

FIGURE 5.1 Components of the Interaction Patterns of the Activity Phase

Practitioner ⟷ Participant

Place

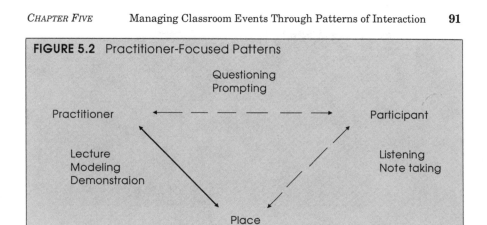

FIGURE 5.2 Practitioner-Focused Patterns

the contextual variables of the community, classroom, school, curriculum, text, problem, or data. The primary interaction is between the participant and the place. For example, in science class, the participant may be presented with five rocks and directed to determine whether they are igneous, sedimentary, or metamorphic. The activities employing these patterns are described in Chapter Eight. This interactional pattern is represented in Figure 5.3.

Participant-Focused Patterns. These patterns represented activities which take their form from or are focused by the participant. In these activities, the primary interaction is between the participant and the place. Although the primary interaction is between the participant and the place, as was evident in the "place-focused patterns," the key distinction of this pattern is degree of control of the activity by the participant/learner. For example, while the practitioner may provide the overall context, such as "writing" or constructing an experiment to discover properties of iron, the participant initiates the activity by generating the content or developing a strategy to address the place or problem. Activities employing these interactional patterns are described in Chapters Nine and Ten. This pattern is represented in Figure 5.4.

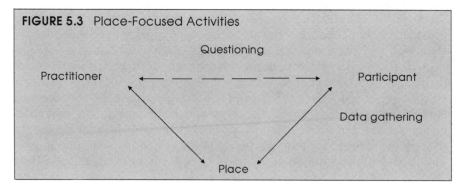

FIGURE 5.3 Place-Focused Activities

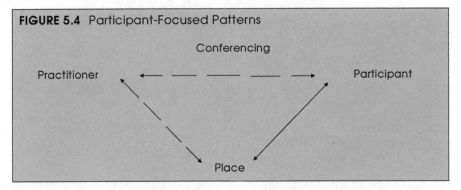

FIGURE 5.4 Participant-Focused Patterns

Conferencing

Practitioner ←— —— —— —— —→ Participant

Place

The three basic interactional patterns described will serve as the framework for the remainder of the book. In each of the remaining chapters, one of the three sets of patterns will be discussed.

Objective Four: *To Describe Instructional Strategies or Techniques That May Occur During Any Form of Student-Teacher Interactional Patterns Evident in the Activity Phase*

Although a wide range of strategies and techniques may be applied within each of these patterns, some teaching methods can be used throughout the phases. Williams (1981) contends that not only is there a wide variety of teaching methods available for use in all classrooms, but that each teacher responds differently in the classroom, applying methods in a unique way related to teaching style. Through selecting certain methods, teachers can communicate that the goal of instruction is "learning" rather than "work" (Marshall, 1987).

In *scaffolding* (Applebee and Langer, 1983), a technique that cuts across the patterns described, the teacher provides support to the student while performing the task. Scaffolding provides students with the support they need to carry off the task successfully. Through the use of instructional scaffolds, teachers determine the difficulties a new activity may pose, select activities to overcome the difficulty, and structure the activity as a whole to make the strategies explicit. Through scaffolds, the student's intended outcome is supported (Searle, 1984). The use of scaffolding to support classroom interactions will be illustrated in later chapters (Eight and Nine).

Dialogue is another technique which may be used throughout the three sets of interaction patterns. Dialogue is "collaborative interaction carried out through language" (Genishi, McCarrier, and Nussbaum, 1988). Informative dialogue begins with the students' difficulties which occur as they address academic tasks or problems (the place). Through dialogue, teachers can promote thinking by providing stimulating questions. In addition, Genishi et al. suggest that teachers can encourage development through dialogue by generating changes in oral and written language (that is, making decisions about when something is "teachable" and when it is not). The structure of dialogue, however, remains child centered, with teaching occurring as children use materials, work with others, see demonstrations, and talk with teachers.

In each of the interaction patterns described, teachers participate and use multiple intertwined strategies. Marshall (1987) suggests that the teacher increase the awareness of the importance of the activity through framing the lesson to provide initial motivation. Throughout the activity, attention is refocused and redirected to support the learning orientation. Responsibility for learning and evaluation is shared, which usually amounts to the teacher making efforts to increase student ownership of the learning process.

As noted in our discussion of facilitative teaching in Chapter Two, the use of "wait time" has been found to be extremely influential in student-teacher interactional patterns (Mirenda and Donnellan, 1986). In a comprehensive review of wait time studies, Rowe (1986) defined two types of wait time: the amount of time teachers wait for a student's reply after asking a question and the amount of time teachers wait to ask another question after a student responds. A short wait time has significant consequences for students in the class. Typically, when a teacher uses a short wait time for a response, a small number of students are responsible for a majority of the responses. By extending wait time to 3 seconds, Rowe reported an increase in the number of students who actively participate in the instructional interaction. An extended wait time also yields more thoughtful and elaborate responses from students, greater attention to other students when they were responding, a reduction in failures to respond, and an increase in students' confidence in their answers. Rowe also found effects for teachers including greater flexibility in their responses, an increase in the types of questions requiring more elaborate student responses, and improvements in expectations for student responses.

Finally, Rowe suggested that the changes which occur when wait time is increased can be best understood through a model of classroom interaction as a game between the teacher and a set of students. The moves in this game include structuring (giving directions, describing procedures), soliciting (asking questions), responding, and reacting. As in most games, satisfaction is high when all players have access to the moves. In a classroom with short wait time, the teacher is in control of three of the moves: structuring, soliciting, and reacting. However, by increasing wait time, students have access to all four moves, thus yielding a more positive classroom interaction.

Tobin (1986) notes another benefit to increases in wait time particularly when the content or subject matter is more difficult. A longer wait time gives students an opportunity to think about what the teacher has said and assimilate that new knowledge into previously held information. For teachers, a longer wait time provides an opportunity to make decisions about courses of action (such as rephrasing a question, calling on another student, moving on to another activity). Tobin's study of teacher wait time in sixth and seventh grade math and language arts lessons supports Rowe's findings regarding an increase in questions requiring elaborate answers and improvements in the quality of teacher-student interaction. Tobin suggests that by maintaining an average wait time of from 3 to 5 seconds, the quality of the learning environment can be improved, accompanied by enhanced student achievement.

Objective Five: *To Describe the Interactions That Occur in the Closure Phase of Classroom Events*

In contrast to a view of the "closure" phase as summarization and review of an instructional activity, most studies examined transitions between activities rather than report specific interactions which occur during closure. One reason for this lack of information could be the difficulty in determining boundaries between activities (e.g., Doyle, 1984). Kallison (1986), for example, describes organizational behaviors that cut across lessons which result in improvement in student achievement. These behaviors include (1) identifying the organizational structure of the lesson at the beginning of the instructional activity, (2) using transitional statements which draw attention to the organizational structure of an instructional activity, (3) making statements which point out similarities and differences between parts of a lesson, and (4) using a summary at the conclusion of a lesson to clarify relationships.

Types of closure activities may include review in the form of guided or independent practice during which the teacher circulates among students to check for their understanding of new information. Others have suggested that lessons begin with a review (through homework check, as described by Rosenshine and Stevens, 1986) or as a part of an advance organizer (Lenz, Alley, and Schumaker, 1987). Despite the lack of research, we suggest that when new information is presented during an instructional activity, the teacher should end the interaction with a brief review and summarization.

In his observation of student teachers of classes grades 1 through 9, Arlin (1979) noted that teachers who are effective managers have been observed to mark beginnings and endings of activities clearly. Student teachers who did not notice the impending end of a class session would often fail to "wrap up" the lessons which frequently resulted in dismissing students with chaotic results. Doyle's work with junior high school English teachers (1984) supports Arlin's finding that successful managers had distinct patterns and clear signals for opening and closing lessons. (Recall the "stop and freeze" signal used by the teacher in the Shultz and Florio, 1979 study.) What follows is a more detailed discussion of interactional patterns that occur during transitions between activities.

Objective Six: *To Recognize the Pattern-to-Pattern Flow That Occurs During Classroom Events*

As Yinger (1979) suggests, most of the school day is spent in activities. There is a flow between activities which can be facilitated through improving transitions. Arlin (1979) defines transition as "a teacher-initiated directive to students to end one activity and to start another" (p. 42). Smith (1984) suggests that effective transitions are usually initiated and ended by a clear, verbal statement made by the teacher, and supported by unambiguous, nonverbal signals such as changes in posture and level of bodily activity. Teachers who prepare their students for transition in advance are also more likely to be successful, as noted in the first situation described at the beginning of the chapter ("It's time to begin to wrap up your groups. You have 5 minutes; then we're back as a whole class"). Instructions during transitions are usually issued in logical order and in small, discrete units. Teachers who effectively use transitions usually wait for instructions to be carried out before continuing to the next segment of work. Remaining on task and avoiding extraneous matters facilitates transitions. Finally, a general awareness of students' activities is necessary when moving from activity to activity.

Breakdowns in transitions seriously impede the flow of activities in a classroom. Effective and efficient transitions seem particularly troublesome for beginning teachers. However, the use of clearly established routines to facilitate transitions would result in smoother flow between activities. Leinhardt, Weidman, and Hammond (1987), in their study of six expert teachers, found that most routines were used during transition times. Management routines such as "line up" and "no talking" were most prevalent during transitions. Support routines such as "take out/put away" and "collect/distribute" were also heavily used, as were preparatory routines such as "wait to start." As Arlin (1979) suggests, the use of advance preparation, "wrapups," wait time before proceding to the next activity, and followthrough on teacher directives appears to facilitate smooth transitions. We would add that clearly established routines for these teacher behaviors would help to maintain the pattern-to-pattern flow between classroom events. Finally, teachers who spend time explaining and rehearsing such routines at the beginning of the school year are more likely to be successful in managing classroom activities throughout the year (Emmer, Evertson, and Anderson, 1980; Evertson, and Emmer, 1982; Evertson, Emmer, Sanford, and Clements, 1983).

SUMMARY

The purpose of this chapter was to introduce the notion of patterns of interaction which occur in classrooms. First, three phases of classroom events were briefly described: preparation, activity, and closure. The explicit presentation of advance organizers was recommended during preparation activities. By providing students with the purpose of an activity as well as information about what is to occur during the instructional event, student attention and participation is facilitated. A clear summary or wrapup during the closure phase of an activity is also recommended.

Three forms of interaction patterns can be observed during the activity phase of an instructional event. Each pattern consists of the practitioner (whoever assumes the role of the teacher for that event), the participant (learner), and a place (data, material, or instructional problem to be addressed). These patterns are distinguished by the focal point of the activity. Practitioner-focused patterns represent activities such as traditional expository teaching. Place-focused patterns and participant-focused patterns revolve around the participant's confrontation with the place or instructional problem. The distinction, in this case, is based upon where the problem originated. For example, participant-focused patterns involve activities such as writing workshop or generating a project idea. Place-focused patterns are typically set by the teacher and involve activities such as inquiry learning and inductive thinking.

A further distinction can be shown through the following examples. A practitioner-focused pattern might include a teacher lecturing on features of rocks while students listen and take notes. A place-focused pattern involves the teacher setting the problem. In this example, the teacher would set out five different rocks and ask the students to determine whether they are igneous, sedimentary, or metamorphic. The teacher might then guide the students to classifying the data or material (the rocks) through experimentation. A participant-focused pattern might include a situation in which a student would like to do a science fair project on the rock formations characteristic of his community.

There are a number of strategies and techniques that can be used across patterns of interaction. Scaffolding, or providing supports to students as they work through activities, was briefly mentioned. The use of dialogue and wait time was also described and the benefits of these techniques were presented. Finally, the pattern-to-pattern flow of activities was discussed. It was noted that smooth transitions between classroom events are facilitated through the effective use of routines.

REVIEW QUESTIONS

1. Describe the advantages of the use of advance organizers during the preparation phase of a classroom events. What are characteristics of effective advance organizers?
2. Three patterns of interactions among practitioner, participant, and place were described. How are the patterns alike? What distinguishes the patterns from each other?
3. Suggest a situation in which a classroom event might include all three patterns. Describe potential benefits and/or problems involved in using all three patterns in one lesson.
4. The extension of "wait time" frequently yields positive benefits to students and teachers. List advantages to students. How does the teacher's interactional style change when wait time is extended?
5. Transitions between instructional activities are sometimes difficult for beginning teachers. Suggest several techniques that a teacher might use to provide for smooth transitions between classroom events.

APPLICATION ACTIVITY

Yinger (1987) refers to a "language of practice" as models of thinking and acting employed by practitioners to accomplish tasks at hand effectively. By grounding discussion of interactional patterns in the actions which teachers perform, it is expected that readers will learn to recognize patterns and design instructional activities which are most effective in facilitating student learning. In this activity, you will attempt to determine patterns of interaction used by a classroom teacher during the activity phase of lessons.

This activity will be completed in over several days of observation. First, you will be asked to make global observations of interactions during a specific time period. After gaining a sense of what is happening during that time period, more focused observations will be required.

Initial, Global Observations

Select an observational period that involves the presentation of a specific content. It might be most beneficial to observe during math, science, or social studies periods. Describe the "actors" and the problem (data, material) evident in the instructional event. How does the teacher manage to engage the students in the content? Do all students participate? Of the three patterns described in the chapter, what pattern is most evident?

Focused Observations

After you've established the most frequently used patterns, select one pattern for more focused observations. Given the techniques mentioned in the chapter, describe how the teacher uses scaffolding to support student learning. Does the teacher use "wait time" effectively? Finally, describe how the teacher makes transitions between activities. To what extent are routines used in transitions? Are these routines similar to those routines used in transitions between other activities?

Summarize your response by describing the personal discoveries made as you became more focused in your observations. Does looking for patterns help you make sense of the classroom events?

REFERENCES

APPLEBEE, A. N. & LANGER, J. A. (1983). Instructional scaffolding: Reading and writing as natural language activities. *Language Arts, 60,* 168–175.

ARLIN, M. (1979). Teacher transitions can disrupt time flow in classrooms. *American Educational Research Journal, 16,* 42–56.

AUSUBEL, D. P. & ROBINSON, F. G. (1969). *School learning: An introduction to educational psychology.* New York: Holt, Rinehart and Winston.

DOYLE, W. (1984). How order is achieved in classrooms: An interim report. *Journal of Curriculum Studies, 16,* 259–277.

EMMER, E. T., EVERTSON, C. M., & ANDERSON, L. M. (1980). Effective classroom management at the beginning of the school year. *Elementary School Journal, 80,* 219–231.

EVERTSON, C. M., & EMMER, E. T. (1982). Effective management at the beginning of the school year in junior high classes. *Journal of Educational Psychology, 74,* 485–498.

EVERTSON, C. M., EMMER, E. T., SANFORD, J. P., & CLEMENTS, B. S. (1983). Improving classroom management: An experiment in elementary school classrooms. *Elementary School Journal, 84,* 173–188.

GENISHI, C., MCCARRIER, A. & NUSSBAUM, N. R. (1988). Research currents: Dialogue as a context for teaching and learning. *Language Arts, 65* (2), 182–191.

KALLISON, J. M. (1986). Effects of lesson organization on achievement. *American Educational Research Journal, 23*, 337–347.

LEINHARDT, G., WEIDMAN, C., & HAMMOND, K. M. (1987). Introduction and integration of classroom routines by expert teachers. *Curriculum Inquiry, 17*, 135–176.

LENZ, B. K., ALLEY, G. R., & SCHUMAKER, J. B. (1987). Activating the inactive learner: Advance organizers in the secondary content classroom. *Learning Disability Quarterly, 10*, 53–67.

MACLENNAN, S. (1987). Integrating lesson planning and class management. *ELT Journal, 41*, 193–197.

MARSHALL, H. H. (1987). Building a learning orientation. *Theory into Practice, 26*, 8–14.

MIRENDA, P. L., & DONNELLAN, A. M. (1986). Effects of adult interaction style on conversational behavior in students with severe communication problems. *Language, Speech, and Hearing Services in the Schools, 176*, 126–141.

PALINCSAR, A. S. (1986). The role of dialogue in providing scaffolded instruction. *Educational Psychologist, 21*, 73–98.

REIS, E. M. (1986). Advance organizers and listening comprehension in retarded and nonretarded individuals. *Education and Training of the Mentally Retarded, 21*, 245–251.

ROSENBERG, M. S. (1986). Maximizing the effectiveness of structured classroom management programs: Implementing rule-review procedures with disruptive and distractible students. *Behavioral Disorders, 11*, 239–248.

ROSENSHINE, B., & STEVENS, R. (1986). Teaching functions in M. C. Wittrock (Ed.), *Handbook of research on teaching* (pp. 376–391). New York: Macmillan.

ROWE, M. B. (1986). Wait time: Slowing down may be a way of speeding up. *Journal of Teacher Education, 37*(1), 43–50.

SEARLE, D. (1984). Scaffolding: Who's building whose building? *Language Arts, 61*, 480–483.

SHULTZ, J., & FLORIO, S. (1979). Stop and freeze: The negotiation of social and physical space in a kindergarten/first grade classroom. *Anthropology and Education Quarterly, 10*, 166–181.

SMITH, H. A. (1984). The marking of transitions by more and less effective teachers. *Theory Into Practice, 24*(1), 57–62.

SUCHMAN, J. (1964). Studies in inquiry training. In R. Ripple & V. Rockcastle, (Eds.), *Piaget rediscovered* (pp. 105–108). Ithaca, NY: Cornell University Press.

TABA, H., DURKIN, M. C., FRAENKEL, J. R., & MCNAUGHTON, A. H. (1971). *A teacher's handbook for elementary social studies: An inductive approach*. Reading, MA: Addison Wesley.

TOBIN, K. (1986). Effects of teacher wait time on discourse characteristics in mathematics and language arts classes. *American Educational Research Journal, 23*, 191–200.

TRUAX, R. R., BAUER, A. M. & SAPONA, R. H. (1988). *A language of practice for special education*, Working paper. University of Cincinnati.

WILLIAMS, R. O. (1981). What teaching methods when? *Theory into Practice, 19*, 82–86.

YINGER, R. (1979). Routines in teacher planning. *Theory into Practice, 18*, 163–169.

YINGER, R. J. (1987). Learning the language of practice. *Curriculum Inquiry, 17*, 293–318.

CHAPTER SIX

Direct Instruction and Mastery Learning

SITUATION

Setting: Fourth grade classroom, beginning of mathematics class.

Teacher: Okay, we're ready to begin. You need to have your papers from yesterday ready to check. Let's go around the group, and each of you take a turn giving us the answer to the problem. Let's start with Michael.

Michael: Number 1, 24.

Teacher: Fine. Luis?

Luis: Eighteen.

Teacher: Alright. Next?

Melanie: Thirteen.

Teacher: [Pauses, nods to next student] Next?

James: Five.

Teacher: Let's put it on the board. James, work through it with me. Everybody, watch the process we're using to work this problem.

*　　　*　　　*

In this example, the teacher opens her lesson with a direct instruction "teaching function" (Rosenshine, 1983). She begins with a daily review, checking the previous day's work, and re-teaching an error. Direct instruction and mastery learning, the activities described in this chapter, focus heavily on basic skills achievement and use student achievement as the basic measure for judging the worth of a given teaching technique (Bickel and Bickel, 1986).

A central message of direct instruction activities is the empowerment of the teacher, who is actively, directly engaged in the teaching-learning process (Bickel and Bickel, 1986). In view of the teacher's power and control in these activities, they should be applied cautiously and with ongoing self-evaluation. Cazden, Cox, Dickinson, Steinberg, and Stone (1979) contend that teaching is an assumed role which involves communication of information that the teacher knows and the learner does not. Teaching, then, is an asymmetrical relationship: it is a performance that requires the complementary performances of at least one other person who is willing to be taught. McDermott (1982) goes so far as to say that teaching is invariably a form of coercion. In order to teach, students must trust that the teacher's coercion is in their best interest.

Given the teacher's power and control within direct instruction activities, perceptions of the teacher's activities should be monitored carefully. Miramontes, Cheng, and Trueba (1984) found a mismatch between what a teacher reported was occurring in her classroom and what was actually occurring. Whereas the teacher felt she was actively teaching and students were not taking advantage of the opportunity, the researchers found an uncoordinated classroom program providing virtually no instruction.

In this section, two representations of teacher-focused activities are presented. In Chapter Six, direct instruction and mastery learning are explored. In Chapter Seven, behavioral techniques, and the application of these techniques within a self-regulated learning perspective, are described. Although related in terms of the primary instigator of events (i.e., the teacher), direct instruction and behavioral strategies vary in their research base and implementation.

Although the activities described in Chapters Six and Seven are teacher focused, teaching-learning behaviors that occur in any classroom are the products of interactions of the inhabitants of that classroom with one another and with their environment (Copeland, 1982). Copeland cautions teachers beginning to implement new teacher-focused activities that a period of negotiation will occur during which students and teacher sort out their relationships within the activities. He questions research studies on teacher effectiveness that assume that conditions in classrooms are the result of the teacher's influence. In incorporating the activities in this section into your agenda for management, it is important to remember that students and the task at hand are integral components of activities within the teacher-focused patterns.

The reader should also note that this and the following two sections include information that will assist teachers as they set up an overall management agenda for their classrooms. The application activities at the end of each section (in this case, following Chapter Seven) will focus on issues that arise when the overall agenda is somehow disrupted. That is, the framework for dealing with behavioral issues (mentioned in Chapter Three) will provide a focal point for some of the application activities.

The primary purpose of this chapter, as has been noted, is to explore the rationale and research base for activities related to direct instruction and mastery learning. Following examples of implementation of these activities, information will be provided to help the reader evaluate and incorporate these activities into an overall classroom management agenda. Finally, the application activity is designed to assist the reader with observations of instructional events which involve practitioner-focused patterns. The activity is intended to help the reader to recognize the interrelationships among the practitioner (in this case, the teacher), the participants (students), and instructional problem.

SELF-EVALUATION

Please indicate agreement or disagreement with each of the following statements:

1. Careful attention to instructional materials is critical in all teacher-focused activities.
2. The managerial role of the teacher is critical in activities involving direct instruction.
3. Teachers often focus on "covering" materials rather than emphasizing student mastery of materials.
4. Proponents of mastery learning believe that almost all students can learn if they are taught under appropriate conditions.

5. Teachers should always review and reteach concepts and skills before introducing new skills.
6. Teachers should provide carefully worded feedback to student responses.
7. Direct instruction as an approach to teaching requires clear and unambiguous presentation of materials.
8. Teachers should be aware of the artificial nature of some teacher-focused activities and take steps to ensure natural conversational interactions.

KEY WORDS

direct instruction

demonstration

guided practice

feedback

mastery learning

correctives

OBJECTIVES

After completing this chapter, you will be able to:

1. Describe a rationale and research base for direct instruction and mastery learning.
2. Describe research based examples of direct instruction and mastery learning.
3. Prepare and evaluate direct instruction and mastery learning activities to incorporate into your classroom management agenda.
4. Describe the role of direct instruction and mastery learning activities within the context of practitioner- focused interactions.

Objective One: *To Describe a Rationale and Research Base for Direct Instruction and Mastery Learning*

Direct Instruction. Direct instruction refers to patterns of teacher behavior that are correlated with increased student academic performance (Rosenshine and Stevens, 1984). Direct instruction focuses on the teacher and his or her classroom organization with a particular emphasis on how instructional time is used in the classroom. The predominant focus of direct instruction is on learning, with an emphasis on engaging students in academic tasks for a large percentage of time and providing a positive social climate with a high rate of success (Joyce and Weil, 1986).

The cornerstone of direct instruction is the systematic, explicit teaching of academic skills, strategies, and behaviors to students (Gersten, Carnine, and Woodward, 1987; Gersten, Woodward, and Darch, 1986). A key principle in designing direct instruction programs is that teacher presentation and materials must be clear and unambiguous. In direct instruction, a teacher (1) explains a new concept or skill to a large group of students, (2) tests their understanding by practicing under teacher direction, and (3) provides continued practice under teacher guidance.

Rosenshine and Stevens (1984) found that low-performing students repeatedly show high academic achievement when their teachers follow a consistent practice of demonstration, guided practice, and feedback. They suggest, based on their findings, that teachers provide demonstrations using clear, controlled presentations of new materials. Guided practice allows the teacher to ask questions of students, to check for understanding and to provide feedback. Students then work on activities directly related to the new material in independent practice. The use of explicit teacher organization behaviors has been related to increased student achievement by Kallison (1986) who found that explicit organization of the lessons leads to increased achievement.

Rosenshine's (1983) work provides several suggestions for teacher presentation. Materials should be presented in small steps so that one point can be mastered by students before they proceed to another. Many varied examples of new skills or concepts should be provided. In addition, the teacher should model or give narrated demonstrations of the learning task, avoiding digressions and staying on topic. Any difficult points should be reexplained.

Throughout the research on direct instruction, the managerial role of the teacher is emphasized. Student engagement in the activity, for example, was found to be higher when teachers moved directly into the learning task rather than making personal statements to set the tone of the activity (Brophy, Rohrkemper, Rashid, and Goldberger, 1983). In addition, teachers determine the content of what their students learn. Brophy (1982), in his study of the discrepancy between the intended curriculum and the curriculum which students learn, found that teachers may tend to "cover" material rather than teach it to mastery. He found that one of the primary tenets of direct instruction, finding out what students know before teaching, is essentially ignored in practice, with teachers being heavily dependent on commercial publishers for activity content.

Mastery Learning. Mastery learning is an approach to learning based on the philosophy that under the appropriate instructional conditions, virtually all students can learn well what they are taught (Guskey, 1980). Mastery learning is based in part on Carroll's (1963) model for school learning, which suggests that a student's aptitude for a subject was related to the amount of time required by the student to learn the material to a given level. If a student is allowed the time he or she needs to learn a subject, and participates in activities designed to learn the subject, then he or she should learn the subject to the desired level.

Bloom (1976) extended Carroll's work suggesting that if students are presented with structured learning opportunities and more opportunities to learn, a majority of students could learn to mastery. He outlined feedback and corrective procedures which divided the material to be learned during the school year into smaller learning units. The teacher paces these units following instruction with a test or quiz. Corrective activities are assigned following interpretation of the results of the test or quiz. After the completion of these correctives, a second test is administered to ascertain the success of the correctives and to assure student mastery.

Guskey (1987) suggests that mastery learning expresses the belief that all students can learn when provided with conditions that are appropriate for their learning; in order to be called mastery learning, activities must include feedback and correctives with an integration of activities and evaluation.

Objective Two: *To Describe Examples of Teacher-Focused Classroom Structures and Activities*

Direct Instruction. Rosenshine (1983) has provided the most detailed discussed of direct instruction activities in the classroom. He describes these activities as "teaching functions." The six teaching functions are listed in Table 6.1. These functions were derived from a series of research studies exploring teacher presentation and the related student achievement.

REVIEW. The first function Rosenshine describes is that of daily review, which involves checking the previous day's work and reteaching if necessary. The teacher checks homework and reteaches areas where students demonstrated errors, in order to make sure that the

TABLE 6.1   Rosenshine's Teaching Functions

1. Review
2. Presentation of new content or skills
3. Initial student practice
4. Feedback and correctives
5. Student independent practice
6. Weekly and monthly reviews

Source note: This table was constructed from an article by B. Rosenshine, "Teaching Functions in Instructional Program," *Elementary School Journal, 83,* 335–351, 1983. The table does not exist in the original publication.

students are ready to continue with the next lesson. Rosenshine suggests that these activities can be completed through group checking, students' checking other's papers, or teacher questions.

PRESENTING NEW CONTENT AND SKILLS.   During the initial presentation of content, Rosenshine suggests that teachers begin with an overview of the material to be covered. At that point, the teacher should proceed in small steps, and at a rapid pace. Detailed or redundant instructions and explanations are provided as teachers perceive they are needed. As teachers are presenting new skills, however, old skills should be practiced until they are mastered.

To be effective, Rosenshine suggests that material be presented in small steps, with the emphasis on one concept at a time. Topics should be covered to closure before an additional topic is introduced. Organization of presentations is the key, with the emphasis on the group mastering a topic or step before proceeding to the next.

INITIAL STUDENT PRACTICE.   Initial student practice should include frequent questions and overt practice with the teacher and materials. Rosenshine suggests frequent prompts and comprehension checks from the teacher. All students should have a chance to respond to teacher questions and receive feedback. This initial practice should be continued until the students seem firm in the process and a success rate of 80 percent or higher is attained.

To be most effective, Rosenshine suggests that initial student practice include frequent questions with specific answers asked by the teacher. Both group responding and calling on individual students should be used. The teacher should check on the students' understanding frequently.

FEEDBACK AND CORRECTIVES.   In this teaching function, the teacher provides feedback to students, particularly when they are correct, but hesitant. The teacher analyzes student errors as a means of providing feedback on his or her instruction, as to the nature of corrections and reteaching necessary. Corrections may include simplifying questions, giving clues, explaining or reviewing steps, or reteaching the last steps. When necessary, the teacher may need to reteach using smaller steps.

The effective teacher asks new questions when students' responses are correct, quick, and firm. If a student's response is correct, but hesitant, the teacher should provide short feedback. If the response is incorrect, but careless, the teacher should correct the response and move on. When the student's incorrect response is due to a lack of knowledge of the facts or process, the teacher should provide hints and ask the student additional questions.

STUDENT INDEPENDENT PRACTICE. Independent practice assures that students are firm and automatic in their responses. This practice is usually implemented through seatwork, during which the student practices overlearning. Teachers should develop a way of monitoring student attention during seatwork, which may include circulating throughout the room or using a teacher's aide.

Effective independent practice relies on managing the procedures of seatwork. The practice activities should vary and should be carefully prepared. The teacher should direct the class through the first problems, and the activities should directly follow guided practice. The teacher should circulate during seatwork and should vary the activities with cooperative as well as individual practice.

WEEKLY AND MONTHLY REVIEWS. The final teaching function described by Rosenshine, *weekly and monthly reviews*, involves rechecking student performance and reteaching when necessary.

Direct Instruction. Gersten, Carnine, and Woodward (1987) note that the phrase "direct instruction" is used as a generic term, with meanings ranging from any type of structured teaching to a system for effective classroom management. Thus far, we've presented Rosenshine's notion of teaching functions and the activities associated with them. The term "Direct Instruction" has been associated with a specific instructional methodology and a particular set of carefully designed and validated curriculum materials developed by Engelmann and his associates (Carnine and Silbert, 1979; Engelmann and Carnine, 1982; Silbert, Carnine, and Stein, 1981).

Gersten, Carnine, and Woodward (1987) describe Direct Instruction as a "complex way of looking at all aspects of instruction—from classroom organization and management to the quality of teacher-student interactions, the design of curriculum materials, and the nature of inservice teacher training" (p. 48). The critical features of Direct Instruction are listed in Table 6.2.

TABLE 6.2 Critical Features of Direct Instruction

1. Academic instruction through explicit step-by-step strategies (or modeling of effective performance)
2. Requirement of mastery of each step in the process
3. Corrections for student errors
4. Gradual fading of teacher-directed activities to independent work
5. Systematic practice with a range of examples
6. Cumulative review of newly learned concepts

Source note: This table was paraphased from R. Gersten, J. Woodward, and C. Darch, "Direct Instruction: A Research Based Approach to Curriculum Design and Teaching," *Exceptional Children, 53*(1), 17–31, 1986. Reprinted with permission from The Council for Exceptional Children and the authors.

In contrast to Rosenshine's general teaching functions, Direct Instruction includes curriculum materials that provide teachers with clear and unambiguous information regarding the most effective means for correction of student errors, the range of examples needed to ensure mastery of a concept, and carefully worded scripts for instruction and practice of a new skill (Gersten, Carnine, and Woodward, 1987). Not all Direct Instruction materials are scripted, however. For example, the *Direct Instruction Mathematics* (Silbert, Carnine, and Stein, 1981) consists of suggestions for lesson design, a means of analysis and modification of commercial materials, as well as information about presentation techniques. Brown (1985), in her review of *Direct Instruction Mathematics*, observed that teachers would need a considerable amount of training before using the program. Gersten et al. (1987) also noted that support for teachers (through consultants of "instructional facilitators") as they implement a Direct Instruction approach is necessary for continued professional development.

MASTERY LEARNING. Guskey (1987) describes three components of mastery learning: the learning objectives, the learner, and instruction. To be effective, there should be a good "fit" or congruence among these three components. What the student is taught, and how he or she is taught, must be congruent with the specified learning objectives. There must also be a match between the instructional procedures and what has been determined necessary for students to learn.

Key to mastery learning is the use of feedback and correctives. As we mentioned earlier, mastery learning is based on the premise that all children can learn when provided with conditions that are appropriate for their learning. After developing units of instruction and completing initial teaching, the teacher tests the students. Students then are given precise information on their learning progress at regular intervals throughout the instructional sequence.

Guskey maintains that feedback must be both diagnostic and prescriptive. It must be paired with corrective activities which offer an instructional alternative, rather than more of the same instruction which has already been ineffective for the student. In addition, the teacher should develop enrichment activities for students who attain mastery from the initial teaching.

Viewing mastery learning as a teach-test-prescriptive instruction process demonstrates that it can be broadly implied. Guskey suggests that teachers do not have to make dramatic changes to use mastery learning. He contends that the changes required to implement mastery learning may be relatively modest.

Objective Three: *To Prepare and Evaluate Direct Instruction and Mastery Learning Activities to Incorporate into Your Classroom Management Agenda*

Both direct instruction and mastery learning focus on the teacher's activities in instruction. The emphasis in direct instruction is on designing and implementing clear, concise presentations, followed by feedback and practice. The emphasis in mastery learning is on appropriate instruction for individual students supported through feedback and prescriptions for instruction.

In planning and evaluating direct instruction and mastery learning activities, teachers should remain aware of the complexity of classroom activities. Leinhardt and Putnam (1987) demonstrate the complexity of teacher-focused activities through their analysis of how students grapple with lessons. They suggest that students use specific cognitive structures which affect just how well they understand the instructional activity. Students must employ:

1. An action system, which enables them to respond appropriately during the activity (i.e., when to respond as a group, when to raise hands to speak, when to watch the teacher or attend to the assignment).

2. A lesson parser, which enables them to recognize and the components of the lesson (i.e., the advance organizer, initial presentation, guided practice, feedback).

3. An information gatherer, which assists the student in using an explanation schema, a way of attending, and a system to select and focus on the essential pieces of the lesson.

4. A knowledge generator, which selects and focuses skills and assists in compiling new knowledge from selected information.

5. An evaluator, which assists students in monitoring their own comprehension of the activities.

Student participation in teacher-focused activities, then, is a complex process of determining what is occurring, tracking the parts of the activity, and figuring out what is to be learned and learning it.

During the initial presentation of both direct instruction and mastery learning, Marshall (1987) suggests that the teacher should frame the activity to provide initial motivation. The first presentations should be used to focus and redirect attention and support the learning orientation. Teachers should be proactive in helping students understand that the goal of instruction is learning rather than simply work. This focus on learning may be reinforced through instructing students on the cognitive plans they need to complete the task, rather than the actions of the task (Marx and Walsh, 1988).

In both direct instruction and mastery learning, classroom learning activities make use of the constructive qualities of errors. Rohrkemper and Corno (1988) contend that there is a limited benefit of uniform success in the classroom, and effective teachers must consider ways of increasing adaptive learning of students through their use of errors. Errors should be treated instructively, and teachers should share the responsibility for learning and evaluation with their students (Marshall, 1987).

Teachers should be aware, however, of the artificial nature of student-teacher interaction during teacher-focused activities. Mehan (1979) contends that one of the features which distinguishes conversations in classrooms and other educational settings from those in everyday situations is the use of evaluation rather than acknowledgment responses. Teachers ask "known information questions" which impose constraints on interaction. Negative evaluations may be frequent, and the teacher may find himself or herself "searching" for the correct answer. In these situations, the teacher may not actually be eliciting student responses, but the teacher may be creating a response out of a number of potential displays.

Objective Four: *To Describe the Role of Direct Instruction and Mastery Learning Activities Within the Context of Practitioner-Focused Interactions*

Recall from Chapter Five that classroom events occur in three phases: preparation, activity, and closure. We then considered key patterns within the activity phase, one of which was practitioner-focused interactions, the central focus of this chapter (and Chapter Seven). Direct instruction and mastery learning involve techniques and teacher behaviors that cut across all three phases of instructional events. For example, the preparation phase might include teaching functions such as review and the presentation of advance organizers as well as actions which motivate the student and convey the goal of instruction. The closure phase of a classroom instructional event might involve guided practice activities, a final review of lesson content, sharing information about students' learning progress, and evaluation of instruction and student responses to make decisions for future instructional activities.

Within the activity phase of the classroom event, practitioner-focused patterns involve the presentation of instruction or "problem" through a variety of techniques. Prior to the presentation, however, careful planning must occur to ensure the "fit" between the learning objectives, learner needs, and techniques or instructional procedures. Decisions are based on the teacher variables such as expectations and philosophy of teaching and learning, student variables such as communication patterns and developmental level, task variables including the preference value of instructional materials, interest level of the activity, difficulty level of assignments, and setting variables such as persons present, instructional grouping, and opportunities for learning (refer to the framework in Chapter Three).

Suppose that all these variables were considered and that the decision was made to conduct the activity phase of a classroom event using practitioner-focused patterns. The practitioner (teacher in this case) might employ a variety of teaching functions and behaviors from direct instruction or mastery learning approaches. That is, the teacher would provide clear explanations of concepts/skills/strategies, test student understanding, and give feedback to student responses. The participant's role would include the use of prior information about the instructional interaction (obtained through previous interactions with the teacher) to determine when to speak, how to gain recognition from the teacher, and when to watch the teacher (that is, employ the "action system" as described by Leinhardt and Putnam, 1987). The participant is also responsible for determining what is to be learned, linking new knowledge to prior knowledge and monitoring comprehension.

To summarize, the notion of practitioner-focused interactions provides one general pattern for instructional presentations. Within this pattern, a variety of techniques may be used and actions implemented by the classroom teacher. Decisions regarding the selection, implementation, and monitoring of teacher actions are facilitated through a consideration of a framework involving teacher, student, task, and setting variables. The next chapter will describe other techniques which may occur within practitioner-focused activities.

SUMMARY

As stated in Chapter Five, the practitioner (and, as we've described in this chapter, the teacher) presents instructional problems through a variety of techniques. Two of these techniques provided the primary topic for this chapter: activities related to direct instruction and mastery learning. These activities involve teacher control over what is to be learned and focus heavily on basic skills achievement.

Direct instruction involves systematic, explicit teaching of academic skills through clear and unambiguous presentations by the teacher. Rosenshine (1983) suggested a comprehensive list of "teaching functions," including review, presentation of new content through small steps, and initial practice activities, including frequent questions by the teacher, specific feedback on incorrect answers, provision for independent practice, and weekly or monthly reviews. Direct Instruction as developed by Engelmann and his associates (Engelmann and Osbourne, 1977; Silbert, Carnine, and Stein, 1981) involves a specific instructional methodology and particular set of carefully designed and validated curriculum materials.

Mastery learning is an approach to learning based on the belief that almost all students can learn when they are provided with conditions that are appropriate for their learning (Guskey, 1987). As with direct instruction, the role of carefully paced instruction along with specific feedback and correctives is emphasized. Teachers should consider the "fit" or congruence between the learner, learning objectives, and instruction as they plan learning activities within a mastery learning framework.

Although this chapter concerned teacher activities and related instructional techniques and materials, the role of the student within the complexity of classroom interactions was recognized. Given the considerable teacher control over the learning process within this pattern, the reader is cautioned to be aware of the difficulties students might have in figuring out what is to be learned and learning it.

REVIEW QUESTIONS

1. The techniques and approaches described in this chapter heavily emphasized the teacher's presentation of information. Suppose you were asked to design a mathematics lesson involving adding two digit numbers with carrying (e.g., 47 + 28). Describe some initial decisions you must make as you begin to plan the lesson. What suggestions for the presentation of instruction should you consider?

2. Describe the major distinction between Rosenshine's use of the term "direct instruction" and the meaning associated with the term "Direct Instruction."

3. Contrast the mastery learning approach with direct instruction techniques. How are they similar?

4. In some classroom settings, there is great anxiety associated with mistakes or errors. Describe a contrasting philosophy about errors, that is, the emphasis on constructive qualities of errors as noted in direct instruction and mastery learning activities.

5. Both the direct instruction and mastery learning approaches involve teacher control over what is to be learned. How can teachers guard against a tendency to emphasize "covering" materials in a commercial curriculum without regard to the student? What can teachers do to ensure recognition of the student's role within teacher-focused interactional patterns?

APPLICATION ACTIVITY

The focus of this chapter was on actions used by teachers within their overall classroom management agenda. When disruptions to this agenda occur, the teacher is then faced with analysis of an instructional or behavioral issue. Following this analysis, the teacher may repair or revise the agenda or abandon a particular pattern to concentrate on another pattern (e.g., move from practitioner-focused activities to participant-focused interactions). The purpose of this activity is to examine a practitioner-focused pattern in an attempt to determine what techniques are used by the teacher as he or she implements a lesson.

In the last activity, you (the reader) made global as well as more focused observations about the patterns used by a classroom teacher. The process of moving from global to more focused observations might be helpful for this activity, also. After observing instruction across several content areas within a classroom, select an observational period in which the teacher is presenting new content. Use the following questions to guide your observations.

Observations of the Overall Instructional Agenda

A. *Describe the Context for the Lesson*

❖ What is the instructional problem or "place" (as we've defined in our patterns)? What materials did the teacher use to support this instructional activity?

❖ Describe the participants. Is the lesson presented to the entire class or to a small group? What is the developmental level of the participants?

❖ Include any other pertinent information that would help a naive observer gain a sense of the context of the instructional event (e.g., setting variables, task variables as described in Chapter Three).

B. Discuss the Techniques and Approaches Used by the Practitioner (Teacher)

❖ List the "teaching functions" used by the teacher during the interaction. Determine the amount of time spent on functions such as *review, presentation,* and *guided practice.* How was the instructional presentation organized? Did the teacher present new information in small steps and provide time for guided practice of new skills? If you did not observe step-by-step instruction, was the content more conducive to another style of presentation?

❖ How did the teacher ensure student mastery of the content? In your opinion, were there some students who did not seem to comprehend the basic content of the lesson? What evidence led you to form that opinion?

C. Consider the Relationships Among the Practitioner, Participants, and Problem Within the Practitioner-Focused Pattern

❖ How much teacher control was involved in this lesson? Describe the statements made by the teacher to motivate students (e.g., how did the teacher describe the goal of the lesson to the students). Determine whether the teacher spent most of the time lecturing about the new information or content. How did the teacher monitor student participation? What did the teacher do to monitor his or her own presentation?

❖ How active a role did the participant play in the interaction? Did the participant's role change depending upon the phase of the instructional event (preparation, activity, closure)? Were there some students who did not participate? If so, offer some hypotheses as to why certain students did not take part in the interaction (e.g., Did the students know the teacher's expectations for participation? Did they know how to participate? Was the content too simple or too difficult?)

❖ Describe the role of the instructional problem within the practitioner-focused pattern you observed. Were the materials challenging and interesting? How well did the instructional problem "fit" with lesson objectives and the learner?

As always, support your comments with specific examples. Provide some closure to this activity either through a summary or some concluding comments. Comment on whether the use of a pattern provided a useful frame for considering the instructional agenda.

REFERENCES

BICKEL, W. E., & BICKEL, D. D. (1986). Effective schools, classrooms, and instruction: Implementation for special education. *Exceptional Children, 52,* 489–500.

BLOOM, B. S. (1976). *Learning characteristics and school learning.* New York: McGraw-Hill.

BROPHY, J. (1982). How teachers influence what is taught and learned in classrooms. *Elementary School Journal, 83,* 1–13.

BROPHY, J., ROHRKEMPER, M., RASHID, H., & GOLDBERGER, M. (1983). Relationships between teachers' presentations of classroom tasks and students' engagement in those tasks. *Journal of Educational Psychology, 75,* 544–552.

BROWN, V. L. (1985). Direct Instruction Mathematics: A framework for instructional accountability. *Remedial and Special Education, 6*(1), 53–58.

CARNINE, D., & SILBERT, J. (1979). *Direct instruction reading.* Columbus, OH: Charles E. Merrill.

CARROLL, J. B. (1963). A model for school learning. *Teachers College Record, 64,* 723–733.

CAZDEN, C., COX, M., DICKINSON, D., STEINBERG, Z., & STONE, C. (1979). "You all gonna hafta listen" Peer teaching in a primary classroom. In W. A. Collins (Ed.), *Children's language and communication* (pp. 183–231). Hillsdale, NJ: Lawrence Erlbaum.

COPELAND, C. D. (1982). Teaching-learning behaviors and the demands of the classroom environment. In W. Doyle & T. L. Good (Eds.), *Focus on teaching* (pp. 83–97). Philadelphia: Temple University Press.

ENGELMANN, S., & OSBOURNE, J. (1977). *Distar language II.* Chicago: Science Research Associates.

ENGELMANN, S., & CARNINE, D. (1982). *Theory of instruction: Principles and applications.* New York: Irvington.

GERSTEN, R., CARNINE, D., & WOODWARD, J. (1987). Direct Instruction research: The third decade. *Remedial and Special Education, 8*(6), 48–56.

GERSTEN, R., WOODWARD, J., & DARCH, C. (1986). Direct instruction: A research-based approach to curriculum design and teaching. *Exceptional Children, 53,* 17–31.

GUSKEY, T. R. (1980). Mastery learning: Applying the theory. *Theory into Practice, 19,* 104–108.

———. (1987). The essential elements of mastery learning. *Journal of Classroom Interaction, 22*(2), 19–22.

HOOD, L., MCDERMOTT, R., & COLE, M. (1980). "Let's try to make it a good day"—Some not so simple ways. *Discourse Processes, 3,* 155–168.

JOYCE, B., & WEIL, M. (1986). *Models of teaching* (3rd ed). Englewood Cliffs, NJ: Prentice Hall.

KALLISON, J. M. (1986). Effects of lesson organization on achievement. *American Educational Research Journal, 23,* 337–347.

LEINHARDT, G., & PUTNAM, R. T. (1987).   The skill of learning from classroom lessons. *American Educational Research Journal, 25*, 557–587.

MARSHALL, H. H. (1987).   Building a learning orientation. *Theory into Practice, 26*, 8–14.

MARX, R. W., & WALSH, J. (1988).   Learning from academic tasks. *Elementary School Journal, 88*, 207–219.

MCDERMOTT, R. P. (1982).   Social relations as contexts for learning in school. In E. Bredo & W. Feinberg (Eds.), *Knowledge and values in social and educational research* (pp. 252–270). Philadelphia: Temple University Press. (Originally published in *Harvard Educational Review, 47*(2), 198–213, 1977.)

MEHAN, H. (1979).   "What time is it, Denise?": Asking known information questions in classroom discourse. *Theory Into Practice, 18*, 285–294.

MIRAMONTES, O., CHENG, L. R., & TRUEBA, (1984).   Teacher perceptions and observed outcomes: An ethnographic study of classroom interactions. *Learning Disability Quarterly, 7*, 349–357.

ROHRKEMPER, M., & CORNO, L. (1988).   Success and failure on classroom tasks: Adaptive learning and classroom teaching. *Elementary School Journal, 88*, 297–312.

ROSENSHINE, B. (1983).   Direct Instruction. In T. Husen & T. N. Postlethwaite (Eds.), (Vol. III, pp. 1395–1400). *International Encyclopedia of Education*. Oxford: Pergamon Press.

————. (1983).   Teaching functions in instructional program. *Elementary School Journal, 83*, 335–351.

ROSENSHINE, B., & STEVENS, R. (1984).   Classroom instruction in reading. In P. D. Pearson (Ed.). *Handbook of reading research* (pp. 745–798) New York: Longman.

SILBERT, J., CARNINE, D., & STEIN, M. (1981).   *Direct instruction mathematics*. Columbus, OH: Charles E. Merrill.

CHAPTER SEVEN

Behavioral Procedures and Self-regulated Learning

SITUATIONS

Setting: Kindergarten, the beginning of the second week of school, end of the morning session.

Teacher: Boys and girls, it's time to listen. [Waits for students to stop all activity.] Thank you. You're all good listeners today. It's clean up time, so each of you needs to put your activity away. As you clean up, I'll be coming around to check your sticker cards [moves to first student].
Marco, let's see your sticker card. Let's count.

Marco: One, two, three, four, five.

Teacher: Nice job, Marco. You have stickers for all five of our activities today. You may listen to a story in the reading corner with the headphones.

Marco: Neat.

Teacher: [Moving to next student] Okay, Elizabeth, let's see your sticker card.

Elizabeth: I got three.

Teacher: You may go to the puzzle table or look at books.

Elizabeth: I want headphones.

Teacher: Not today, Elizabeth. People with five stickers can get a drink and "go to headphones" [use headphones]. How can you get five stickers tomorrow?

Elizabeth: Listen. Finish my activities. Follow directions.

Teacher: Right, Elizabeth. I'll remind you so you can try hard to earn five stickers tomorrow.

*   *   *

Setting: Sixth grade history class, three school days before midterm exams.

Teacher: In three days we'll be having the midterm examination. [Students moan.] Don't panic. We're going to begin to review today. Remember our strategy? Let's work through it in order to help you get ready.

Mickey: I know the first step! You ask yourself, "What am I supposed to do?"

Teacher: Great. But what might be a step before starting the strategy? What should you do after a teacher announces a test or a midterm? [No responses.] How about asking the teacher what topics will be covered on the test?

Joan: They never tell us. They just say "Study everything."

Teacher: Let's think about the strategy. I'd do as Mickey suggested. I'd ask, "What am I supposed to do?" and I would answer myself, "Be able to recognize the main ideas of the history units so far." What's our next step? Marti?

Marti: Look at the alternatives.

Teacher: Not quite yet. I'd ask "What is my plan? or How can I do it?" Any ideas? Mickey?

Mickey: First, I'd get together all the study sheets and review them.

Teacher: That's a fine idea, but it's not really a plan. I'd think about a series of steps, like (1) gather my study sheets, (2) pick out key concepts, (3) outline them, (4) memorize them, and (5) test myself. What else should you do as you work through the plan?

Joan:	I'd ask myself "Am I using my plan?"
Teacher:	Absolutely. And the last step of the strategy?
Mickey:	Evaluate. I'd ask myself "How did I do?" After I gave myself a test, I could tell how I did by checking my answers.

*   *   *

Setting: Eighth grade American history class; advance organizer (list of activities to be covered during the period) is on the board.

Teacher:	Ingrid, your comments about Kennedy's handling of the Cuban missile crisis were well taken. [Turns to the board, crosses off third activity on the list.] Now, let's move on to item 4. [Stops suddenly after looking at her watch.] Oh, I don't know where the time goes during this period. I see that we've got 7 minutes left in the period. What shall we do?
Tony:	How about giving us time to start our projects?
Teacher:	That's one idea, Tony. [Looking at the board] You see, I had planned to discuss two more points before giving you time to start your projects. I guess I didn't do such a great job planning today's class.
Ingrid:	That's okay, so our discussion got a little off track—it was interesting.
Teacher:	Thanks for your kind comment, but we have only a few days left before the chapter test. We could skip items 4, 5, and 6 and spend the remainder of the class period reviewing Chapter 5. You need to be familiar with those topics because they're on the test, so we'd have to be sure to address those issues tomorrow. On the other hand, we could take some time to discuss ideas for your projects.
Chris:	We've got a big game this weekend. Couldn't we get a head start on our projects?
Teacher:	[Pausing, appears to be thinking, evaluating alternatives.] Let's talk about the projects.

*   *   *

Setting: Third grade class, students lining up to go to lunch.

Robbie:	[Loudly] Hey, stop pushing me James!

James:	Kathy's standing too close to me!
Kathy:	I am not! [James accidentally steps on Robbie's foot as he turns toward Kathy]
Robbie:	Ouch! I'll slug you if you do it again!
James:	I couldn't help it, she made a face at me.
Teacher:	It seems like Robbie has a problem. We could go back to our seats and line up again. Or... [pauses]. How about if you use our strategy, Robbie?
Robbie:	[Grimaces, says softly] I'd rather step on his foot.
Teacher:	[Ignores Robbie's comment] What's the first step?
Kathy:	Ask myself "What is my problem?"
Teacher:	[Nods to Robbie] Robbie, go ahead.
Robbie:	What is my problem? James pushed me and stepped on my foot.
Teacher:	Fine. What's the next step?
Robbie:	[Looks at the cues on the bulletin board] What is my plan? Punch him [smiles as he says this].
Teacher:	That's one possibility, but think of the consequences.
Robbie:	Just kidding. I'd tell him to stay in his place in line. Or I could move behind Kathy.
Teacher:	Those are excellent alternatives. Suppose you chose to get behind Kathy. What's the next step?
Robbie:	I'd ask myself, "Am I using my plan?" That's easy, cause I've already moved.
Teacher:	And, finally? What would you do next?
Robbie:	I'd ask myself, "How did I do?"
Teacher:	[Turns to the class] How would Robbie know how he did with his plan?
Kathy:	If he made it to the lunch room without hitting anyone?
James:	If he got all his points and got to go outside for recess?
Teacher:	Sure. Well, we've worked through Robbie's problem using the strategy. Maybe next time you can think about your lining up problems in a positive way.

These four situations contrast the teacher-focused activities which are described in this chapter: behavioral procedures and those procedures designed to promote self-regulated learning. All these activities trace their roots back to behavioral learning theory which suggests that what an individual does, rather than why the individual exhibits the behavior, is of primary importance. The role of the teacher is to manage the learning environment to reinforce behaviors which increase successful learning and to decrease behaviors which are less productive through the application of behavior management principles. Techniques and strategies which fall under the rubric of self-regulated learning emphasize the learner's role in the learning process and are designed to foster student skills in "learning how to learn."

SELF-EVALUATION

Indicate whether you agree or disagree with each statement:

1. Behavioral procedures should be applied when a student disrupts instruction by talking out.
2. Clear definitions of behavior must be developed prior to attempting the behavior change process.
3. Teachers should consider the intrusiveness of behavioral procedures and implement the least restrictive procedures when dealing with nonconventional behavior.
4. Monitoring one's behavior is an effective means of producing long-term behavior changes.
5. The use of contracts should be considered for students in the upper elementary grades.
6. The use of token economies is most effective when students select the types of reinforcers.
7. The ultimate goal of most behavioral procedures is to transfer control of the behavior from external reinforcers to the student.
8. Strategies for academic tasks and activities such as solving division problems and managing disruptive behavior should be taught to all students.

KEY WORDS

behavioral principles

behavioral procedures

reinforcement

extinction

stimulus change

self-regulated learning

cognitive behavior modification

self-monitoring

self-instruction

contingency contract

token economy

OBJECTIVES

After completing this chapter, you will be able to:

1. Describe a rationale and research base for behavioral procedures and techniques involving self-regulated learning.
2. Describe research-based examples of the application of behavioral procedures.
3. Describe research-based examples of techniques and procedures associated with cognitive behavior modification.
4. Prepare and evaluate behavior modification and self-regulated learning activities to incorporate into your classroom management agenda.
5. Describe the role of behavioral procedures and techniques/strategies associated with self-regulated learning within the practitioner-focused interactional pattern.

Objective One: *Describe a Rationale and Research Base for Behavioral Procedures and Techniques Involving Self-regulated Learning*

Behavioral Procedures. Sulzer-Azaroff and Mayer (1977) suggest that the application of behavioral theory consists of behavioral principles (rules governing behavior) and behavioral procedures (specific teaching and behavior management techniques based on behavioral principles). In view of the classroom-based nature of this text, our discussion will focus on behavioral procedures rather than on principles.

Beginning in the late 1950s, teachers began to apply behavioral procedures, such as contingency management and programmed materials, in the classroom. The application of these procedures has been referred to as behavior modification (sometimes softened to behavior management), social learning techniques, or applied behavior analysis.

In addition, some teacher preparation programs traditionally associate classroom management with discipline, thereby leading to an emphasis on disruptive behavior of students (Doyle, 1986). Behavioral procedures are considered an efficient and effective means for dealing with individual behavior problems.

Joyce and Weil (1986) summarize the assumptions of the theory behind behavioral techniques. First, behavior is lawful and responds to variables in the individual's environment. Once a behavior has occurred, the probability that it will occur again depends on responses from the environment. Any response which enhances the probability that the behavior will occur again is called a reinforcer.

Behavior, in the behavioral frame of reference, is observable and definable. Nonconventional behaviors are felt to be acquired through learning and, in the same manner, can be "unlearned" through applying behavioral procedures. Joyce and Weil contend that behavioral goals are specific, discrete, and individualized. Procedures for encouraging new behaviors involve setting specific, individualized behavioral goals, determining personal reinforcers, and applying behavioral techniques consistently. The role of personal history is deemphasized. However, an individual's past learning history plays a role in that undesirable behaviors may have been reinforced in the past. Joyce and Weil contend that in this model, the emphasis is on the responses in the environment which are producing or maintaining the behavior. After determining this, the teacher can develop a plan to modify the behavior.

Learning, then, when applying behavioral procedures, depends on the responses in the environment. Managing those responses becomes the primary operating procedure in the classroom. In managing reinforcement (those responses which increase behaviors) Shea and Bauer (1987) suggest five principles:

1. Reinforcement occurs when the specific behavior is demonstrated.
2. Reinforcement follows the behavior immediately.
3. Early in the behavior management program, the specific behavior should be reinforced each time it occurs.
4. Once the specific behavior is at the desired level, reinforcement should occur intermittently.
5. Social reinforcers are always applied concurrently with tangible reinforcers.

These principles of reinforcement describe the ways in which teachers can manipulate the "functional relationship" (Wolery, Bailey, and Sugai, 1988) between behavior and the responses which maintain it. Vargas (1977) suggests that the basis of teaching in this model is identifying the behavioral procedures and reinforcers that will change the behavior. A functional relationship exists when behavior change is demonstrated to occur as a function of the teaching procedures, reinforcement, or some other response.

The process of managing this functional relationship is usually referred to as a behavior change process (the steps of this process are summarized in Table 7.1). The first step in the process is the identification of the behavior to be changed. As discussed earlier, one of the premises of the behavioral model is that behaviors are observable and can be defined. A behavior which is measurable can be counted reliably by several different observers. Making this definition adequately clear is essential in the next step of the process, collecting and recording baseline data. In this step, the level of the behavior before applying a procedure is recorded.

Recent research has increased the emphasis on the initial information teachers gather about behaviors before applying a behavioral procedure. Carr and Durand (1985) suggest that these initial steps should include identifying and assessing the educational situations in which the behavior problems reliably occur. Once the behavior is defined in this way, it is possible to describe the social and communicative function of the behavior, and select more conventional behaviors to be reinforced to replace the behavior. In this way, what could have been a program to decrease a nonconventional behavior may emerge as a program to increase a more conventional behavior.

After determining the level of the behavior, reinforcers should be identified. Shea and Bauer suggest that the two most effective means of selecting behaviors for an individual student are to observe the student to see what reinforcers he or she selects and to ask the student what he or she prefers. After reinforcers are determined, procedures are implemented. Again, documentation of the student's behavior during the procedure is recorded. Any

TABLE 7.1 Steps in the Behavior Change Process

1. Select the target behavior.
2. Collect and record baseline data.
3. Identify reinforcers.
4. Implement procedures.
5. Evaluate procedures.

Source note: This table was adapted from T. M. Shea and A. M. Bauer, *Teaching Children and Youth with Behavior Disorders,* 2nd edition, p. 234. Englewood Cliffs, NJ: Prentice Hall, Inc., 1987. Reprinted with permission of the publisher.

procedure should be consistently applied for at least ten school days. The final step, which occurs throughout the procedure process, is that of evaluation. By collecting and charting procedure data, teachers can evaluate the effectiveness of the behavior change process through comparison with the baseline process.

Shea and Bauer (1987) suggest a continuum of behavioral procedures (see Figure 7.1). The least restrictive procedure, *positive reinforcement of appropriate behavior*, refers to the nonspecific praise and reinforcement which teachers usually provide throughout the school day. Examples include comments such as "Good working," "You are all being good students," or "Nice job." For some students, however, this general reinforcement may not be adequate. These students would require the next level on the continuum, *positive reinforcement of specific behaviors*. This procedure involves the teacher making explicit statements. Rather than stating "Congratulations on passing classes so well," the teacher would state "Congratulations on passing classes quietly, with your hands to yourselves." In the third step of the continuum, *positive reinforcement of incompatible alternatives*, the teacher reinforces a behavior that cannot occur concurrently with the undesirable behavior. The teacher would reinforce the student for having his or her feet on the floor rather than stating "No kicking."

The next step of the continuum suggested by Shea and Bauer involves systematically ignoring the nonconventional behavior. This behavioral procedure, called *extinction*, involves discontinuing or withholding the reinforcer which has been maintaining a behavior.

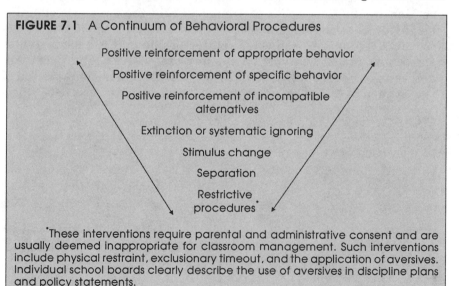

FIGURE 7.1   A Continuum of Behavioral Procedures

Positive reinforcement of appropriate behavior

Positive reinforcement of specific behavior

Positive reinforcement of incompatible alternatives

Extinction or systematic ignoring

Stimulus change

Separation

Restrictive procedures*

*These interventions require parental and administrative consent and are usually deemed inappropriate for classroom management. Such interventions include physical restraint, exclusionary timeout, and the application of aversives. Individual school boards clearly describe the use of aversives in discipline plans and policy statements.

When used consistently and systematically, extinction results in the gradual decrease and elimination of the specific behavior. Behaviors that are ignored in this fashion become nonfunctional and consequently stop. However, when extinction is initially applied, an "extinction burst" may occur, and the behavior being ignored may increase in frequency for a brief period of time before it decreases. In addition, some behaviors, dangerous to the student, others, or the instruction going on in the classroom, cannot be ignored.

Stimulus change involves changing the student's environment so that the behavior no longer occurs. It is more restrictive than those previously discussed in that it fails to deal with the behavior directly, but merely arranges the environment to avoid the behavior. For example, two students who squabble would not be placed in close proximity in the classroom. However, in that this procedure does not address the issue at hand, when students do get together, the squabbling will resume.

Separation, or nonexclusionary time out, is more restrictive in that it prevents the student from participating in his or her educational program. Timeout is an abbreviation for "time out from positive reinforcement" and calls for the teacher to remove the student from a reinforcing environment for a brief period of time contingent on the student's commission of an undesirable behavior (Powell and Powell, 1982). This procedure is quite restrictive and limits the student's access to his or her right to education. In addition, if the classroom is not, in itself reinforcing, timeout or separation will strengthen, rather than weaken, the undesirable behavior. Timeout should not be implemented without careful development of the program with a behavioral consultant, supervisor, and the child's parents. Permission of the child's parents should be obtained. Behaviors which are appropriate for the application of separation are those which require a response to maintain them. Separation should be attempted only after other procedures have been demonstrated to be unsuccessful. Considerations for the application of timeout are presented in Table 7.2.

Three additional procedures which occur across the continuum are shaping, modeling, and cuing. *Shaping* is the reinforcement of successive approximations of behaviors leading to the desired behavior (Shea and Bauer, 1987). The criterion for reinforcement is gradually increased as the student's behavior approximates that desired. *Modeling* involves having the student observe the appropriate response and providing reinforcement for that response. In *cuing* the teacher presents a verbal prompt immediately before the behavior is to occur.

Martens, Peterson, Witt, and Cirone (1986) investigated teachers' perceptions of procedures used in classroom management. Teachers suggested the most effective, easiest to use, and most frequently used

TABLE 7.2 Considerations for the Application of Timeout

1. Carefully define behavior
2. Determine the current level of the behavior
3. Examine the current level of reinforcement in the classroom. If the classroom is not reinforcing for the student, separation will not be successful.
4. Confer with behavioral consultant, supervisor, and the child's parents regarding the procedure and alternative strategies.
5. Obtain parent permission.
6. Select an area which separates the student from the reinforcement of the ongoing classroom activities, but which is within your line of vision. The hall or school office are not appropriate areas and can be quite reinforcing.
7. Keep the separation period short (two to five minutes).
8. Separate the students without scolding or lecturing.

procedures included redirecting the student toward more conventional behaviors through using a cue and manipulating previously contracted rewards. The procedures determined to be least effective and least efficient were those which removed the student from the classroom.

Techniques Related to Self-regulated Learning. Behavioral procedures are very powerful, however, some researchers and teachers became concerned with the emphasis on external control of behavior by elements in the environment. An illustration from the area of special education (specifically learning disabilities) provides a clear example of the changes in teacher attitudes about external control. Years ago, some learning disabilities teachers believed that student learning would be enhanced by limiting any potential distractions from the environment. In some instances this was carried to an extreme, with students working in carrels devoid of any visual or auditory stimulation that might distract them from their work. While structure of this sort might help students complete more worksheets, how did this help students cope with environments outside the classroom? The image of some special education students walking around with portable carrels to help them focus their attention is a rather comical one but is used to illustrate a point. In this example, a more useful procedure would have been to help students learn to monitor their own attention. It is our contention that the teaching-learning process should be guided by the overriding goal of the development of students' ability to regulate their own learning processes.

A belief in the development of self-regulated learning is central to our stance as facilitative teachers. Paris and Oka (1986) describe self-regulated learning as individuals managing "their cognitive abilities and motivational effort so that learning is effective, economical, and satisfying" (p. 103). Corno and Mandinach (1983) suggest that self-regulated learning is the "highest form of cognitive engagement" and includes "specific cognitive activities such as deliberate planning and monitoring which learners carry out as they encounter academic tasks" (pp. 89–90). Techniques and strategies associated with cognitive behavior modification have been used to facilitate the development of self-regulated learning in some students.

The cognitive behavior modification (CBM) perspective emerged in response to an interest in helping students learn to control their own behavior and develop strategies for learning. The term "cognitive behavior modification" has been used to refer to procedures such as "self-control" and "self-instruction," techniques such as "self-monitoring," and strategies used to solve problems (Lloyd, 1980; Meichenbaum, 1977, 1982, 1986a). Cognitive behavior modification varies from behavioral procedures in terms of the involvement of the student. Rather than the "passive student in an active environment," cognitive behavior modification increases student regulation of the learning process. In behavioral procedures, effectiveness and economy are emphasized, with little discussion of learner satisfaction. In addition, the use of cognitive behavior modification is socially valid; the change in behavior is monitored and maintained across several contexts by the learner, rather than by others, and is consistent.

Harris (1982) describes cognitive behavior modification as an integrated, eclectic approach influenced by behaviorism, social-learning theory, cognitive psychology, developmental psychology, and instructional theory. It is based on the belief that thoughts, feelings, and behaviors are interactive and reciprocal in nature. She defines cognitive behavior modification as "the selective, purposeful combination of principles and procedures from diverse areas into training regimens or interventions, the purpose of which is to instate, modify or extinguish cognitions, feelings, and/or behaviors" (p. 5).

Several features are common to procedures and techniques subsumed under the CBM rubric (Lloyd, 1980). First, the "self" prefix indicates that the student actively participates in the procedure (e.g., "self-control," "self-assessment," "self-recording"). Verbalization is a key component of procedures which often involve a strategy (series of steps). In addition to using statements to guide oneself through a strategy, self-control procedures typically involve monitoring and evaluation of the successful implementation of a strategy or technique (Meichenbaum, 1986b). Finally, the training process is initiated by an adult but truly involves the student as a collaborator. That is, the adult teaches by modeling the procedure or technique, supporting the student during the training process (through scaffolding and explicit feedback), and gradually turning over the control of the process to the student (Meichenbaum and Asarnow, 1979).

Self-control procedures can be used to help with the behavior change process in a number of areas. *Self-monitoring* is a technique which involves systematically monitoring one's own behavior. This technique typically requires that the student determine whether a behavior occurred (*self-assessment*) and note it in some way (*self-recording*). These techniques have been used with such diverse behaviors as "talk-outs," on-task behavior, and academic work (such as monitoring the number of math problems solved correctly) (Workman, 1982). In contrast to general techniques, *self-instructional procedures* involve a strategy or set of steps used to guide students through specific tasks. For example, self-instructional training has been used in such diverse areas as reading comprehension (Wong and Jones, 1982), paragraph writing (Harris and Graham, 1985), and solving social problems (Camp and Bash, 1981). Research-based examples will be described in the following section.

Objective Two: *To Describe Research-Based Examples of Behavioral Procedures*

Behavioral procedures have been applied with regard to individual student behaviors and in structuring classrooms. Three classroom structures, based on behavioral principles, have been used frequently. These include token contingency contracting, token economies, and levels systems.

Token Contingency Contracting. A *contingency contract* is an arrangement between teacher and student that designates how an individual is to behave and the consequences for such a change (Wolery, Bailey, and Sugai, 1988). Contingency contracts may be written or oral, and are applied with students who are able to enter into agreements and understand consequences associated with their behaviors.

Classroom contracts have five components (Kazdin, 1975). First, behaviors are clearly and precisely identified. Second, contracts clearly specify the rewards are privileges related to the demonstration of the designated behaviors. The third component is a description of the outcomes associated with failing to meet the expectation. Fourth, bonuses may be built into the contract to increase motivation. Finally, a way of recording the progress of the contract must be included.

Designing a behavior contract includes the following steps (De-Risi and Butz, 1975):

1. Select the behaviors to be addressed. Initially, the teacher would dominate this step. As the student becomes more independent, his or her contribution to the discussion of the behavior addressed should increase.
2. Identify the reinforcers related to contract completion. Again, the teacher initially dominates. However, negotiation emerges as the student progresses.
3. Establish a record keeping system. Teachers may maintain records, or students may self-record.
4. Write the contract in positive, clear terms understood by all parties involved. Contracts should be stated in a positive way. A review date should be included. Signing the contract adds commitment.
5. Implement the contract. During implementation, the contract should be continually reviewed, and evaluated.

Although these steps may be initially dominated by the teacher, students should gradually increase their self-control over the process.

Token Economies. *Token economies* are the most versatile and commonly used behavioral classroom structure (Shea and Bauer, 1987). Token economies are contingency management systems which allow students to earn tokens that can be exchanged at a later time for specific backup reinforcers (Wolery, Bailey, and Sugai, 1988). Designing a token economy includes seven steps (Ayllon and McKittrick, 1982; Kazdin, 1977, 1985; Wolery, Bailey, and Sugai, 1988):

1. Describe the required behaviors in clear, observable terms. These behaviors are the classroom expectations and include both social and academic behaviors.
2. Determine an appropriate token. Tokens may be objects (chips, pennies) or symbols (stars, points). Tokens should be appropriate for the age of the student, easily dispensed, and difficult to counterfeit.
3. Identify items, privileges, and incentives. Tokens are effective because of the backup reinforcers used. A wide variety of reinforcers should also be used to maintain student interest.
4. Plan an exchange system. An exchange plan should include when tokens are exchanged (hourly, daily, weekly), how they are exchanged, and where the exchanges take place.

5. Plan procedures for fading the use of the token economy. As students become more independent, the number of tokens should be decreased, and they should be given intermittently. Student self-management should also be increased as the program continues.
6. Develop a record keeping system. To evaluate and modify the economy to meet student needs, data should be collected.
7. Establish operating procedures. Before implementing the token economy, the teacher should seek approval of the principal and supervisors. Parents should be informed of the program. The teacher should prepare all materials before implementation and market the program to students.

Token economies are not generalizable to other situations unless they are faded (LaNunziata, Hunt, and Cooper, 1984). In order to remain effective, reinforcers should be varied and sufficient, students should be equally involved, and students should be faded off the token system when appropriate.

Levels System. Levels systems are suggested to ensure that the application of token economies is faded (LaNunziata, Hunt, and Cooper, 1984). A level system is an organizational framework within which various behavior management interventions are applied to shape students' social, emotional, and academic behavior to preestablished levels. Within the organizational framework, a wide range of behavioral procedures may be used, including token economies, contingency contracting, and other strategies which are not behavioral in nature (Bauer, Shea, and Keppler, 1986). Levels systems include a description of each level, criteria for movement from one level to another, and the behaviors, expectations, and privileges related to each level. A sample level system is presented in Figure 7.2.

Bauer and Shea (1988) describe ten steps to designing a levels system:

1. Determine the behaviors demonstrated by the students when entering the program. Behaviors should be expressed in a positive way, for example, "Keep hands and feet to self" rather than "no hitting."
2. Determine the terminal-level behaviors for the students for whom the system is designed.
3. Determine the intermediary behaviors between entry and terminal behaviors. In this step, list at least two but no more than four sets of behaviors which evenly distribute expectations between those established for the entry and terminal levels. Write the sets of graduated expectations on separate sheets of paper,

labeled "Level 1" through "Level 4." At this point you may wish to consider a name for your levels.

4. Determine the privileges appropriate for students beginning the program and leaving the program. Evenly distribute privileges among the levels. Remember to plan for fading student supports and increasing personal responsibility for behavior as the student progresses through the system.

5. Develop a mechanism for moving among levels. Students may be required to stay at each level for a minimum period of time, students may contract for a level, students may earn a level through a token economy, or students may independently or as a group determine levels.

6. Design a communication system among students, parents, and others.

7. Determine augmentative systems, such as contingency contracts or token economies. In addition, bonus points may be used for outstanding gains and positive behavior.

8. Determine a monitoring system.

Levels systems are advantageous in that they include fading student supports and increasing self-monitoring as part of the system. However, levels systems may tend to maximize restrictions and seem punitive.

Objective Three: *To Describe Research-Based Examples of Techniques and Procedures Associated with Cognitive Behavior Modification*

As stated earlier, techniques and procedures associated with cognitive behavior modification have been applied to such diverse behaviors as on-task behavior, nonconventional behavior (e.g., talk outs), and academic productivity. Specific strategies have been developed for certain classes of academic problems (e.g., reading comprehension, solving math problems, writing compositions). Other strategies include those designed to help students with social problem solving as well as strategies to assist students with "learning how to learn." Following several examples of self-control techniques and strategies, instructional procedures will be briefly described.

Techniques such as self-monitoring and self-recording have been used to help special education students regulate their behavior. Some students with learning disabilities have difficulty focusing on their work and attending to tasks. Hallahan and his colleagues found that the use of self-monitoring was effective in increasing the on-task behavior of students during independent work periods as well as small-group reading instruction (Hallahan, Lloyd, Kosiewicz, Kauffman, and Graves, 1979; Hallahan, Marshall, and Lloyd, 1981). McLaughlin, Krappman, and Welsh (1985) found similar results when

FIGURE 7.2 GCCSEC Level System

	LEVEL 1	LEVEL II
MAXIMUM LENGTH OF STAY	9 weeks	9 weeks
REQUIREMENTS FOR MAINTAINING LEVEL STATUS	—	80% of possible points (4 of every 5 days)
REQUIREMENTS FOR ADVANCING TO NEXT LEVEL	90% of possible points (45 of 55 days); no more than 10 timeouts	90% of possible points 45 of 55 days; no more than 5 timeouts
ACADEMIC EXPECTATIONS	Starts assignments on command; during weeks 1–5, on task for 15 min of each ½ hr; weeks 6–9, on task 20/30 min of each ½ hr not necessarily consecutively	Starts and completes assignments within specified time; on-task behavior: weeks 1–2—20/30 min; weeks 3–4—25/45 min; weeks 5–9—30/45 min
BEHAVIORAL EXPECTATIONS	Discusses individual goals + class rules with teacher daily; no more than 10 timeouts; bus points + 85% (45 of 50 days)	Independently states individual goals and class rules daily; no more than 5 timeouts; bus points + 90% (4 of 5 days)
SOCIAL SKILLS EXPECTATIONS	Demonstrates ability to participate in supervised actitivy with 1 student; attends daily class meetings; participates in individual activity time	Demonstrates ability to interact appropriately with 2 or more peers at a time without supervision; daily contributions to discussions during class meetings; compliments others at least once a day; daily participation in groups (social skills and vocational education)
PRIVILEGES	Free time using equipment in classroom; special activities with staff members; Level I purchases in class store	Unescorted restroom and drink breaks; sets table at lunch; runs errands within building Level II purchases in class store, snacks and soft drinks at specified times; locker assignment

Offenses resulting in ground level placement:

Physical abuse to peer (3 days)   Physical abuse to staff (5 days)
Running away from assigned area   Destruction of property
Possession of drugs   Setting off fire alarm
Possession of weapons
Excessive swearing (student must be given warning before being placed on Ground Level
    for swearing)

LEVEL III (½ DAY TRANSITION)	LEVEL IV (COMPLETE TRANSITION)	GROUND LEVEL
6–18 weeks	6 weeks	1–5 days
80% of possible points (4 of every 5 days)	90% of possible points (30 of every 35 days)	—
Min.: 90% of possible points (30 of 35 days); Max: 90% of possible points (90/100 days)	Meets criteria established by public school SEH teachers	Level I—80% possible points Level II—85% possible points Level III—90% possible points
Starts and completes assignments within specified time; stays on task independently 30 min at a time	Meets criteria established by public	Same expectations for level below the one student was on prior to offense resulting in Ground Level placement
Self-isolation (no time-outs); assists teacher in selecting appropriate goals; delayed attention from teacher after raising hand; meets criteria established in SEH program in regular school; bus points + 90% (4 of 5 days)	Meets criteria established by public school SEH teachers	Same expectations for level student was on prior to offense resulting in Ground Level; states reason for Ground Level placement and alternative strategies
Daily contributions during class meetings; daily participation in social skills and vocational education groups; encourages peers regularly; meets all criteria established in SEH program in regular school	Meets criteria established in SEH program in regular school	Same expectations for level below the one student was on prior to offense resulting in Ground Level placement
Up to ½–day placement in regular school program; lunch outside of school with staff member once a week; "free" Friday once a month; unsupervised to and from bus—Early transition with 30 consecutive days of + 90%	Includes all privileges used in SEH program in regular school	One-half the amount of free time earned by student prior to offense resulting in Ground Level; restricted choice of activities for free time (no computer, record player, tape recorder, overhead projector); scheduled restroom and drink breaks supervised at all times

Source note: Day Treatment Program Levels System, Greater Clark County Special Education Cooperative, Jeffersonville, IN. Reprinted with permission from the cooperative, Linda Grumley, and Carolyn Weeks.

students with behavioral disorders recorded their on- and off-task behavior. These self-control techniques have also been found effective in helping students control such behaviors as "talk-outs" (Williams and Rooney, 1982; Workman and Hector, 1978). Increases in academic productivity have resulted from techniques such as simply graphing number of correct responses on assignments.

Strategies involving self-instructions have been used for both general and specific problems confronted by students. Wong and Jones (1982) designed a self-questioning technique to help students with reading comprehension activities. Their strategy involved the following questions/steps:

1. Why are you studying this passage for? (so you can answer some questions you will be given later).
2. Find the main idea/ideas in the paragraph and underline it/them.
3. Think of a question about the main idea you have underlined. Remember what a good question should be like (look at the prompt).
4. Learn the answer to your question.
5. Always look back at the questions and answers to see how each successive question and answer provide you with more information (p. 231).

The use of this strategy by learning disabled eighth and ninth graders resulted in improvements in reading comprehension performance.

Other strategies which have been used by special educators include academic attack strategies (Lloyd, 1980) and learning strategies for learning disabled adolescents (Deshler, Alley, Warner, and Schumaker, 1981). Academic attack strategies involve strategies for specific classes of problems (e.g., math strategies as mentioned in Cullinan, Lloyd, and Epstein, 1981). Teachers may also design their own strategies for tasks ranging from looking up a word in a dictionary to comparing grocery store prices (Lloyd and deBettencourt, 1982). Deshler and his colleagues at the University of Kansas Institute for Research in Learning Disabilities developed the Strategies Intervention Model which includes learning strategies for learning disabled adolescents (Schumaker, Deshler, and Ellis, 1986). One aspect of their comprehensive model includes instruction in task-specific strategies which will help students improve their performance in mainstreamed settings (e.g., paragraph writing strategy and test taking).

In contrast to strategies for highly specific problems, Camp and Bash (1981) developed a general problem-solving strategy (the *Think Aloud* program) for students encountering problems in a variety of areas. Following the use of the *Think Aloud* program, an increase in prosocial behavior was shown by students who had previously exhibited aggressive behaviors. The program includes a series of self-instructional questions: (1) What is my problem? or What am I supposed to do? (2) What is my plan? or How can I do it? (3) Am I using my plan? (4) How did I do? (Camp and Bash, 1981, p. 17). The reader will note that this strategy includes a monitoring step (3) and an evaluation step (4). The situation at the beginning of this chapter illustrated the use of these steps to help students generate plans for studying for examinations as well as monitor their progress within the task of studying.

Instructional Issues. Instruction in self-control techniques and strategies typically includes features described by Brown and Palincsar (1982) as components of an "ideal training package...practice in the use of task-appropriate strategies, instruction concerning the significance of those activities, and instruction concerning the monitoring and control of strategy use" (p. 7). Instruction in the actual steps of a strategy or actions required in a self-control technique include steps such as assessment, demonstration, corrections, reinforcement, directed practice, guidance, and independent practice (Lloyd and deBettencourt, 1982). Deshler, Alley, Warner, and Schumaker (1981) presented a similar set of steps: analyze student's current learning habit, describe the strategy, model the strategy, provide for verbal rehearsal of the strategy, practice with controlled materials, and practice with classroom materials.

Instruction in the selection of strategies, monitoring the strategy, and evaluating the outcomes of strategy use are activities associated with the term "metacognition." Flavell (1979) contrasted cognitive and metacognitive goals in the following way:

> you sense (metacognitive experience) that you do not yet know a certain chapter in your text well enough to pass tomorrow's exam, so you read it through once more (cognitive strategy, aimed at the straightforward cognitive goal of simply improving your knowledge)...you wonder (metacognitive experience) if you understand the chapter well enough to pass tomorrow's exam, so you try to find out by asking yourself questions about it and noting how well you are able to answer them (metacognitive strategy, aimed at the metacognitive goal of assessing your knowledge) (pp. 908–909).

Meichenbaum's example (1986) of the thinking which occurs at a party when you suddenly block on someone's name (imagining where you've seen that person before, going through the alphabet to see if you can retrieve the name, deciding to just keep talking and perhaps the name will occur to you) provides an additional illustration of metacognition (generating strategies, selecting a strategy, and monitoring its use).

Thus, in addition to knowledge about techniques and strategies, instruction in self-regulated learning involves metacognitive aspects such as monitoring and evaluating strategy use.

Objective Four: *To Prepare and Evaluate Behavioral Procedures and Cognitive Behavior Modification Activities to Incorporate into Your Classroom Management Agenda*

Behavioral Procedures. Behavioral procedures have contributed to classroom management in terms of increasing task organization and managing the contingencies to maximize learning. However, these procedures may also be used to control students, maintain the student in the role of respondent rather than active learner, and emphasize artificial reinforcers (Donnellan and Kilman, 1986). Implicit in the application of behavioral strategies is the potential controller (the teacher) and the controlled (the student), decreasing student choice and spontaneity (Guess and Siegel-Causey, 1985). Autonomy and choice are characteristics of persons whom society respects; behavioral procedures diligently applied may reduce student demonstration of both of these characteristics (Lipsky and Gartner, 1987).

In the recent past, research on behavior management were dominated by descriptions of ways to decrease behaviors, predominately through punitive procedures (Mesaros, 1983). However, through increased emphasis on the functional analysis of behaviors, punitive contingencies have decreased (Axelrod, 1987). Donnellan and LaVigna (1986) have presented data that demonstrated that a classroom was managed for the entire school year without the use of punishment. Pfiffner, Rosen, and O'Leary (1985) found that all positive consequences, in which students selected their own rewards were most effective in managing student behavior, but recognized the amount of work this placed on the teacher.

In applying behavioral procedures, teacher should be attentive to classroom climate. Marshall (1988), in her description of classrooms as learning places rather than working places, suggests that a work-dominated classroom suggests that students are involved in drudgery and "do work" rather than learn. In addition, teachers should be cautious of cultural differences in determining which behaviors are to be reinforced. The lack of inference suggested by the application of behavioral procedures may be in conflict with the student's cultural behaviors. For example, Delgado-Gaitan and Trueba (1985) describe Mexican-American students who copied each other's work in the classroom. Although contrary to behavior deemed appropriate by the school, this sharing of answers was consistent with the collaborative problem solving and collectivism seen in the students' family life and play.

Techniques Associated with Cognitive Behavior Modification. Fantuzzo, Polite, Cook, and Quinn (1988) in their review of the literature on students in elementary school settings found that student-management interventions resulted in greater treatment effects than did those of teacher-managed interventions. In fact, a significant, positive relationship was found between the number of intervention components that were student-managed and the treatment effect.

Harris (1982) cautions that cognitive behavior modification is not a remedy for all problems confronting students and their teachers, and is, in fact, time demanding. Rooney and Hallahan (1985) argue that while techniques such as self-monitoring have been shown to result in a "narrow band of behavioral changes," cognitive changes have not been demonstrated in the research (p. 47). Kendall (1977) also suggests several issues in the application of cognitive behavior modification. Because of the cognitive skills needed, pretraining may be necessary for some children. In addition, incentives may be necessary to increase and maintain the student's interest. An overriding concern is that of generalization. Kendall suggests that the amount of generalization which occurs depends on the training materials and setting used, whether instruction is predetermined or individualized, and whether concrete rather than conceptual learning is used.

Other researchers have been concerned with the problems of generalization. It has been suggested that instruction in a strategy or technique as well as in metacognitive aspects related to the use of that strategy or technique is not enough. Teachers should model strategies throughout the instructional day, demonstrating "coping" rather than a "mastery" model (Meichenbaum, 1982). In the history class example at the beginning of the chapter, the teacher thought aloud, illustrating how she coped with the problem of not covering all the activities in her advance organizer. She discussed alternative actions and demonstrated her decision-making processes. Ellis, Lenz, and Sabornie (1987) describe this teacher behavior as adopting a metacognitive perspective.

Teachers should also be extremely cautious about the use of self-control techniques and strategies with efficient learners. Strategy instruction may interfere with an efficient learner's already successful strategy. Wong and Jones (1982) note that the performance of students who were efficient readers did not improve with instruction in the reading comprehension strategy. Meichenbaum (1982) also suggests that the teacher listen to the learner's strategies to make sure that the strategy is not already in the learner's repertoire. These concerns support the need for assessment, as a critical step found in most procedures related to strategy instruction.

Objective Five: *To Describe the Role of Behavioral Procedures and Techniques/Strategies Associated with Self-regulated Learning Within the Practitioner-Focused Interactional Pattern*

It is easy to see how behavioral procedures may be used by the practitioner (classroom teacher) to provide initial structure to a classroom environment. In addition, these procedures may be applied to interactions within the practitioner-focused pattern. Often, the problems or issues addressed through the application of behavioral procedures involve student behaviors which are nonconventional. The role of the participant (student) is a rather passive one, with the teacher maintaining control of the interaction in an effort to change the behavior to a more conventional one. While instruction in techniques and strategies associated with self-regulated learning is still carefully controlled by the teacher, the ultimate objective is to transfer this control to the student. The student has a greater, more active role in interactions associated with self-regulated learning. As stated in Chapter Six, the decisions as to which procedures should be used is dependent upon the teacher's stance, the learning objectives, and the "fit" between the student's actions and the goals for instruction.

SUMMARY

The purpose of this chapter was to continue the discussion of procedures and techniques that can assist the teacher in managing the learning environment. Following a brief discussion of a rationale for use of behavioral procedures, examples of teacher activities that are congruent with a behavioral perspective were presented. Principles of reinforcement that teachers can use to manipulate functional relationships between behavior and responses that maintain it were described. The importance of objective definitions of behavior was discussed. Decisions regarding the selection of behavioral procedures should be made with reference to the continuum of procedures described in the chapter. It was suggested that the least restrictive, most efficient procedures be used to guide the student to more conventional behavior.

Concern with external control led to the emergence of techniques associated with cognitive behavior modification. Within this framework, students actively participate in the regulation of their own behavior. Techniques and procedures such as self-monitoring and self-instruction were described. Strategies for certain types of problems (academic and behavioral) were presented in addition to general problem solving strategies. Instructional issues pointed to the need to provide students with a rationale for strategy use as well as information regarding monitoring and control of the strategy.

Finally, decisions to use behavioral procedures or techniques associated with cognitive behavior modification should be based on careful attention to the situations in which the behaviors occur, cultural differences, and in-depth knowledge about the student. That is, a concern with the social and communicative function of the behavior should help teachers develop programs to increase more conventional behavior as opposed to decrease a nonconventional behavior. Attention to cultural differences may illustrate that what seems to be nonconventional may in fact be a culturally determined pattern of interaction. In-depth knowledge about a student's strategies for dealing with problems may point out that those strategies are effective for that learner. Any instruction in teacher-generated strategies may interfere with the student's already efficient strategies.

REVIEW QUESTIONS

1. Identification of the behavior to be changed is the first step in the behavior change process. Describe the consequences of generating a poor or unclear definition of the behavior to be changed. Why is it important to note the educational situation in which the behavior occurs?

2. A continuum of behavioral procedures was suggested. Under what conditions should a restrictive procedure be used? Under what circumstances should teachers use less restrictive procedures? What factors should teachers consider as they make decisions about what procedures should be implemented?

3. The use of techniques and procedures associated with cognitive behavior modification emerged from a belief that the ultimate goal of instruction should be the development of self-regulated learning processes. Compare and contrast this goal with objectives within a behavioral perspective.

4. Explain differences between techniques such as self-monitoring and strategies such as Camp and Bash's Think Aloud program. How are they similar? Why might a teacher use self-monitoring to help a student control his "talk-outs" rather than a self-instructional strategy to control that behavior?

5. In their efforts to structure classrooms to facilitate learning, teachers sometimes use contracts, token economies or level systems. Suggest situations in which each of these procedures may be useful.

6. If our stance includes an emphasis on helping students become self-regulated learners, why don't we just teach all students strategies and techniques to control their learning processes? Support your answer with specific examples from the research literature.

APPLICATION ACTIVITY

This chapter provided suggestions for actions that teachers can use within their overall classroom management agenda. However, if disruptions to this agenda occur, the techniques and procedures described in this chapter may be very useful. The purpose of this activity is to apply parts of the framework mentioned in Chapter Three to generate options for dealing with behavioral questions or issues.

Select a classroom situation in which a student demonstrates a behavior which is less conventional than those of his or her peers. Make this determination based on the observations conducted for the previous application activities. Use the following guidelines for completing this activity. Because of the extensive nature of this activity, it is suggested that items A and B be completed first. Items C and D (most pertinent to this chapter) should be completed following feedback by a peer or instructor.

A. Describe the Behavioral Issue or Question

❖ Describe your perceptions of the issue. What led you to select this particular issue? How did you determine the conventionality of the behavior? Include relevant background information if you have access to it.

❖ Interview the teacher to obtain his or her perceptions of the issue. If possible, interview the student also.

B. Analyze the Issue or Question

❖ Complete an antecedent-behavior-consequence chart. Be sure to provide a clear definition of the behavior.

❖ Analyze the context which surrounds the behavior. Describe the relevant variables: teacher, student, task, and setting variables. (Use the questions in Table 3.4 as a guide.)

❖ Generate hypotheses about the nature of the behavior. Is it attention-getting behavior, a control issue, lack of learning or immaturity? What is the communicative function of the behavior?

C. Generate at Least Two Hypotheses and Define an Agenda to Develop More Conventional Behaviors

❖ For one of the hypotheses, define an agenda using behavioral procedures mentioned in this chapter. Describe why you selected that specific procedure or procedures.

❖ For the remaining hypothesis, use a technique or strategy associated with cognitive behavior modification as the basis for an agenda to develop more conventional behavior. Again, give a rationale for selecting that particular technique or strategy.

D. Summary: Determine Which Agenda Would Be Most Appropriate for Dealing with the Behavioral Issue

❖ Explain the basis (rationale) for your decision. Comment on aspects of the agenda such as the intrusiveness of the procedure as well as the focal point of the control (teacher, student, environment).

❖ Comment on the usefulness of the framework for providing a means for considering behavioral issues or questions.

REFERENCES

AYLLON, T., & MCKITTRICK, S. M. (1982). *How to set up a token economy.* Lawrence, KS: H & H.

AXELROD, S. (1987). Functional and structural analysis of behavior: Approaches leading to reduced use of punishment procedures. *Research in Developmental Disabilities, 8*(2), 165–178.

BAUER, A. M., & SHEA, T. M. (1988). Structuring classrooms through levels systems. *Focus on Exceptional Children, 21*(3), 1–12.

BAUER, A. M., SHEA, T. M., & KEPPLER, (1986). Levels systems: A framework for the individualization of behavior management. *Behavioral Disorders, 11*(1), 28–37.

BROWN, A. L., & PALINSCAR, A. S. (1982). Inducing strategic learning from texts by means of informed, self-control training. *Topics in Learning and Learning Disabilities, 2*(1), 1-17.

CAMP, B. W., & BASH, M. S. (1981). *Think aloud: Increasing social and cognitive skills—A problem-solving program for children* (Primary level). Champaign, IL: Research Press.

CARR, E. G., & DURAND, V. M. (1985). Reducing behavior problems through functional communication training. *Journal of Applied Behavior Analysis, 18,* 111–126.

CORNO, L., & MANDINACH, E. B. (1983). The role of cognitive engagement in classroom learning and motivation. *Educational Psychologist, 18,* 88–108.

CULLINAN, D., LLOYD, J., & EPSTEIN, M. H. (1981). Strategy training: A structured approach to arithmetic instruction. *Exceptional Education Quarterly, 2*(1), 41–49.

DELGADO-GAITAN, C., & TRUEBA, H. T. (1985). Ethnographic study of participation structures in task completion: Reinterpretation of "handicaps" in Mexican children. *Learning Disability Quarterly, 8,* 67–75.

DERISI, W. J., & BUTZ, G. (1975). *Writing behavioral contracts: A case simulation practice manual.* Champaign, IL: Research Press.

DESHLER, D. D., ALLEY, G. R., WARNER, M. M., & SCHUMAKER, J. B. (1981). Instructional practices for promoting skill acquisition and generalization in severely learning disabled adolescents. *Learning Disability Quarterly, 4,* 415–421.

DONNELLAN, A. M., & KILMAN, B. A. (1986). Behavioral approaches to social skill development in autism: Strengths, misapplications, and alternatives. In E. Schopler & G. Mezibov (Eds.), *Social behavior and autism* (pp. 213–237). New York: Plenum Press.

DONNELLAN, A. M., & LAVIGNA, G. W. (1986). Nonaversive control of socially stigmatizing behaviors. *The Pointer, 30*(4), 25–31.

DOYLE, W. (1986). Classroom organization and management. In M. C. Wittrock (Ed.), *Handbook of research on teaching* (3rd ed., pp. 392–431). New York: Macmillan.

ELLIS, E. S., LENZ, B. K., & SABORNIE, E. J. (1987). Generalization and adaptation of learning strategies to natural environments: Part 2: Research into practice. *Remedial and Special Education, 8*(2), 6–23.

FANTUZZO, J. W., POLITE, K., COOK, D. M., & QUINN, G. (1988). An evaluation of the effectiveness of teacher vs. student management classroom interventions. *Psychology in the Schools, 25,* 154–163.

FLAVELL, J. H. (1979). Metacognition and cognitive monitoring. *American Psychologist, 34,* 906–911.

GUESS, D., & SIEGAL-CAUSEY, E. (1985). Behavioral control and education of severely handicapped students: Who's doing what to whom? and why? In D. Bricker & J. Filler (Eds.), *Severe mental retardation: From theory to practice* (pp. 230–240). Reston, VA: The Council for Exceptional Children.

HALLAHAN, D. P., LLOYD, J., KOSIEWICZ, M. M., KAUFMANN, J. M., & GRAVES, A. W. (1979). Self-monitoring of attention as a treatment for a learning disabled boy's off-task behavior. *Learning Disability Quarterly, 2,* 24–32.

HALLAHAN, D. P., MARSHALL, K. J., & LLOYD, J. W. (1981). Self- recording during group instruction: Effects on attention to task. *Learning Disability Quarterly, 4,* 407–413.

HARRIS, K. R. (1982). Cognitive-behavior modification: application with exceptional students. *Focus on Exceptional Children, 15*(2), 1–16.

HARRIS, K. R., & GRAHAM, S. (1985). Improving learning disabled students' composition skills: Self-control strategy training. *Learning Disability Quarterly, 8,* 27–36.

JOYCE, B., & WEIL, M. (1986). *Models of teaching* (3rd ed.). Englewood Cliffs, NJ: Prentice Hall.

KAVALE, K., & HIRSHOREN, A. (1980). Public school and university teacher training programs for behaviorally disordered children: Are they compatible? *Behavioral Disorders, 5*(3), 151–155.

KAZDIN, A. E. (1975). *Behavior modification in applied settings.* Homewood, IL: Dorsey Press.

———. (1977). *The token economy: A review and evaluation.* New York: Plenum Press.

———. (1985). The token economy. In R. M. Turner & L. M. Ascher (Eds.), *Evaluating behavior therapy outcome* (pp. 225–253). New York: Springer.

KENDALL, P. C. (1977). On the efficacious use of self-instructional procedures with children. *Cognitive Therapy and Research, 1,* 331–341.

LaNUNZIATA, L. J., HUNT, K. P., & COOPER, J. O. (1984). Levels systems. *Techniques: A Journal for Remedial Education and Counseling, 1,* 151–156.

LIPSKY, D. K., & GARTNER, A. (1987). Capable of achievement and worthy of respect: Education for handicapped students as if they were full-fledged human beings. *Exceptional Children, 54,* 69–74.

LLOYD, J. (1980). Academic instruction and cognitive behavior modification: The need for attack strategy training. *Exceptional Education Quarterly, 1*(1), 53–63.

LLOYD, J. W., & DEBETTENCOURT, L. J. U. (1982). *Academic strategy training: A manual for teachers.* Charlottesville: University of Virginia Learning Disabilities Research Institute.

MARSHALL, H. H. (1988, April). The classroom as "learning place." In H. Marshall (Chair), *Metaphors of Classroom Research.* Symposium conducted at the annual meeting of the American Educational Research Association, New Orleans, LA.

MARTENS, B. K., PETERSON, R., WITT, J. C., & CIRONE, S. (1986). Teacher perceptions of school-based interventions. *Exceptional Children, 53,* 213–223.

MCLAUGHLIN, T. F., KRAPPMAN, V. F., & WELSH, J. M. (1985). The effects of self-recording for on-task behavior of behaviorally disordered special education students. *Remedial and Special Education, 6*(4), 42–45.

MEICHENBAUM, D. (1977). *Cognitive-behavior modification: An integrative approach.* New York: Plenum Press.

——. (1980). Cognitive behavior modification with exceptional children: A promise yet unfulfilled. *Exceptional Education Quarterly, 1*(1), 83–88.

——. (1982). *Teaching thinking: A cognitive- behavioral approach.* Invited address to the Society for Learning Disabilities and Remedial Education. Austin, TX: Society for Learning Disabilities and Remedial Education.

——. (1986a). Cognitive-behavior modification. In F. H. Kanfer & A. P. Goldstein (Eds.), *Helping people change: A textbook of methods* (3rd ed., pp. 346–380). New York: Pergamon Press.

——. (1986b). Metacognitive methods for instruction: Current status and future prospects. In C. A. Maher & M. Schwebel (Eds.), *Facilitating cognitive development: International perspectives, programs, and practices* (pp. 23–32). New York: The Haworth Press.

MEICHENBAUM, D., & ASARNOW, J. (1979). Cognitive-behavioral modification and metacognitive development: Implications for the classroom. In P. C. Kendall & S. D. Hollon (Eds.), *Cognitive-behavioral interventions* (pp. 11–35). New York: Academic Press.

MESAROS, R. A. (1983). A review of the issues and literature regarding positive programming and contingency procedures for use with autistic children. Unpublished manuscript, University of Wisconsin-Madison.

PARIS, S. G., & OKA, E. R. (1986). Self-regulated learning among exceptional children. *Exceptional Children, 53,* 103–108.

PFIFFNER, L. J., ROSEN, L. A., & O'LEARY, S. G. (1985). The efficacy of an all positive approach to classroom management. *Journal of Applied Behavioral Analysis, 18,* 257–261.

POWELL, T. H., & POWELL, I. Q. (1982). The use and abuse of using the timeout procedure for disruptive pupils. *The Pointer, 26*(2), 18–22.

ROONEY, K. J., & HALLAHAN, D. P. (1985). Future directions for cognitive behavior modification research: The quest for cognitive change. *Remedial and Special Education, 6*(2), 46–51.

SCHUMAKER, J. B., DESHLER, D. D., & ELLIS, E. S. (1986). Intervention issues related to the education of LD adolescents. In B. Y. L., & J. K. Torgesen (Eds.), *Psychological and educational perspectives and learning disabilities* (pp. 329–365). New York: Academic Press.

SHEA, T. M., & BAUER, A. M. (1987). *Teaching children and youth with behavior disorders.* Englewood Cliffs, NJ: Prentice Hall.

SULZER-AZAROFF, B., & MAYER, G. R. (1977). *Applying behavior analysis procedures with children and youth.* New York: Holt, Rinehart and Winston.

VARGAS, J. (1977). *Behavioral psychology for teachers.* New York: Harper & Row.

WILLIAMS, R. M., & ROONEY, K. J. (1982). *A handbook of cognitive behavior modification procedures for children.* Charlottesville: University of Virginia Learning Disabilities Research Institute.

WOLERY, M., BAILEY, D. B., & SUGAI, G. M. (1988). *Effective teaching: Principles and procedures of applied behavior analysis with exceptional students.* Boston: Allyn & Bacon.

WONG, B. Y. L., & JONES, W. (1982). Increasing metacomprehension in learning-disabled and normally achieving students through self-questioning training. *Learning Disability Quarterly, 5*, 228–240.

WORKMAN, E. A. (1982). *Teaching behavioral self-control to students.* Austin, TX: Pro-Ed.

WORKMAN, E., & HECTOR, M. (1978). Behavior self-control in classroom settings: A review of the literature. *Journal of School Psychology, 16*, 227–236.

CHAPTER EIGHT

Cooperative Learning, Inductive Thinking, and Discussion

SITUATIONS

Setting: First grade classroom, students seated on rug on floor around teacher.

Teacher:	Today we're going to begin decorating the classroom for open house. What kind of things can we do to make the room nice for moms and dads?
Joel:	Paper chains.
Teacher:	That's a really good idea. Anything else?
Martina:	Pictures of us.
Michael:	Pictures of all of us saying "Hi."
Martina:	A big picture of all of us saying "Hi."
Teacher:	What a neat idea! A poster of all of us waving or saying "Hello." I think we can work that out.
Terri:	Flowers. On paper.
Teacher:	I think we can make flowers, too. Let's work on those three ideas. Who are my group leaders

today? [Students raise hands.] Martina, you're a group leader, and you wanted to think about a poster. Would five other people interested in working on a poster, a big picture of all of us saying "Hi," stand. [Six students stand.] I think six will still be okay. You poster people can go back to the math area. Marcus, you're a leader; what would you like to work on?

Marcus: Paper chains. All colors.

Teacher: I'll see what colors we have. How about three or four "chain" people? [Four students stand.] You folks can go to the reading area. And our "flower children"? Is that okay with you, Elaine. You're our last leader.

Elaine: Fine. You guys all want to make flowers?

*   *   *

Setting: Middle school, sixth grade science class.

Teacher: It's time for each pair of students to report. Let's all settle down so they can share. [Pauses.] Marissa and Marco?

Marissa: We sorted the leaves we were assigned into three groups. The first group were ovals; they didn't have any finger or branchy parts sticking out. The second group were the ones that had finger or branchy parts that stuck out that were pointed, like maple leaves. The last group were the ones that had finger or branchy parts that stuck out that were rounded off.

Teacher: What did you two do with the ginko leaves?

Marco: Well, we put it with our oval ones, because it didn't have any of those branchy parts. But it didn't really fit there, because it wasn't oval. So, we put it into its own group until we gather more leaves.

Teacher: I think you two were thinking. Maybe the ginko needs some more investigation.

*   *   *

Setting: High school literature class.

Teacher: Today we're going to begin our discussion of *Taming of the Shrew*. We're going to be using the case method which we've used before to discuss a problem which I'll be giving you in a minute. Let's review what we do in discussing a "case." First? [Turns to students.] Michael?

Michael: We have to define the problem.

Teacher: Our problem is: "Would the male-female relationships in *Taming of the Shrew* be seen the same way today in view of womens' liberation?" Then what...Renée?

Renee: We have to pose a hypothesis.

Teacher: Then? [Nods toward student in front row.]

Melanie: We have to find information from other areas to support us, like social studies, the paper, books and stuff.

Teacher: Then you draw your conclusion. Finally, each discussion group will select an individual to argue their case and a devil's advocate. Questions?

*   *   *

In each of these examples, the data, problem, or material is the focus of the interaction. In each of the activities described in this chapter, students are presented with information, posed a problem, or provided materials or topic. From this "stuff" or task, the interaction emerges. The role of the teacher is to facilitate students' interaction with the task, rather than direct it.

In many classrooms, activities that are grounded in data, materials, a problem, or the "place," the community or setting involved have been known as "work." However, though this allusion to work is deeply ingrained in our language and traditions, Marshall (1988) contends that it is an inaccurate metaphor. Using the metaphor or "workplace" for the classroom alludes to a sense of drudgery, in which the goal is to "do work" rather than learn. Unlike classrooms, the goal of the work setting is to produce a product or service for the benefit of the employer. In classrooms, learning is based on expertise and knowledge to be shared and a desire to help others construct knowledge. Classrooms, Marshall concludes, should be learning places, not workplaces.

In looking at classrooms as learning places, "what is learned" emerges as a primary concern. Doyle (1988), however contends that the "task" is missing in most descriptions of teaching. The concept of the task, he maintains, includes four aspects: (1) the goal state or product, (2) the problem or set of conditions or resources available to accomplish the task, (3) the operations involved in assembling and using resources to reach the goal state or product, and (4) the importance of the task in the overall scheme of things in the classroom.

Tasks can be described in many ways. Doyle suggests that tasks have a cognitive level, which refers to the cognitive processes students are required to use in accomplishing it. Work may be familiar (that is routinized, recurring exercises) or novel (assignments for which students are required to assemble information and operations from several sources in ways that have not been explicitly presented by the teacher). In the teacher-focused activities of the previous section, familiar tasks were emphasized. In the data/materials/place—focused activities of this section, novel tasks are employed.

While the activities described in this section are focused on the data/materials/place, the role of teacher and students cannot be forgotten. The teacher affects the tasks, and thus students' learning, by defining and structuring the "work" involved (Doyle, 1988). Classrooms are comprised of not only the tasks, but task conditions, which include the teacher's control of instruction, the time allocated, and the social system of the classroom (Marx and Walsh, 1988). In some cases, the very physical presence of the teacher may be a major barrier to the development of the students' interactions. These activities are simply additional considerations for incorporation into your agenda for management.

SELF-EVALUATION

Indicate whether you agree or disagree with each statement:

1. The emphasis on competition and independent work results in few opportunities for students to work together on academic projects in many classrooms.
2. Cooperative learning is only possible among students with great social and communicative skills.
3. Controversy within cooperative learning interactions should be avoided.
4. Cooperative learning results in academic gains and improvements in relationships among students.
5. Teaching concepts is much more efficient than helping students learn to develop and generate their own concepts and ideas.
6. Students contribute to each other's learning during discussions.
7. Teachers must carefully plan, monitor, and control discussion activities to accomplish specific goals.

KEY WORDS

inductive thinking

inquiry

discussion

OBJECTIVES

After completing this chapter, you will be able to:

1. Describe a rationale and research base for cooperative learning, inductive thinking, and discussion.
2. Describe research based examples of cooperative learning, inductive thinking, and discussion.
3. Prepare and evaluate cooperative learning, inductive thinking, and discussion.
4. Describe the role of cooperative learning, inductive thinking, and discussion within the context of data/materials/problem—focused interactions.

Objective One: *To Describe a Rationale and Research Base for Cooperative Learning, Inductive Thinking, and Discussion*

Cooperative Learning. Cooperative learning has its origins in the group investigation learning described by Thelen (1960). Thelen suggests that through group problem solving, students acquire knowledge and become participants in a more effective social group. In his concept of group learning, three concepts emerge: (1) inquiry, (2) knowledge, and (3) the dynamics of the learning group.

Thelen suggests that central to *inquiry* is a puzzle, a problem to be solved. The role of the teacher is to provide the problem situation, but students as a group identify and formulate the problem and work toward a solution. The goal of inquiry is the development of *knowledge*, which Thelen describes as the application of information and principles drawn from past experience to present experience. The *dynamics of the learning group* must be workable; the group must be large enough to provide diversity and small enough for individual participation, and share enough common values that communication is possible.

Joyce and Weil (1986) suggest six phases of group investigation. First, students must encounter a puzzling situation. This situation may either emerge or be provided by the teacher. In the second phase, students as a group explore their reactions to the situation. In the third phase, students formulate the study task and structure their activities, which they pursue independently and as a group in the fourth phase. Fifth, students pause to analyze their progress and process, and determine which aspects of the activity should be recycled in the sixth phase.

Thelen's early contention about the role of communication has recently been supported through research. Kalkowski (1988) pursued the hypothesis that cooperative learning group communication is the mediator of cooperative learning. In a case study of the application of cooperative learning in a school with a large bilingual population, Kalkowski analyzed cooperative communication in view of individual contributions. She found that the social-emotional communication occurred most frequently in the communication in the cooperative groups, followed by other communication types (i.e., procedural supply, information supply, information request). Kalkowski contends that social and emotional communication may be the key medium through which cooperative learning's positive social and learning effects occur.

Cooperative learning has been contrasted with competitive and traditional instructional strategies among a wide range of students. Cooper, Johnson, Johnson, and Wilderson (1980) found that cooperative learning activities increased interpersonal attraction among students who were initially prejudiced against each other on the basis of ethnicity, sex, or ability. Academic achievement gains and increases in self-esteem were found among mainstreamed handicapped students in classes which employed cooperative learning techniques (Madden and Slavin, 1983). Cooperative learning activities have been found to promote interaction and encouragement among handicapped and nonhandicapped students (Johnson and Johnson, 1981). These increases in positive interaction among handicapped and nonhandicapped students were found to generalize to unstructured class and school activities (Johnson, Johnson, Warring, and Maruyama, 1986).

Inductive Thinking. Inductive thinking activities in the classroom were developed by Taba (1966). Taba contended that thinking could be taught using specific teaching "strategies" applied in sequence. These strategies include (1) concept formation, (2) interpretation of data, and (3) the application of principles.

Concept formation, the first inductive teaching strategy, involves engaging students in a series of questions. Through questions, students identify the information which is relevant to the problem, group information, and develop names for these groups. Through concept formation, students increase their conceptual system, practicing differentiation, identifying common properties, and determining a hierarchy among groups.

Interpretation of data, the second in the sequence of three strategies, again uses teacher questions. Initially, the teacher questions students in a manner that they identify the critical relationships among aspects of the data. Next, students explore relationships, from which, in the third step, they make inferences.

The third strategy, *application of principles*, also involved three sets of activities. First, students are assisted in predicting consequences and formulating hypotheses. Students then begin to explain and support their predictions and hypotheses, which they verify.

As learning tasks require students to form concepts, interpret data, or generalize, the teacher applies the appropriate strategy. Although this pattern of interaction may appear teacher initiated, the nature of the learning task dictates the activity. In this way, inductive learning activities are data/place/problem focused.

Discussion. Discussion involves dialogue among students on a specific topic or question. Gall and Gillett (1981) suggest that discussion is an activity that involves a group of persons, usually in the roles of moderator and participant, who communicate with each other. They contend that there is a reciprocal influence in groups in that students learn not only from the teacher, but from each other. One of the strengths of the discussion method, as suggested by Gall and Gillett, is that it helps teachers to see individual student's interpretations of issues, problems, and subject matter content. Discussions are task/problem/data focused, in that they are driven by the content, topic, or question.

Through these activities, students develop an ability to share and evaluate information, develop the ability to separate emotional arguments from reasoning, and formulate personal views of give-and-take. Gall and Gillett (1981) also contend that discussion can be motivating for both student and teacher. Students participate in sharing knowledge, and through that sharing, teachers can evaluate students' level of understanding.

There are several reasons why teachers may be hesitant to use discussion, and from these concerns, a rationale for using the activity emerges. Gall and Gillett suggest that teachers may infer that because students may not participate in traditional class activities, they may not participate in discussion. In addition, teachers may fear that the clamor and movement which occur in classrooms during discussion may be viewed as "poor control" and "poor teaching." Finally, teachers may argue that they have too much material to cover to allow student discussion.

Those teachers may be concerned about students' reticence, with the teacher's support, students do discuss. The "loss of control" which may seem evident in classrooms in which discussion are used may be viewed as a sharing of instructional responsibility and learning. In the first situation which opened this chapter, for example, the teacher was not in control of the way in which the classroom would be decorated for Open House. However, through guiding the discussion, creative, practical ideas emerged. Teachers who effectively use discussion facilitate and reinforce active participation by the students, without stepping in to "lead." In "having too much material to cover," teachers forget that some skills, such as problem solving cannot be taught without discussion and independent attempts to share opinions and perceptions.

Objective Two: *To Describe Research-Based Examples of Cooperative Learning, Inductive Thinking, and Discussion*

Cooperative Learning. Several cooperative learning strategies have been described in the literature. These include group investigation (Sharan and Hertz-Lazarowitz, 1980), Co-op Co-op (Kagan, 1985), jigsaw learning (Aronson and Goode, 1980), and circles of learning (Johnson and Johnson, 1975).

Group investigation (Sharan and Hertz-Lazarowitz, 1980) emphasizes the interdependence among groups. In group investigation activities, all members of the class are assigned to the same general area of study, but each group is responsible for researching a single topic related to that area. Students are encouraged to join the group of their choice, depending on their interests. In their groups, students plan the investigation, pursue their topic of study, and present a report.

Co-op Co-op (Kagan, 1985) is similar to group investigation, but provides more structure to the activity. A class discussion is initially conducted by the class, which is then subdivided into subtopics for the small groups. Before groups begin to work on their academic goals, team-building exercises are used to facilitate cooperative interactions among their group members. Each group then further subdivides the topic to be explored by individual students. Students present the research on their individual topics to the group, and after discussion, individual information is integrated to prepare a presentation for the entire class.

In *jigsaw learning* (Aronson and Goode, 1980), students are divided into heterogeneous groups. Each person in the group is given access to only one part of the lesson (i.e., one person may have the information about a country's social customs, another religious beliefs, another food). Each student is responsible to learn the assigned part of the lesson thoroughly and teach it to all other members of the group. Students from different groups, having the same material to learn, meet in counterpart groups to discuss their part of the lesson before attempting to teach their peers.

Circles of Learning (Johnson and Johnson, 1975) also employs heterogeneous groups, integrating students in ability, sex, ethnicity, and if applicable, handicaps. The classroom is arranged so that students in each group sit in a circle facing each other. A complete set of materials is provided to each group, with individual students responsible for sharing information and materials and for helping each other learn. Individual tests and grades are given, but group rewards or grades may be given for group products.

Inductive thinking. Taba's curriculum (Taba, Durkin, Fraenkel, and McNaughton, 1971) provides a clear example of the use of inductive thinking activities in classrooms. In contrast to the emphasis of traditional social studies curricula on content and suggested activities, Taba's curriculum attempts to balance emphases on content, learning processes, and the learner. This "balance" is maintained through her development of a system of teaching and learning using key themes (concepts) and strategies for students in grades 1 through 8. Sample concepts include causality (focusing on events, multiple causes of events, and the use of this information to predict future events), conflict (focusing on interrelationships among individuals and groups, how conflict is characteristic of the growth and development of individuals and groups, the notion of resolving conflicts, compromise), cooperation, cultural change, differences, interdependence, and power.

The development of inquiry processes, creative thinking, hypothesis generation, and evaluating hypotheses by checking available data are all skills that are highly valued in the Taba curriculum. As students move through levels of this curriculum, learning activities related to the themes become more complex and challenging. Students take on greater responsibility for making interpretations and inferences based on information discussed and presented. Taba observed that such tasks are often difficult for students who have been conditioned to obtain information directly from textbooks. Therefore, the teacher's role is to support the development of processes such as interpreting data and inferencing, gradually withdrawing this support as students become more independent learners.

Discussion. Several applications of discussion method are presented in the literature. They include issue-oriented discussions, problem solving discussions (Gall and Gillett, 1981), and the case method (Graham and Cline, 1980).

In *issue-related discussions*, the focus is students' discussion of their personal opinions on public issues. The objective of these discussions is to increase students' awareness of their own opinions and those of others. Through the discussion, students begin to analyze and evaluate opinions and to modify their own opinions through analysis and evaluation. In addition, teachers may ask students to come to a consensus, increasing the demands of the discussion (Gall and Gillett, 1981).

Problem-solving discussions can be used to solve both concrete and abstract problems, ranging from discovering how to determine different weights of objects to planning a class party. Gall and Gillett suggest several criteria for these discussions. They suggest that the quality of the solution should be assessed, as well as the commitment that students have toward the solution. The third criterion, which emerges in brainstorming, is involved in the quantity of solutions used. Gall and Gall (1976) found that discussion groups were more effective than individuals in solving problems which require students to draw on their peers for assistance, develop multiple solutions, and commit to a course of action.

The *case method* (Graham and Cline, 1980) is a more structured discussion activity, used to lend reality to indirect experience, focus on concrete problems, develop decision making skills, broaden students' experiences, and help students see varying points of view. In the case method, students work from actual documents, created materials, audio-visual materials, or simulations, to develop, support, and evaluate hypotheses. In the case method, the student assigns materials which the students examine. Students then discuss the case together, reach a decision, and present their hypotheses. The role of the teacher is that of facilitator, with the students developing their own hypotheses and arguments.

Objective Three: *To Prepare and Evaluate Cooperative Learning, Inductive Thinking, and Discussion*

Cooperative Learning. Bohlmeyer and Burke (1987) provide a framework for considering cooperative learning techniques. Considering the variables which they describe provides teachers with a process for structuring cooperative learning activities which are compatible with their classroom context and classroom management agenda. The variables which Bohlmeyer and Burke discuss are outlined in Table 8.1.

A teacher's initial consideration in preparing cooperative learning activities is the nature of the *subject matter* which will be ad-

TABLE 8.1 Variables to Be Considered in Preparing Cooperative
Learning Activities

1. Subject matter
2. Nature of student interdependence during the activity
3. Nature of interaction among groups during the activity
4. Basis of designating groups
5. Basis of determining evaluation and reward
6. Managing the physical environment

Source note: This table was constructed from an article by E. M. Bohlmeyer and
J. P. Burke, "Selecting Cooperative Learning Techniques: A Consultative Strategy
Guide," *School Psychology Review, 16*(1), 36–49, 1987. The table does not
appear in the original publication.

dressed. Bohlmeyer and Burke suggest that the teacher consider
whether the activity be used to address basic academic skills. Other
options for cooperative activities include using cooperative learning
activities to deal with narrative factual material such as that presented in social studies activities. A third consideration is to use
cooperative learning activities to explore and discuss conceptual subject matter.

The *nature of student interdependence during the activity* must also
be considered. Students may be continually interdependent on each
other for practice, drill, and developing understanding throughout the
activity. As an alternative, the interdependence may be more developmental in nature, with students beginning the activity more independently and gradually increasing the amount of interdependence.

The *nature of interaction among groups during the activity* may
be adapted to the individual classroom context. Groups may be cooperative, assisting each other in achieving the goals of the activity.
Groups may also function independently, working toward criteria on
goals which are independent of those of other groups. In *designating
the groups* themselves, the teacher may select members, students may
self-select based on social attraction, or students may self-select based
on the topic considered. The *basis for evaluation and reward* may be
for individual participation or based on the product of the group.

Managing the physical environment for cooperative learning activities may force modifications in the physical learning context.
Desks and work areas may need to be rearranged; changing the
arrangement must take into account noise levels and distractions
which may be caused by several groups actively discussing topics. The
preparation on the part of the teacher will be different; rather than
planning the actual activity, the teacher plans the "problem" or puzzle,
provides resources and materials, and trouble shoots the interactions.

Preparation, then, may incorporate brainstorming questions which may emerge, potential difficulties in social interactions, and acquiring appropriate materials. In view of the unique materials and resources needs of cooperative learning activities, funding the activities may emerge as an issue.

Besides the physical context, the social context of the classroom should be considered. Slavin (1983) suggests that groups should be balanced. Students should be encouraged to help all members of the group master the material or participate so that their group has the created group success. In addition, students may need to adjust to the shift in the teacher's role from source of information to consultant in interactions.

Inductive Thinking. Joyce and Weil (1986) describe several variables to be considered in preparing and evaluating inductive thinking activities. They suggest that the three teaching strategies Taba describes strongly resemble each other. In each strategy, the teacher questions students, to guide them from one phase of the activity to the next. Careful consideration, however, must be given to the timing of moving students to the next phase. Joyce and Weil, for example, caution teachers about moving prematurely from the concept-formation strategy, because data may not have been appropriately identified. However, staying in this phase too long may lessen the students' interest.

In inductive thinking, the classroom atmosphere is cooperative. A teacher remains the initiator of the phases, yet as mentioned earlier, the task is the focus of the interaction. The teacher's primary mental task is to monitor how students are processing information, and to respond with appropriate questions. The strategies can be used in any curriculum that has large amounts of data that needs to be organized, such as social studies. The teacher's role is to help students process the data in developmentally complex ways (Joyce and Weil, 1986). Joyce and Weil contend that although Taba's strategies were developed for social studies, they can be applied to a variety of areas.

Using inductive thinking activities is particularly helpful in facilitating students' development in looking at more than one aspect of data. Through using inductive thinking, students can learn to categorize and build concepts on those categories (Joyce and Weil, 1986).

Discussion. Effective discussion depends on a range of variables. The ideal *group size* is five members, which means teachers typically have either several discussions going concurrently or have one discussion occurring while the remainder of the class observes. *Seating arrangements* must vary from rows facing the instructor, with circles being the most helpful for discussion. Chairs rather than desks are more amenable to discussion.

Gall and Gillet suggest several skills for facilitating the discussion process. These skills include

1. Maintaining an open discussion in which students feel free to say what they think.
2. Listening to others and keeping the discussion focused.
3. Analyzing different points of view.
4. Evaluating the effectiveness of the discussion.

Taba suggests that the classroom climate set by the teacher is a critical factor in effective discussions (Taba, Durkin, Fraenkel, and McNaughton, 1971). The teacher must maintain enough control to prevent a chaotic flow of unrelated ideas yet maintain openness to encourage a high degree of student contribution. Pacing is also important; Taba recommended that teachers wait five seconds for comments to allow time for students to think (refer to Chapter Five for a discussion of wait time). She also described the role of questioning skills to support effective discussions. For example, opening questions should be carefully selected to set the focus of the discussion. Other types of questions include "lifting questions," which move the discussion from one point to another ("There's another point to be considered. What is it?"), "extending questions," which broaden participation by allowing students who might not generate topics of discussion to contribute by extending the ideas of others ("What do you feel about John's idea?"), and "clarifiers" which not only facilitate discussion flow but also serve to encourage students to develop questioning skills ("Is there a better way we could describe this?").

Objective Four: *To Describe the Role of Cooperative Learning, Inductive Thinking, and Discussion within the Context of Data/Materials/Problems–Focused Interactions*

As noted in Chapter Five, all interactional patterns within the "activity" phase of an instructional event involve the practitioner (whoever is assuming the role of the teacher), participants (whoever is assuming the role of the learner), and the data/task/materials or problem around which the instructional event is organized. The key distinction noted in this chapter involves the focus of the pattern: the interaction between the data or materials and the participant within the instructional event. The teacher plays a supportive role within this interaction; the level of support will differ depending upon the goal of the instructional event, the data/material/problem, and the participant. Typically the practitioner sets up the problem in certain instructional events (e.g., selecting the tasks to be accomplished through cooperative learning activities, providing the topic for discussion). Teachers may use a variety of techniques such as scaffolding and questioning to support the interaction. In the first grade classroom situation mentioned at the beginning of this chapter, the teacher set the stage for the interaction (e.g., choosing the task of decorating the room) and acknowledged students' ideas. She set up groups for specific tasks, which were to be carried out through cooperative learning interactions.

As the instructional event proceeds, the practitioner's role may lessen, as participants exert greater influence on the interaction (e.g., as they move discussions to a particular point or select strategies for attacking problems within cooperative learning tasks). In the middle school example, the students reported on the results of their investigation indicating their use of inductive thinking to group the leaves into specific categories. The teacher's comments in the final example involving high school students suggest that the students will use the case method to generate solutions to a problem. If we were to observe the discussion that followed, we might see examples of intense student interaction with the data with minimal teacher role in the interaction.

In addition to the goal of greater academic progress, the use of data-focused interactions will have a major impact on the development of communicative competence. Activities such as cooperative learning, discussion, and strategies related to inductive thinking require students to interact with one another by taking on, maintaining, or relinquishing various roles within the interaction (e.g., group leader, listener, active contributor to discussion, reactor to comments). Students will learn to manage controversy and seek concurrence, both of which lead to questioning of one's views and more active searches for information (Johnson and Johnson, 1985). It is for these reasons that data-focused activities provide powerful learning opportunities both in the academic and social/communicative development.

SUMMARY

This chapter outlined three activities which teachers could use to facilitate interactions between students and the data/problem/materials within the instructional event. Although the focus of the instructional event is on the data/problems/materials–student interaction, the teacher's role is critical. In addition to setting the event (through activities within the "preparation" phase), initially, the teacher may provide greater direction within the activities. Ultimately, the goal is to help students actively participate in discussions, handle controversy (and perhaps seek concurrence) within cooperative learning groups, and carry out inductive thinking activities with minimal support from the teacher.

Cooperative learning, inductive thinking, and discussion activities frequently result in improvements in academic skills. More important, engaging in these activities seems to facilitate communication skills as well as changes in student self-esteem. Positive interactions among group members support the development of relationships between handicapped and nonhandicapped students.

The curriculum developed by Taba is designed to help students develop skills in processes such as concept formation, interpretation of data, and application of principles. The teacher supports the learner's development of skills in organizing information, generating hypotheses, and making inferences from information. Although her curriculum was designed for social studies, the strategies and activities can be easily applied to other content areas in which data may be organized and interpreted. In keeping with our focus on facilitating communicative competence, discussion provides another important means for supporting the data/problems/materials–student interaction. Taba strongly advocates discussion as a means for teachers to help students develop inductive thinking. As with cooperative learning, discussion encourages students to learn from each other.

One might ask why activities such as cooperative learning and inductive thinking are not typically observed in classrooms. Relinquishing total control of the instructional event by focusing on the interaction between participant and problem/task may be difficult for teachers. Shifts in attitudes required for the creation of classroom environments supportive of cooperative learning activities may also be problematic (Graves and Graves, 1985). Graves and Graves recommend that teachers acknowledge the gradual process of developmental change necessary for students to participate fully in cooperative learning activities. Teachers, too, should acknowledge changes in their skills in supporting discussions or designing inductive thinking activities. For those teachers who have, or are attempting to develop, a facilitative stance, cooperative learning, inductive thinking, and discussions provide powerful means for accomplishing the goal of facilitating the development of self-regulated learners.

REVIEW QUESTIONS

1. Describe cooperative learning. What types of instructional activities would seem most conducive to the use of cooperative learning in classrooms? Why might some students resist this type of activity?

2. Suppose you encountered a teacher who seemed reluctant to try cooperative learning activities in the classroom. What potential benefits of cooperative learning might you point out to that teacher?

3. Two important learning processes advocated by Taba are interpretation of data and formulating hypotheses about data. Taba suggested that these processes are developed through activities and discussions about information (what we would call "data/problems/materials–student interaction). How might you argue with someone who (a) believes that content issues are most important in the areas of social studies and science and (b) strongly believes in instruction through reading texts and content-driven curriculum activities?

4. Facilitating discussions to achieve specific goals is sometimes an extremely difficult task. Describe some contextual considerations one must address in preparing discussion activities. How structured should the discussion interaction be? What is the role of teacher flexibility in the support of discussion?

5. Attempting cooperative learning activities involves risks for teachers and students who are most familiar with instructional activities involving competition and independent learning. Describe several examples of risks from both the teacher's and students' perspective. What can teachers do to minimize those risks?

APPLICATION ACTIVITIES

Given the typical emphasis on competition and independent work, it may be difficult to observe and participate in cooperative learning, inductive thinking, or discussion activities in classrooms. Therefore, consider the following three options:

A. Observe Data/Problem/Task–Student Interactions

It might be possible to find a classroom activity which involves cooperative learning, discussions, or inductive thinking. Describe the context of the instructional event (refer to Chapter Three if necessary). Who are the participants? What is the problem/task/materials that shapes the interaction? Next, describe the roles of the participants. How much support of the interaction is needed? Finally, comment on changes in the interaction as the event proceeds. For example, suppose a group of students were given the task of planning a journey to the moon. How did the interaction change as students move from initial planning stages to the solution of the problem? How much support did the teacher provide as the interaction proceeded? Summarize your assignment by commenting on what the students gained from the interaction.

B. Design a Cooperative Learning Activity

Using the classroom in which you've conducted your observations, design an interactional event which includes cooperative learning activities. This event could involve planning a party (focusing on students' communicative competence, dealing with controversy and seeking consensus) to an academic task such as determining relationships between two cultural groups' concern for special needs students. Select two students and describe their roles within the interaction. Generate possible scenarios for the event: hypothesize how those students might react to the activity. What level of support may be necessary for the successful outcome of the activity you selected? Describe potential problems with the interaction. Following consideration of alternative activities which may be used to accomplish the same goal, summarize your assignment by commenting on the benefits of focusing on the data/problem/materials–student interaction.

C. Participate in a Cooperative Learning Activity

Select three colleagues who are familiar with this text. Rather than work on this assignment independently, complete option A or B as a cooperative learning activity with your colleagues. Audio- or videotape the interaction so that you can observe your interactions at a later date. When you review the tape, comment on changes in the interaction as the event proceeded. Was there equal participation by all members of the group? Were the roles carefully delineated and explicitly described or did the roles emerge as the interaction proceeded? How did the complexity of the problem seem to influence the interaction? Summarize by commenting on your personal reaction to completing the assignment through cooperation with colleague as opposed to the assignments in previous chapters independently.

REFERENCES

ARONSON, E., & GOODE, E. (1980). Training teachers to implement jigsaw learning. In S. Sharan, P. Hare, C. Webb, & R. Hertz-Lazarowitz (Eds.). *Cooperation in education* (pp. 47–81). Provo, UT: Brigham Young University Press.

BOHLMEYER, E. M., & BURKE, J. P. (1987). Selecting cooperative learning techniques: A consultative strategy guide. *School Psychology Review,* *16*(1), 36–49.

COLE, D. A. (1986). Facilitating play in children's peer relations. *American Educational Research Journal, 23,* 201–215.

COOPER, L., JOHNSON, D. W., JOHNSON, R. & WILDERSON, F. (1980). The effects of cooperative, competitive, and individualistic experiences on interpersonal attraction among heterogeneous peers. *The Journal of Social Psychology, 11,* 243–252.

DOYLE, W. (1988). Work in mathematics classes: The context of students' thinking during instruction. *Educational Psychologist, 33*(2), 167–180.

GALL, M. D., & GALL, M. (1976). "The discussion method." In *Seventy-fifth yearbook of the study of education* (pp. 166–216). Chicago: University of Chicago.

GALL, M. D., & GILLETT, M. (1981). The discussion method in classroom teaching. *Theory into Practice, 19,* 98–102.

GRAHAM, P. T., & CLINE, P. C. (1980). The case method: A basic teaching approach. *Theory into Practice, 18,* 112–116.

GRAVES, N. B., & GRAVES, T. D. (1985). Creating a cooperative learning environment: An ecological approach. In R. Slavin, S. Sharan, S. Kagan, S. Hertz–Lazarowitz, R. Webb & R. Schmuck (Eds.), *Learning to cooperate, cooperating to learn* (pp. 403–436). New York: Plenum Press.

JOHNSON, D. W., & JOHNSON, R. T. (1975). *Learning together and alone.* Englewood Cliffs, NJ: Prentice-Hall.

———. (1985). The internal dynamics of cooperative learning groups. In R. Slavin, S. Sharon, S. Kagan, R. Hertz-Lazarowitz, C. Webb, & R. Schuck (Eds.), *Learning to cooperate, cooperating to learn* (pp. 103–124). New York: Plenum Press.

JOHNSON, R. T., & JOHNSON, D. W. (1981). Building friendships between handicapped and nonhandicapped students: Effects of cooperative and individualistic instruction. *American Educational Research Journal, 18,* 415–423.

JOHNSON, D. W., JOHNSON, R. T., WARRING, D. & MARUYAMA, G. (1986). Different cooperative learning procedures and cross-handicap relationships. *Exceptional Children, 53,* 247–252.

JOYCE, B., & WEIL, M. (1986). *Models of teaching* (3rd ed.). Englewood Cliffs, NJ: Prentice Hall.

KAGAN, S. (1985). Co-op Co-op: A flexible cooperative learning technique. In R. Slavin, S. Sharan, S. Kagan, S. Hertz-Lazarowitz, R. Webb, & R. Schuck (Eds.), *Learning to cooperate, cooperating to learn* (pp. 437–462). New York: Plenum Press.

KALKOWSKI, P. (1988).   Communication in cooperative learning groups. Paper presented at the AERA National Meeting, New Orleans.

MADDEN, N. A., & SLAVIN, R. E. (1983).   Effects of cooperative learning on the social acceptance of mainstreamed academically handicapped students. *Journal of Special Education, 17,* 171–182.

MARSHALL, H. H. (1988, April).   The classroom as "learning place." In H. Marshall (Chair), *Metaphors of Classroom Research.* Symposium conducted at the annual meeting of the American Educational Research Association, New Orleans, LA.

MARX, R. W., & WALSH, J. (1988).   Learning from academic tasks. *The Elementary School Journal, 88,* 207–219.

SHARAN, S., & HERTZ-LAZAROWITZ, R. (1980).   A group investigation method of cooperative learning in the classroom. In S. Sharan, P. Hare, C. Webb, & R. Hertz-Lazarowitz (Eds.), *Cooperation in education* (pp. 14–46). Provo, UT: Brigham Young University Press.

SLAVIN, R. E. (1983).   *Cooperative learning.* New York: Longman.

———. (1985).   An introduction to cooperative learning research. In R. Slavin, S. Sharon, S. Kagan, R. Hertz-Lazarowitz, C. Webb, & R. Schuck (Eds.), *Learning to cooperate, cooperating to learn* (pp. 5–15). New York: Plenum Press.

TABA, H. (1966).   *A teacher's handbook for elementary social studies.* Reading, MA: Addison Wesley.

TABA, H., DURKIN, M. C., FRAENKEL, J. R., & MCNAUGHTON, A. H. (1971). *A teacher's handbook for elementary social studies: An inductive approach* (2nd ed.) Reading, MA: Addison Wesley.

THELEN, H. (1960).   *Education and the human quest.* New York: Harper & Row.

CHAPTER NINE

Student-Focused
Group Activities

SITUATIONS

Setting: Second grade classroom, a reading group of six students. The teacher is seated in the circle with the students.

Teacher: We've been working on questioning all this week. We read, then we asked questions. What words do we use to begin questions?

Melanie: "W" words.

Teacher: [Repeating response] "W" words. What are some "W" words?

Stephen: Who, what, where.

Josh: When.

Teacher: Two more? [Students pause.] We have who, what, where, when...

Tammy: How and why.

Teacher: [Nods to acknowledge Tammy's response] We're going to read, and work on our questions. Melanie, would you like to lead us first?

Melanie: [Reads first paragraph of "Three Billy Goats Gruff." Pauses. Then asks student next to her] Tammy, how many Billy goats were there?

*   *   *

Setting: Fourth grade classroom, one-half of the class is seated on the floor in a circle, the other half at desks working.

Teacher: Luis, let's talk about your goal.

Luis: I'm going to make sure I bring in my math homework.

Teacher: Did you achieve that goal?

Luis: Yes. I gave it to Ms. T. this morning and it was even signed.

Teacher: Thanks, Luis. Anyone want to comment as to whether Luis met this goal?

Margie: He did, I saw him. And Ms. T. put his name on the "Superstar" chart.

Teacher: Thanks, Margie. Luis, I agree that you must have achieved this goal. In my notebook I have down that you have met this goal all week. Think it's time for another?

Luis: Okay, I'll bring in reading homework.

Teacher: Anyone like to talk about this new goal for Luis?

Sylvia: I don't think it's a good goal. He does his reading homework. A goal is something you're trying to do, and he's doing that already.

Teacher: Other comments?

Cindy: I don't think it's a good goal. Too easy.

Teacher: Luis, group members feel that this really isn't a very good goal. What do you think?

Luis: Maybe I'll work on something besides homework. Maybe I'll work on trying new games in gym.

*   *   *

Setting: Ninth grade composition class; students are writing during "writing workshop." Teacher is also writing. After about 5 minutes, the teacher decides to circulate among the students. The teacher stops first at Marcus's desk.

Marcus: Mr. L. I'm hung up on this piece of writing.

Teacher: [Looking directly at Marcus rather than at the paper] I recall from yesterday's discussion that the piece was about an encounter with a cat. What kind of help do you need?

Marcus: I found a problem when I was sort of reading it outloud to myself, so let me do that. "The three students paused, looking at the cat—no I changed that to 'marveling at the cat,' grasping the map in their hands."

Teacher: The problem?

Marcus: I can't put the part about holding the map in the right place. If I say, "The three students paused, grasping the map, looking at the cat..." it sounds funny.

Teacher: You're right, it does sound awkward. Remember last week when Richard discussed his problem during share time. He's been working on editing phrases to eliminate the clutter.

Marcus: Now I remember! What if I put the part about looking at the cat closer to "the three students"?

Teacher: How does that sound?

Marcus: "Three students looking at the cat, held the map." Or how about "The three students holding the map paused"? And whichever one is more important, the cat or the map, I set aside. Right?

Teacher: Sounds like a good solution.

In each of these three situations, the primary focus of the interaction involves the student. In the first example, reciprocal teaching, the "teacher" role is one shared by students. Initially, the teacher sets the context or boundary for the instructional event and maintains a rather directive role as the interaction with the text is modeled. The ultimate goal, however, is that the students will assume the role of teacher as they work through strategies related to reading comprehension. Reciprocal teaching, then, can be considered a student-focused interaction pattern because the direction or movement of the interaction ultimately depends on the students. In the second example, that of a "pow-wow," personal goals and evaluation are student focused. The third example represents writer's workshop, in which students initiate their own writing activities; the teacher serves as a consultant to the student and a peer writer.

In this section, student-focused activities are described. In these activities, the primary focus of the instructional event is the students' interaction with the data/materials/problem. While the teacher might set the context and general boundaries of the instructional event, the data/material/problem is generated by the student. The teacher's role is one of support (as with other interactional patterns). In these activities, students are assisted in attaining personal integration, effectiveness, and self-evaluation by the teacher (Joyce and Weil, 1986).

Student-focused activities may need to be introduced slowly among students who have experienced primarily teacher-focused activities. Scobie (1983) describes a continuum, in which the teacher begins by directing students, moves to contracting with them, and continues on to delegating to them. In this manner, students gradually gain control of their own learning and behavior (which is in keeping with our ultimate goal of helping students become self-regulated learners).

Dialogue occurs throughout student-focused activities. Genishi, McCarrier, and Nussbaum (1988) describe dialogue as "collaborative interaction carried out through language." Dialogue occurs as students use materials, work with others, observe, and talk. Dialogue stems from problems which children meet as they interact with data/materials/problems.

The two chapters in this section reflect the diversity of activities which are student-focused. The purpose of Chapter Nine is to explore the rationale and research base for three instructional events: reciprocal teaching, class meetings, and writer's workshop. Following examples of the implementation of these activities, information will be provided to help the reader evaluate each of these events for possible inclusion into an overall classroom agenda. Given that this pattern is "student focused," the reader is asked to pay particular attention to the role of the teacher within each of these interaction patterns.

In Chapter Ten, individual and small-group activities, such as peer collaboration and interviews, are presented. Throughout these activities, students remain the most important factor influencing the interaction, that is, the major determiner of the nature and direction of the activity.

SELF-EVALUATION

Indicate whether you agree or disagree with each statement:

1. Student-focused interactions within an instructional event require minimal involvement of the teacher.
2. "Thinking aloud" and working through novel problems are powerful means for helping students become self-regulated learners.
3. There is little difference between cooperative learning activities and instructional events such as class meeting and reciprocal teaching.
4. Teachers are often hesitant to rely on peer interaction and small-group activities because of a fear of losing control of the classroom.
5. The nature of student-focused activities requires students to have adequate skills in the areas of reading and writing.

KEY WORDS

reciprocal teaching

writing workshop

class meeting

pow-wow

OBJECTIVES

After completing this chapter, you will be able to:

1. Describe a rationale and research base for reciprocal teaching, class meetings, and writer's workshop.
2. Describe research-based examples of reciprocal teaching, class meetings, and writer's workshop.
3. Prepare and evaluate reciprocal teaching, class meetings, and writer's workshop.
4. Describe the role of reciprocal teaching, class meetings, and writer's workshop within the context of student-focused interactions.

Objective One: *To Describe a Rationale and Research Base for Reciprocal Teaching, Class Meetings, and Writer's Workshop*

Reciprocal Teaching. Reciprocal teaching is an instructional procedure which involves a dialogue between teachers and students for the purpose of constructing the meaning of the text (Palincsar, 1986a, Palincsar and Brown, 1986). This dialogue is based on verbal exchange, in which one individual acts in response or reaction to a second individual. Another key feature of the reciprocal teaching dialogue is the expectation that all participants in the interaction will take turns assuming the role of teacher. Moreover, this instructional method is a collaborative learning procedure designed to improve students' comprehension of text through influencing how students interact with situations involving reading passages (Palincsar, 1986a, 1986b; Palincsar and Brown, 1986; Palincsar, Stevens, and Gavelek, 1988). Reciprocal teaching, then, helps students learn to apply strategies and regulate their own learning.

In reciprocal teaching, the teacher's role is that of an expert providing the support necessary to move students from acquiring skills, into various levels of competence, and eventually to mastery. The teacher initially leads the instruction, modeling and providing explanations which render the strategies explicit, concrete, and overt. Gradually, students begin to share the leadership role taking turns acting as the group leader or teacher (Palincsar, 1986a, 1986b; Palincsar and Brown, 1986; Palincsar and Brown, 1987; Palincsar, Stevens, and Gavelek, 1988). In the situation at the beginning of the chapter, the teacher conducted an initial review of the questioning strategy and turned the interaction over to a student who led the interaction.

Palincsar and her colleagues have developed four strategies shared by participants in a reciprocal teaching situation (all of which are related to reading comprehension): predicting, question generating, summarizing, and clarifying. In *predicting*, students present hypotheses about what the author will discuss next in the text. *Question generating* gives students an opportunity to identify information which provides the content for valid questions. *Summarizing* is group identification of the most important content of the paragraph. The last goal, *clarifying*, involves having students recognize that there may be many reasons why the text is challenging the students (Palincsar and Brown, 1986).

The use of reciprocal teaching has resulted in improvement of students' reading comprehension scores (Palincsar and Brown, 1984). In addition, qualitative improvements in the students' dialogue were noted. These results suggest that students were able to internalize the strategies and apply them to monitor their reading comprehension (Palincsar and Brown, 1984).

Class Meeting. Class meetings were introduced by William Glasser (1965) who maintained that helping students develop problem-solving skills must be done socially, in groups. In *Reality Therapy*, he suggested that human problems are the result of failing to have met the need for love and the need for self-worth. In classrooms, "love" is demonstrated by helping and caring for each other. Feeling loved increases an individual's self-worth. Glasser also assumed that through a commitment to change, students can fulfill their needs.

Reality therapy classroom meetings require (1) personal involvement, (2) facing reality, and (3) learning alternatives to the way in which one currently behaves. *Personal involvement* is essential for students to learn that they are valuable and capable and that there are others (the teacher) who can assist them in meeting their needs. *Reality* is necessary to establish a standard of behavior. *Learning better ways to behave* involves being responsible to fulfill your needs in a way that does not deprive others of the ability to fulfill their needs. Through these requirements, the teacher and student become personally involved in schooling.

Little research has been conducted on Glasser's reality therapy group meetings. However, Shearn and Randolph (1978) found no relationship between application of the model and any increase in students' self-concept or on-task behavior.

Writer's Workshop. Graves (1983) describes writer's workshop as a style of instruction in which writing is treated as a laboratory or studio subject. It involves the organization of a classroom environment to facilitate writing development. Atwell (1987) suggests that writer's workshop is "less a program than a way of life" (p. 17). In contrast to more traditional writing instruction such as creative writing exercises, a "literate environment" is established which supports students as they become writers.

Graves (1985) suggests that the teacher teaches most by showing how he or she learns. In the atmosphere of a studio environment, such as writer's workshop, teachers and students write together and learn from each other. A "process" approach to writing development is maintained, in which meaning is emphasized and skills are addressed only in the context of the students' writing. The environment is highly predictable, and supportive, enabling students to take risks with their writing. The studio nature of writer's workshop encourages peer interaction, which leads to sharing ideas, taking risks with various styles of writing, and "charging" the environment with an enthusiasm for writing (Atwell, 1987).

Objective Two: *To Describe Research-Based Examples of Reciprocal Teaching, Class Meetings, and Writer's Workshop*

Reciprocal Teaching. Classroom-based studies of the use of reciprocal teaching as an instructional intervention involved an examination of improvements in students' reading comprehension. In addition, dialogues were examined to note changes in students' abilities to employ the strategies. Palincsar and her colleagues report that students' ability to summarize, question, clarify, and predict improved markedly through the application of the reciprocal teaching procedure. Quantitative improvements on comprehension measures were found to be large, reliable, and durable. In addition, the students' improved skills generalized to classroom settings (Palincsar, 1986a; Palincsar and Brown, 1984, 1986; Palincsar, Stevens, and Gavelek, 1988). Palincsar and Brown (1986) reported that after five years of using the technique, substantial changes in dialogue, comprehension, and generalization of the skills occurred. They used reciprocal teaching in large and small groups, as well as during peer tutoring. As a result of their studies, they contend that reciprocal teaching can be used in content areas such as science.

Initial studies of reciprocal teaching were conducted with small groups of junior high students (five students) who were enrolled in remedial reading classes. Since then, this procedure has been implemented with larger groups of students (ranging in number from seven to fifteen). Current research has focused on the implementation of reciprocal teaching with first grade students who were identified by their classroom teachers as at risk for academic difficulty. In contrast to initial studies that focused on changes in the dialogue over time and differences among groups who received the intervention and those who did not, features of the dialogue and scaffolded instruction provided by the teacher and peers are currently being examined.

Palincsar and Brown (in press) suggest that an important feature of reciprocal teaching involves modeling processes which successful readers use to comprehend text. The teacher makes the process explicit by modeling what to do when encountering an unfamiliar word, for example. Another critical feature is the use of scaffolded instruction to support students as they gradually develop strategies to lead the group interaction. Palincsar and Brown observed teachers who invited the first grade students to participate as they collaboratively constructed the meaning of the text, provided the necessary support of the dialogue, and withdrew support as students internalized the strategies.

Palincsar and Brown's work with first graders revealed that dialogues became less teacher-directed as the study progressed. In addition, students were better able to monitor their understanding of text (e.g., requesting clarifications). Further evidence of internalization of the strategies came from anecdotal reports from teachers. They observed that children used the strategies in contexts other than the listening comprehension lessons involved in the study. Finally, researchers noted qualitative differences in dialogues which were also reflected in varying gains on comprehension assessments (Palincsar and Brown, in press). These differences will be described in the following section.

Class Meeting. Two frameworks for class meetings will be described: Glasser's class meeting and Morris's (1982) pow-wow.

Glasser describes the *class meeting* as a time when students and teachers collaboratively join in discussion of behavioral, personal, and academic problems. The meetings are structured to develop solutions rather than discuss problems. The emphasis is on clear, honest sharing of feelings in a nonevaluative way. Issues and questions are addressed through assessing the reality of the solutions and the concept of personal choice to commit to the solution.

In the class meeting, the teacher must encourage a climate of acceptance and involvement. Then a problem or issue is brought up by either student or teacher. The students make personal judgments about the issue and identify alternatives. In concluding the meeting, students make a public commitment, which they know will be reevaluated later.

The *pow-wow* serves as a classroom support group for students who are developing more conventional behavior. The pow-wow requires each student to determine his or her own behavioral goal. In the pow-wow, each student states a personal goal. The group leader asks the student first, and then the rest of the group, if the student has met his or her goal. The student then is asked whether he or she has met the goal. The student then makes a new goal, which is evaluated by the remainder of the group. The student then may change the goal. As the situation at the beginning of the chapter illustrates, group members carefully suggested that Luis select a different goal, one that is more meaningful to the student. The goal is written on a chart which is kept in the classroom, and peers are asked for suggestions in helping the student make the goal. Each student in the group then makes one positive statement about the student making the goal. The process continues until all students have developed a goal.

Morris maintains that there are several advantages to using the pow-wow. Students are involved in developing their own goals. In addition, students learn to think about what events bring about certain behaviors. Through evaluating other students, students become more attentive to the classroom environment. Finally, through the "positives," students improve their self-image.

Writer's Workshop. The use of a studio concept for writing instruction grew out of a series of studies conducted by Graves and his colleagues (Graves, 1983; Sowers, 1985). Since then, teacher-researchers such as Atwell (1987) have described their personal journeys as they attempted to create a writer's workshop in their classrooms. All of the writers suggest three key ideas which are central to the development and support of writer's workshop. First, writers need *time* to write. Graves (1985) advocates a minimum of four class periods a week (30 minutes each period) to provide students with regular blocks of time necessary for their development. Second, *ownership* of writing is critical. Teachers should trust students to generate their own topics rather than using story starters or imposing guidelines for writing. Teachers may inadvertently take ownership of student work by suggesting specific revisions or formats for writing. Therefore, giving students ownership requires teachers to listen to students in order to help them discover what they want to do. The third key aspect is *response*. Teachers should respond to student writing as they conduct conferences throughout the writing process (as opposed to the more traditional response of written comments after the writing is complete). Response from peers is also important and may occur during group share time or at the point of publication. In preparation for publication, more opportunities for response are available as students edit their work, share writing pieces with peers, and submit work to teachers for final edits.

Atwell (1987) describes additional ideas borrowed from other researchers which contributed to the writer's workshop as she implemented it in her classroom. The conventions or mechanics of writing is best learned through in the context of students' writing. To enhance and facilitate writing development, writers need to read from a variety of genre. (Graves also recommends surrounding students with literature). Atwell contends that students need to observe adults who are experienced writers. In this manner, students may watch as teachers encounter such difficulties as generating topics and selecting topics. Finally, she recommends that teachers continue to observe and learn from their students' writing.

The predictability and routine of the interactions within the writer's workshop strongly support writing development. Atwell (1987) organizes her writing workshop into four parts. She begins with a brief *minilesson* presented to the entire class. The content of these minilessons is based on student need and revolves around issues such as topic search and selection, instruction in conventions (e.g., using quotations to mark dialogue), and process issues such as revising and editing. Next, Atwell holds a *status-of-the class conference* to check where each student is in the writing process (e.g., start new topic, first draft, self-edit, publish). Following the status check, students write as the teacher circulates among the students and confers with them about their writing. During the *conference*, the teacher expects students to describe what the piece is about, where they are in the writing, and what help they might need (Graves, 1983). The teacher asks questions without making judgments about the writing, thereby allowing students to maintain ownership of their writing. Conferencing also helps students acquire the language of writers (Sowers, 1985). Rather than referring to their writing as right, wrong, or messy, students learn to look at the information within their writing or examine their work for accurate use of writing conventions. Finally, the workshop concludes with *group share* time during which students may share their work with the class. Students may use this time to gain other perspectives on their work, to share a successful technique, or to celebrate a completed work. The structure and organization of writer's workshop contributes to the development of a community of learners in which students and teachers work together to discover the excitement and power of writing.

Objective Three: *To Prepare and Evaluate Reciprocal Teaching, Class Meetings, and Writer's Workshop*

Reciprocal Teaching. A specific instructional process is described for teachers who use reciprocal teaching (Palincsar and Brown, 1986). Initially the teacher defines and provides rules to assist students in learning the strategies (predicting, question generating, summarizing, and clarifying). Throughout this period of instruction, the teacher models the strategies used and provides guided practice for the students. Later, the teacher provides support for interactive dialogues as students assume responsibility for leading discussions. In order to focus the interaction on comprehension of the text, Palincsar (1986a) recommends that the teacher select materials so that students are not (1) hindered by decoding the text and (2) using materials representative of those that students are expected to use in school.

In addition to modeling strategies such as predicting, clarifying, summarizing, and questioning, the teacher should make explicit the processes of encountering difficulties in the text. Palincsar and Brown (in press) describe this as "having the knowledge of an expert but experiencing the comprehension activity as a novice might" (pp. 24–25). The essence of reciprocal teaching, however, is the use of dialogue to transfer the control and responsibility for the reading process from the teacher to the student. As students become responsible for the dialogue, the teacher assumes the role of coach, fading out modeling, providing feedback, and promoting self-evaluation (Palincsar, 1986b).

In their review of dialogues of first grade teachers, Palincsar and Brown (in press) observed three types of statements: instructional/modeling statements, prompting statements, and reinforcing statements. Students who continued to receive a high percentage of prompting statements from the teacher throughout the study did not show as much gain in comprehension scores as students whose teacher gradually reduced her role in the dialogue (permitting students to engage in the dialogue independently). This clearly illustrates the importance of withdrawing scaffolds for the dialogue as students learn to use the strategies. Relinquishing control of the interaction to students may be difficult for some teachers, yet the transfer of control within the reciprocal teaching procedure is an important example of facilitative teaching (refer to Chapter Three).

Class Meeting. During Glasser's *class meeting*, the teacher must demonstrate a stance which projects a warm, personal relationship with each student. In addition, he or she must remain nonjudgmental while supporting students in developing more responsible alternatives. The teacher must also work to support the group as a whole as it identifies, selects, and follows through alternatives. Group discussion techniques, described in Chapter Eight, may assist the teacher in working with students.

The pow-wow emphasizes interaction of the whole group. All students must remain involved; if one student leaves the group, the pow-wow stops and everyone waits until he or she returns. In addition, the whole group must attend to the person speaking. Morris suggests that the pow-wow should include a cross section of students who remain together for some period of time. The goals which students develop should be observable and measurable. Morris also suggests that teachers should not expect results in a short period of time and shouldn't be afraid to modify the process.

Writer's Workshop. Organizing the classroom to support writer's workshop requires careful attention to both physical and social contexts. A physical context which "invites" students to write includes a variety of materials (different kinds of paper, writing implements, supplies such as stapler and scissors) and furniture arrangements to facilitate individual writing and small group discussion. A positive social context is created through the opportunities for and predictability of teacher and student interaction (e.g., conferences, sharing time). For example, Graves (1983) wrote about a teacher who set the tone of his room, clearly indicating to students that their ideas were valued. He also suggested that greater opportunities for teacher-student interaction within the workshop setting would lead to a greater willingness on the part of students to take risks and meet challenges within their writing.

Both Graves (1983) and Atwell (1987) advocate predictable patterns of teacher-student interaction to support writing development. Atwell, for example, described a pattern of response to students' writing as "always beginning with the writer's meaning, with ideas and information, then reflecting, concentrating on one or two concerns, nudging, waiting, and coming back" (pp. 71–72). Graves suggests that teachers follow the student by asking questions which encourage thinking about writing. Teachers should also wait for and listen carefully to student responses. As illustrated in the situation at the beginning of the chapter, the teacher listened to the student's concerns and helped him to generate a solution to his problem.

The social context of writer's workshop provides important occasions for peer interaction. Atwell (1987) suggests that the writer's workshop provides opportunities for social relationships to be brought into the classroom and put to work. Students know who is an expert on a certain topic or writing style, and freely consult one another. While the teacher may need to show students how to confer with peers without being judgmental or sarcastic, students become enthusiastic about writing and are supportive of each other's work.

Within the writer's workshop, teachers and peers provide scaffolds to support student writing development. In reciprocal teaching the teacher models how a novice might interact with unfamiliar text; the teacher in writer's workshop shares his or her personal writing process with students. Graves (1983) describes this as modeling within the context of natural predicaments, becoming writers together. For example, the teacher might begin a piece of writing (using an overhead projector or large chart paper) by generating a list of topics. The teacher verbalizes his or her thoughts as a topic is selected. Similarly, the teacher might talk through the process of abandoning that topic after verbalizing several unsuccessful attempts at writing a lead.

Gradually, the teacher withdraws support as students learn to trust their judgments and maintain responsibility for their writing. For example, if one views conferencing with the teacher as a form of scaffolding, then an important goal may be to have students learn to have conferences with peers or with themselves. Atwell (1987) provides students with guidelines for such conferences, which are based on the types of questions and discussion that take place during conferences with the teacher. Atwell describes another method she uses to provide an initial scaffold for the writing process that is withdrawn as students assume control over their writing. During an introduction of writer's workshop, Atwell explains a poster which includes guidelines for "What Writers Do" (e.g., find an idea, draft one, confer, revise, confer, self-edit). This poster remains in class for two or three weeks. Atwell removes these guidelines because she feels strongly that students need to make decisions about the writing process in terms of their own writing. This is a clear illustration of a facilitative stance, in which the ultimate objective for the teacher is to promote the development of writers.

Objective Four: *To Describe the Role of Reciprocal Teaching, Class Meetings, and Writer's Workshop in the Context of Student-Focused Activities*

The distinction between the interaction patterns described in Chapter Eight (data/materials/problems-focused interactions) and the student-focused interactions may be viewed by some readers as rather subtle at first glance. In both Chapters Eight and Nine, the primary emphasis of each pattern is on the interaction of the student with the task/materials/problem. In both cases, the teacher's role is primarily one of support, with the type and level of support varying according to student need. The importance of a facilitative, highly communicative environment and a shared responsibility for teaching and learning is similar for both types of interactional patterns.

The key distinction between the activities described in Chapter Eight (cooperative learning, inductive thinking, and discussions) and those in this chapter relates to the impact of specific influences on path or direction of the interaction. In data/materials/problem–focused interactions, the data or task exerts the greatest influence on the interaction. If, in the course of a science experiment, students inadvertently mixed two chemicals yielding an unexpected outcome in the data, the instructional activity is likely to take a path different from the activity in which students kept the chemicals properly stored. Suppose students were given the task of determining the type of rocks from a set of samples. If the samples were all of one kind of rock, the instructional event would take a certain path. If two samples were clearly metamorphic, the need for inductive thinking would be reduced. In a discussion of various influences on the settlement of the American West, the students would be limited in their discussion by the content of the problem. All these examples suggest the role of the data in imposing or influencing direction of the instructional interaction.

In contrast to the limitations placed on the interaction by the data or materials, the student is the primary determiner of the direction or path of student-focused interactions. For example, in reciprocal teaching and class meeting, the responses made by other students in the group clearly impact on the direction of the interaction. If a student selects a goal during a class meeting that seems too simplistic (as in the illustration at the beginning of the chapter), the interaction takes a path which would differ if all students selected realistic goals. In writer's workshop, the writing process (thinking, planning, discussing) is clearly the primary factor influencing the interaction.

Finally, the following image might serve to illustrate the importance of the student within student-focused interactions. Sowers (1985) cited Levi-Strauss's description (1966) of "the tinker who constructs with whatever materials come to hand for ends that may be altered as new and interesting components come into view" (p. 340). While the materials clearly influence the construction, it is the student who makes decisions about how to proceed and determines direction of the interaction.

SUMMARY

Student-focused activities such as reciprocal teaching, class meetings, and writer's workshop emphasize the students' interaction with some task, material, or problem. In each activity, the teacher maintains a supportive role, which varies as students move from dependence on the teacher's scaffolds to control of the interaction (self-regulated learning). Critical to each of the activities described in this chapter is the classroom context which encourages peer interaction.

Reciprocal teaching is an instructional procedure which has been used to promote reading and listening comprehension skills. Instruction takes place in small groups, with strategies initially modeled by the teacher. Through reciprocal exchanges among the participants, each student ultimately assumes the role of leader or "teacher" in the interaction. The process of reciprocal teaching has been used to facilitate the acquisition of comprehension monitoring and comprehension fostering strategies such as predicting, questioning, clarifying, and summarizing.

Class meetings have been used to help students develop problem-solving skills. Within these meetings, students discuss behavioral, personal, and academic problems with the ultimate focus on developing solutions. Other meetings, such as the pow- wow, provide support for students who are developing more conventional behavior. During these meetings, students determine personal goals and discuss them with the group. Other potential benefits to students related to class meetings include active involvement in selecting goals, attention to classroom events which might contribute to certain behaviors, and development of a more positive self-image.

Writer's workshop is a style of instruction in which writing occurs in a studiolike environment. This environment is designed to support students' writing development by (1) providing time to write on a regular basis, (2) permitting ownership of the writing, and (3) responding to student work in a manner that challenges and encourages development. Teachers and students create and maintain a literate environment in which they write and share ideas. The structure of a writer's workshop includes a minilesson, a check on students' writing status, writing/conferring, and a time to share their work with others. As with reciprocal teaching and class meetings, the social context is extremely important. Peer interaction is viewed as another means of supporting writing development.

In the examples described in the chapter, the teacher actively participates either by setting the initial boundaries of the interaction or through providing scaffolding to promote student development. The data/materials/problem also assumes an important role in the interaction. In student-focused activities, a primary factor influencing the interaction is students and their responses to their own work or to one another. In reciprocal teaching, the student assumes the role of the teacher or group leader to learn reading or listening comprehension strategies. Other students' responses to questions from the group leader influence the interaction significantly. The same is true for class meetings, in which students react to each others' goal selections or collaboratively generate solutions to problems. In writer's workshop, students' involvement with their own writing as well as discussions with others about their work affects the interaction.

REVIEW QUESTIONS

1. Describe the similarities between reciprocal teaching, class meeting, and writer's workshop. How are the teacher's roles different from the teacher's roles in the activities mentioned in Chapter Eight (cooperative learning, inductive thinking, and discussion)?

2. Both cooperative learning activities and writer's workshop involve intense student involvement in the interaction. Compare and contrast these two activities with respect to the role of the student.

3. The data/materials/problem component of the interaction plays an important role in the activities presented in Chapters Eight and Nine. Describe how reciprocal teaching might change or remain the same if the instructional problem related to a science experiment rather than reading comprehension. How might a cooperative learning interaction change if the problem involved a writing activity?

4. List three important features of a classroom environment that would facilitate activities such as reciprocal teaching, class meeting, and writer's workshop. Comment on why some teachers might be hesitant to use these activities in their classroom.

APPLICATION ACTIVITIES

This chapter described several activities in which the primary focus of the interaction was on the student. Because it might be difficult to find examples or participate in reciprocal teaching, class meetings, and writer's workshop activities, several options for activities are suggested here.

A. Use a Class Meeting Format to Set Goals for a Behavioral Issue

The purpose of this activity is to design and implement an instructional event using a class meeting format. Select a small group of students in a classroom in which you are familiar. Use Morris' "pow-wow" as a framework for the interaction. Ask students to select a behavioral issue to serve as the data/materials/problem for the meeting. Try to ensure that the issue is one which is easily discussed among the group (e.g., the problem of cafeteria noise level or unkempt lockers or desks that disturb the teacher). (Note: If you are unable to serve as group facilitator, ask the teacher in the classroom in which you are observing to implement the activity.)

Observe the interactions among the students. (It might help to audiotape the interaction for more detailed analysis.) Describe your role (or the teacher's role) as group facilitator. How much scaffolding or control of the interaction did you (or the teacher) provide? Did all group participants share equally in the interaction? If there were some students who tended to dominate the activity, make some hypotheses as to why this domination occurred. Summarize your comments with some guesses as to how the outcome of the meeting might have differed if the activity had been carried out as a cooperative learning task.

B. Discuss the Possibility of Starting Writer's Workshop

The purpose of this activity is to examine the impact of teacher stance on opinions regarding student-focused activities. The activity involves interviewing a teacher to determine his or her reaction to the use of writer's workshop in his or her classroom. First, generate a description of writer's workshop (including the key factors and principles mentioned in the chapter). Share this information with the teacher. Ask the teacher what he or she thinks would be some possible outcomes of attempting to implement writer's workshop in his or her classroom.

As you interview the teacher, try to determine aspects of his or her stance that might support a writer's workshop. Observations of the teacher's interactional patterns in the classroom should also assist you in determining whether the teacher might be "open" to creating a classroom environment similar to writer's workshop. For example, does the teacher allow students to make decisions about any aspects of their classroom activities? Is the teacher more directive in his or her interactions? Summarize your comments with statements about the impact of stance on student-focused activities.

REFERENCES

ATWELL, N. (1987). *In the middle: Writing, reading, and learning with adolescents.* Upper Montclair, NJ: Boynton/Cook.

GENISHI, C., MCCARRIER, A. & NUSSBAUM, N. R. (1988). Research currents: Dialogue as a context for teaching and learning. *Language Arts, 65,* 182–191.

GLASSER, W. (1965). *Reality therapy.* NY: Harper and Row.

GRAVES, D. H. (1983). *Writing: Teachers and children at work.* Portsmouth, NH: Heinemann.

———. (1985). All children can write. *Learning Disabilities Focus, 1*(1), 36–43.

JOYCE, B., & WEIL, J. (1986). *Models of teaching* (3rd ed.). Englewood Cliffs, NJ: Prentice Hall.

LEVI-STRAUSS, C. (1966). *The savage mind.* Chicago, IL: The University of Chicago Press.

MORRIS, S. M. (1982). A classroom group process for behavior change. *The Pointer, 26,* 25–28.

PALINCSAR, A. S. (1986a). Metacognitive strategy instruction. *Exceptional Children, 53,* 118–124.

———. (1986b). The role of dialogue in providing scaffolded instruction. *Educational Psychologist, 21,* 73–98.

PALINCSAR, A. S., & BROWN, A. L. (1984). Reciprocal teaching of comprehension-fostering and comprehension-monitoring activities. *Cognition and Instruction, 1,* 117–176.

———. (1986). Interactive teaching to promote independent learning from text. *The Reading Teacher, 37,* 771–777.

———. (IN PRESS). Classroom dialogues to promote self-regulated comprehension. In J. Brophy (Ed.), *Teaching for understanding and self-regulated learning* (Vol. 1). New York: JAI Press.

PALINCSAR, A. S., & BROWN, D. A. (1987). Enhancing instructional time through attention to metacognition. *Journal of Learning Disabilities, 20,* 66–75.

PALINCSAR, A. S., STEVENS, D. D., & GAVELEK, J. R. (1988, April). *Collaborating in the interest of collaborative learning.* Paper presented at the annual meeting of the American Educational Research Association, New Orleans, LA.

SCOBIE, R. (1983). Situational teaching: Fostering self-direction in the classroom. *Curriculum Inquiry, 13,* 130–150.

SHEARN, D. F., & RANDOLPH, D. L. (1978). Effects of reality therapy methods applied in the classroom. *Psychology in the Schools, 15,* 79–83.

SOWERS, S. (1985). Learning to write in a workshop: A study in grades one through four. In M. Farr (Ed.), *Advances in writing research.* Volume 1: *Children's early writing development* (pp. 297–342). Norwood, NJ: Ablex.

CHAPTER TEN

Student-Focused
Small-Group
and Individual Activities

SITUATIONS

Setting: Third grade classroom, students are working in pairs, with desks pushed together, on the floor, grouped at the table.

John:	Read that first sentence to me again, C. J.
C.J.:	"The moon was pushing up from the hills." This just isn't right. I want it spookier.
John:	It's okay.
C.J.:	No it's not. I need a different word. Pushing isn't right.
Teacher:	What are you two gentlemen discussing today?
John:	Part of my story isn't working. I need a different word. Look [gives paper to teacher].
Teacher:	Why don't you two list words that mean about the same thing as pushing and see if you can find one that will work better. Try some...

John: Shoving...

C.J.:   Poking...

John: That's the word I couldn't think of, poking! [John scratches out pushing and writes in poking.]

              *   *   *

Setting: Junior high school, after school, student is seated at a desk; teacher is seated next to her.

Teacher: Thanks for coming back after class, Lucy. I thought we should talk about what happened today during class.

Lucy: What do you mean?

Teacher: From where I was sitting, it seemed that you were looking out the window, tapping your pencil, and moving around a lot.

Lucy: I guess I'm just kind of jumpy.

Teacher: You're kind of jumpy...

Lucy: Yeah, I have a lot on my mind, and I'm just sort of ...of jumpy.

Teacher: Can you tell me a little more about what's on your mind?

Lucy: All this high school testing stuff. I mean, I really want to go to the college prep program, and I can do the work, but this testing stuff just isn't fair.

Teacher: It isn't fair?

Lucy: I do good work, I work hard. And if I screw up on just one test, I can't go, or they put me on a waiting list and I wait forever.

Teacher: The high school testing which is coming up is making it hard for you to work. What can we do to make you feel less "jumpy"?

              *   *   *

Given the emphasis on individual work and independent activities in most American classrooms, very few schools permit students to help each other with classwork on a regular basis (Cooper, Marquis, and Edward, 1986). Yet, learning that occurs "out of school" often depends upon shared experiences and collaboration (Resnick, 1987). Cooper, Marquis, and Ayers-Lopez (1982) suggest that interaction with peers can serve to support cognitive development, with peers serving as resources for one another. In Chapter Eight, we observed that cooperative learning activities, as instructional strategies, often led to improvements in students' social development. The focus of this chapter, however, is to explore the opportunities presented by student-focused interactions. Earlier, we described cooperative learning as an instructional strategy that involves peer interaction. However, within cooperative learning activities, the overall objective is set by the teacher and the interaction is heavily influenced by the data/materials/problem. Activities involving peer interaction are peer initiated or focused and can occur in a variety of data/materials/problems.

Within student-focused activities such as peer collaboration, the teacher's role is a supportive one. In some instances, the presence of the teacher may inhibit certain types of interaction. For example, in their description of activities to facilitate play in children, Cole (1986) found that even the physical presence of the teacher may be a major barrier in social development. He found the most successful strategy to be providing initial training, and then stepping back to allow students to resolve their own difficulties in a more normal manner.

In some cultures, student collaboration is an accepted home and play behavior, in which students collectivize their learning experiences (Delgado-Gaitan and Trueba, 1985). "Unsanctioned talk" can become a time of working on intellectually challenging tasks (Dyson, 1987). In a series of case studies, Dyson demonstrates that students spontaneously collaborated with one another to create extended stories and seriously critiqued the logic of those stories. She contends that conventional definitions of "on" and "off" task may need to be extended to include peer collaboration.

In this chapter, the opportunities for learning through the use of individual and small-group focused patterns, including collaboration, are described. In contrast to activities involving peer interaction, interviews emphasize the individual as the focus of the interaction. They are used to examine an incident with the student, to help the student understand his or her own perceptions and feelings. The goal of the interview process is increased self-knowledge and self-understanding. Research-based examples of peer interaction and interviews will be discussed followed by ideas related to how teachers can design an environment and plan activities which support peer interaction and the use of interviews.

SELF-EVALUATION

Indicate whether you agree or disagree with each statement:

1. Collaborating with peers to complete tasks reduces the amount of work for each member of the collaborative group.
2. Collaborative interactions require that students maintain equality in the interaction in order for collaboration to be effective.
3. Discussion of topics and information that is "off task" detracts from the collaborative process.
4. Working together to solve problems or confront specific issues jointly is most effective through implementing an interview process.
5. Teachers less skilled in reflective or active listening should not attempt to discuss highly sensitive issues with students during the interview process.

KEY WORDS

peer collaboration

interview

nondirective interview

OBJECTIVES

After completing this chapter, you will be able to:

1. Describe a rationale and research base for peer collaboration and interviews.
2. Describe research-based examples of peer collaboration and interviews.
3. Prepare and evaluate peer collaboration and interviews.
4. Describe the role of peer collaboration and interviews within the context of data/materials/problem focused interactions.

Objective One: *Describe a Rationale and Research Base for Peer Collaboration and Interviews*

Peer Collaboration. Peer interaction and the development of peer relationships serves as a "context of special promise for development" (Cooper, Marquis, and Edward, 1986, p. 274). Learning to get along with peers, sharing, cooperating, or competing, all involve the development of skills, behaviors, and communication styles that serve us as adults in our culture (Garvey, 1986). Why is it, then, that in some classroom settings students are penalized for being "off task" when such conversations often serve to support cognitive, social, and communicative development?

Dyson (1987) argues that peer talk is valuable for communicative and cognitive development. She notes that this talk permits students to assume conversational roles that are different from student-teacher talk. She maintains that during collaborative activities (in this case, creation of narratives through drawing and writing), peers may serve as an interested audience for the student, or help each other critique the frames which they are constructing. In addition, through collaboration, students may become more aware of anticipating the reactions of others in their activities. Students are more likely to ask questions of their peers, challenge ideas and make suggestions to one another. She comments that "the social life of the children energized rather than interfered with the academic curriculum" (p. 416), concluding that conversations or "time off task" served as opportunities for student development.

Peer interaction may take a number of forms. One form of interaction of current research interest is "peer collaboration." Cooper, Marquis, and Edward (1986) describe collaborative activities as the sharing the power of directing the activity, that is, sharing or alternating the teacher role or not assuming a leader-follower pattern. Their observations of peer learning activities led to the development of a continuum of interactive patterns ranging from solitary activity to collaborative interactions. The various forms of interaction will be described later in this chapter.

Daiute (1986) suggests that collaborative learning activities center on the Vygotskyian (1972) concept that children are more successful in developing their thinking and communication skills if they model them directly on social interactions. She notes that when two writers work together, they produce better texts than either one does alone. In her descriptive study of collaborative writing, she found that collaborating students maintained important features in their individual work, while increasing complexity, fluency, and accuracy in mechanics. Daiute suggests that explicit negotiation which takes place in collaborative writing could assist students in developing more complex inner talk. During collaborative writing, students exchange information both subtly and explicitly.

Student-focused activities such as those involving collaboration (whatever the form) seem to provide opportunities for the development of communicative competence. In the following sections, more in-depth information about the forms of interaction and discussions of how teachers might support activities involving peer interaction will be presented.

Interviews. An interview is a specific pattern of verbal interaction, which is initiated for a specific purpose and focuses on a specific content area (Kahn and Cannell, 1957). In this section, two interview styles are described, Redl's "life space interviewing" and Rogers's nondirective interviews. Teachers are cautioned, however, that these techniques may be viewed as outside of the realm of the classroom teacher. Teachers are urged to use their supervisors or behavioral consultants to assist them if they feel that these strategies are needed to work effectively with a student.

Life-Space Interviews. Redl (1959) suggests that the life space interview is a way of structuring an incident in a student's life so that the issue confronting the student can be addressed. In Redl's point of view, the life space interview may be used for one of two purposes: the clinical exploitation of life events and emotional first aid. However, a single interview may address both purposes.

Clinical exploitation of life events occurs when the teacher uses a behavioral incident to explore with the student a consistent behavioral characteristic. In exploiting life events, the teacher may help the student become more aware of his or her unconventional perception of a situation or a consistently less effective way in which the student is dealing with a situation. The life-space interview may be used to help the student become more aware of social standards, and reactions and pressures of the group. In *emotional first aid,* the life-space interview may serve to reduce the student's frustration, support the student in an emotionally charged situation, or restore a strained student-teacher relationship. Emotional first aid can help the teacher reinforce behavioral and social limits and realities, and help the student develop solutions to working and learning in the group.

Nondirective Interviews. The *nondirective interview* is based on the work of Rogers (1982). Rogers contends that positive relationships enable persons to grow and that the role of the teacher is that of facilitator and helper. The teacher's role is to facilitate student exploration of new ideas about their lives, work, and relationships. Rogers assumes that students are willing to be responsible for their own learning. Open sharing and honest communication are essential in using the nondirective interview.

Through the nondirective interview, the teacher mirrors students' thoughts and feelings through reflective comments. The purpose of the interview is to raise the students' consciousness of their own perceptions and feelings, helping them clarify their ideas. The goal of the nondirective interview is increased self-understanding and self-knowledge within the security of an empathetic relationship (Joyce and Weil, 1986).

Objective Two: *To Describe Research-Based Examples of Peer Collaboration and Interviews*

Peer Collaboration. Research on peer interaction suggests that students may assume various roles within collaborative activities. Following a description of a continuum of roles, two specific examples of peer collaboration activities will be discussed: those surrounding writing in classrooms and those surrounding computer learning.

Cooper, Marquis, and Edward (1986) observed students ages 5 through 12 in a Montessori school that encouraged collaboration as part of students' learning experiences. Five forms of peer learning clearly illustrate the diversity of interaction styles evident in collaborative activities. Some students engaged in *solitary activity*, working alone and declining offers of assistance from others. Others assumed the role of *onlooker*, observing others, occasionally making comments and suggestions, yet not engaged in their own work. Cooper and her colleagues commented that this form of interaction may be helpful in helping the "onlooker" learn from the more skilled children. In the *parallel-coordinate* form in interaction, two children work on their own projects, yet may contribute suggestions or ideas to the other person. This style of interaction seemed to assist students in maintaining attention to their individual tasks. Furthermore, ideas and suggestions occurred within conversational exchanges which covered a range of academic and nonacademic topics.

Guidance involves a form of interaction in which one student assumes the role of teacher, offering help and directing the activity. A variation of this occurs when one student requests help from another, initiating the interaction. Finally, Cooper and her colleagues observed instances of *collaborative interaction*. The collaboration occurred either through the completion of associated projects that shared the same goal (thematic collaboration) or through interrelated projects that accomplished a shared goal (differentiated collaboration). This variation in peer learning interactions was also noted by Stodolsky (1984), who described the following types of peer instructional work groups: completely cooperative, cooperative, helping obligatory, helping permitted, and peer tutoring.

Examples of peer collaboration have emerged around journal writing and free writing. In journal writing, Dyson (1987) suggested that the joint activity of journal writing provided a social occasion for children during which they worked together on entries and interacted about their separate activities. During the joint activities, the students extended the boundaries of their work, critiqued the logic of their own texts, and considered the needs of the audience.

Daiute (1986) described a more structured creative writing experience as the basis of peer collaboration. Students were provided with factual information (on animals, in her reported case) and asked to write around a theme (in her example, on how animals, like people's lives, can be difficult). After writing initial stories independently, the students then shared comments and suggestions about each others' stories. The students discussed character names, plot events, mechanics, and, in that the writing was performed using a word processing program, typing. Students self-reported that writing together was more "fun" and increased their ideas.

Students appear to benefit from collaborative activities in a variety of roles (e.g., onlooker, guidance, collaborative role). When seated next to a peer in an environment in which collaboration is encouraged, students may contribute information and ideas to one another (Cooper, Marquis, and Edward, 1986). The teacher's role in supporting this process will be described later on in the chapter.

Interviews

LIFE-SPACE INTERVIEWS. Two systematic studies have explored the application of life-space interviews in educational settings. Reilly, Imber, and Cremins (1978) used the life-space interview in a resource room setting. The use of the interview was related to increases in students' conventional behavior. The technique was also found to be manageable in this setting. DeMagistris and Imber (1980) also used the activity with strong positive effects, but in so far as their study involved students with severe behavioral disorders in a residential treatment, their findings may have limited application in a school setting.

NONDIRECTIVE INTERVIEWS. Rogers (1982) maintains that during nondirective interviews, the teacher abdicates the role of decision maker, and enters the role of facilitator who focuses on the students' comments and reactions. The teacher is not the knowledgeable advisor, but a partner in the problem-solving processes.

Joyce and Weil (1986) suggest that the nondirective interview may be applied in several types of problem situations: personal, social, and academic. In any application of the activity, the teacher must be willing to accept that the student is capable of directing himself and solving his own problems. The teacher assists a student in developing personal awareness in an atmosphere of safety and acceptance.

Objective Three: *To Prepare Peer Collaboration and Interviews*

Peer Collaboration. As with other instructional events, peer interaction activities are greatly influenced by variables in the classroom context (refer to Chapter Three). Certain types of tasks lend themselves to interaction (e.g., writing on computers, science and social studies activities). These activities or projects provide opportunities for students to assume various roles (Garvey, 1986; Stodolsky, 1984). Context variables include the teacher's attitude toward peer teaching, organizational features of the school and prior experience with collaboration (Garvey, 1986).

Within all the interaction patterns (described in earlier chapters), the teacher's role is critical. Cooper, Marquis, and Edward (1986) describe the teacher's role as providing "supportive guidance." In some cases, younger children may need help in setting goals. They might need explicit instruction in group work (e.g., turn-taking, acknowledging participation from all the students). Cooper et al. suggest that teachers observe for situations in which one student manipulates the group or when students have difficulty pacing their work. The teacher should also be aware of the diversity of forms that collaboration may take (ranging from solitary activity to shared work). Cooper and her colleagues suggest that the "occurrence of peer learning depends upon the important interplay of teacher sanction and children's developmental readiness" (p. 293). In the situation at the beginning of the chapter, the students appeared to be contributing ideas to the interaction. The teacher provided some support through questioning, yet stepped away to let the students resolve their problem.

As with writer's workshop, the teacher can facilitate peer learning by permitting students to develop areas of expertise and help those students share this expertise with others (Cooper, Marquis, and Ayers-Lopez, 1982). Daiute (1986) suggests a more active role on the part of the teacher, ensuring that a collaborative pair is working and highlighting discussion points and ideas. Dickinson (1986) acknowledges the role of the teacher providing opportunities for cooperation and peer learning, as did Dyson (1987). Finally, Forman (1987) suggests that teachers help children learn to regulate their own peer relations, help mediate disputes, continue to be sensitive to cultural issues.

Project STRETCH (1980) suggests that teachers consider four sets of variables when planning peer collaborative activities. These variables include (1) matching students who will collaborate, (2) selecting the appropriate setting, (3) preparing students to collaborate, and (4) managing the logistics of the collaboration.

When *matching students who will collaborate*, students should be a part of or contribute to the relationship. Students who collaborate should be comparable in size and age and able to communicate with their partners. Teachers should avoid pairing "stars" with less outstanding students.

In *selecting the appropriate setting,* teachers should decide whether the collaborative activity will be one-to-one or small group in nature. Teachers should be conscious of each student's needs; some students may find collaborative activities intrusive and distracting rather than facilitating. Providing students with alternatives may gradually increase their comfort level in collaborative activities.

When *preparing students* to collaborate, the teacher should make clear the goals of the activity. Students may also need teacher assistance in developing listening skills and expressing themselves in a collaborative relationship.

There are several *logistical concerns* when students are collaborating in the classroom. Space may be an issue, with noise level emerging as a problem when several individuals are collaborating. The teacher should be explicit concerning the responsibilities of the collaborators in the activity. The teacher should remain available to supervise the activities and provide support when needed.

Daiute (1986) suggests that teachers can further enhance collaborative learning by making sure that the pair is working effectively and highlighting points which seem to recur in their discussions. In addition, in that some of the points of discussion may be quite subtle, the teacher can assist students through explicitly describing, restating, and summarizing more subtle points.

Garvey (1986) observes that the collaborative process may be affected by factors beyond the student's control (e.g., physical appearance, handicaps, personal name). In these cases, the teacher may have to assume a more active role in facilitating the collaborative process. Dyson (1987) notes that there may be some students whose interest in social interaction may distract them from academic tasks, while other students may have difficulty finding a comfortable niche in the peer group (as in Garnica, 1981).

Interviews

LIFE-SPACE INTERVIEWS. Morse (1980) outlines a series of steps that occur during a life space interview. An interview usually begins as a result of a specific incident. The teacher then encourages the student to state his personal perception of the situation. The teacher must determine if the incident is an isolated happening or a significant part of a recurring issue.

During the life-space interview, the teacher listens to those involved in the incident as they construct it. No moralizing or attacking takes place. Even though the students' perceptions are accepted, the teacher may suggest alternative perceptions for consideration by the student.

A nonjudgmental resolution phase follows. Some issues may be resolved at this point, and the interview may end here. However, if the problem is not resolved, the teacher may offer his or her view of the issue. Finally, the teacher and student develop an acceptable plan to deal with the present problem and similar problems in the future. A sample life-space interview is presented in Table 10.1.

NONDIRECTIVE INTERVIEWS. Rogers (1982) maintains that nondirective interviews must take place in a setting with the appropriate climate. The teacher must present the stance of warmth, responsiveness, and interest in the student as an individual. Second, the climate should be one in which students are free to express feelings, without

TABLE 10.1 Sample Life-Space Interview

STEP	SAMPLE BEHAVIOR AND VERBALIZATION
Instigating event	Student pulls materials from bulletin board, shredding posters, and so on.
Testing for depth and spread	"Marcia was calling me stupid. You always catch me. You just don't like me."
Content clarification	"I was mad at Marcia for calling me stupid, so I ripped down the posters."
Enhancing a feeling of acceptance	Teacher: "You felt angry at Marcia. Being called stupid when you're trying your best can make you angry."
Avoiding early value judgments	Teacher: "How do you feel about your decision to show that you were mad at Marcia by tearing down the posters?"
Exploring change possibilities	Teacher: "What is a better way to show you're mad at Marcia and to let me know how you feel?"
Resolution	"I could get away from her when she calls me names...I could just ignore her...I could tell you about it...I could tell her she's making me mad and she should stop."

Source note: This table was adapted from T. M. Shea and A. M. Bauer, *Teaching Children and Youth with Behavior Disorders,* 2nd edition, p. 213. Englewood Cliffs, NJ: Prentice Hall, Inc., 1987. Reprinted with permission of the publisher.

fear of lecturing, moralizing, or teacher judgment. Although the student is free to express feelings, he or she is not free to attempt to control the teacher or to act on these feelings. Finally, the interview should be free from pressure or coercion.

The teacher's primary participation in the nondirective interview is in the form of reflective or active listening. Joyce and Weil (1986) indicate that three kinds of teacher comments occur. At the beginning of the interview, the teacher may take the lead through giving the student some indication as to what the topic of discussion should be. However, the teacher should take the lead without making comments following the students statements; the teacher reflects, clarifies, accepts, and demonstrates what the student is expressing. Semidirective responses such as interpretations and approval may also be used sparingly.

In interpretation, the teacher contributes to the interview a comment so that a student who is unable to offer an explanation for his or her behavior may continue the discussion. Approval is usually only given when the student makes genuine growth and progress.

The nondirective interview proceeds through four phases. In the initial phase, the student *releases feelings* (sometimes referred to as catharsis). During this time, the student discharges the feelings surrounding the problem. Through reflective listening, such as that demonstrated in the situation at the beginning of this chapter, the teacher assists the student in clarifying his or her feelings surrounding an issue. *Insight*, the next phase, follows the expression of pentup feelings. The student, through reflective listening, begins to understand reasons for his or her behavior. Through the insight into these reasons, he or she may begin to see more conventional ways of addressing the problems or issues.

Action is the third phase of the directive interview process. The test of the insights which the student gains is a change in action. This action phase is followed by the *integration* phase, during which the student begins to integrate the insights and actions into a more comprehensive way of addressing future problems or issues.

Objective Four: *To Describe the Role of Peer Collaboration and Interviews in the Context of Student-Focused Activities*

By our definition, student-focused activities involve an emphasis on the students' interactions with some instructional problem or material. As with other interaction patterns, the data/materials/problem and the practitioner still play significant roles in the interaction. However, the student or group of students remain the primary factor in influencing the interaction.

The role of the student is easily observed in activities involving collaboration, as shown in the situation at the beginning of the chapter. Certainly some tasks lend themselves to collaborative activities (e.g., writing together using a computer which permits shared viewing as the story is being written, extended projects which involve collaboration as students share information). The classroom context is also particularly important, especially the teacher's acknowledgment and support of conversation during collaborative activities. For example, Cooper and her colleagues (Cooper, Marquis, and Edward, 1986) observed that collaborative exchanges were often embedded in conversation about a variety of topics. An environment which encouraged such conversation was also found supportive of collaboration among kindergarten students (Dyson, 1987). Teachers may need to look more carefully at conversations which appear to be "off task" because frequently such conversational interaction seems to be most conducive to collaborative interaction.

Interviews are frequently used to help students explore and help clarify a particular incident in a student's life. The interaction between the student and the problem is the primary interaction, with very specific roles played by the teacher (practitioner). In the nondirective interview, the teacher mirrors students' thoughts and feelings through reflective comments, which again clearly shows that the student is the primary influencing factor in the interaction.

We have seen how patterns of interaction within the "activity" phase of classroom events involve complex interactions between the practitioner, the participant, and some instructional problem/data/materials. This section (Chapters Nine and Ten) described the student's role in determining the direction of the interaction. Earlier, we discussed an important goal for classroom interaction—the development of students' communicative competence. We also presented our views toward supporting students as they become self-regulated, lifelong learners. Teachers who acknowledge the value of conversation and collaborative interaction will not only permit such interaction in the classroom but also work toward facilitating the students' development of skills which enhance collaborative interactions.

SUMMARY

This chapter included descriptions of two student-focused activities: peer interaction/collaboration and interviews. As with the activities discussed in Chapter Nine, the student (or students) provide the primary impetus or direction of the interaction. Certain types of instructional materials or problems are most supportive of student-focused activities (e.g., projects in science or social studies, writing activities). Although the teacher's role, as with those activities which are data/problems place focused (Section Four), is primarily one of support, the environment is one in which the classroom teacher heavily influences the interaction.

Much of the research on peer interaction and collaboration has involved writing activities. Roles within such activities may vary ranging from the onlooker who may learn through observation of more skilled students to the collaborator who actively contributes ideas to the project. While collaboration adds complexity to the writing process (Daiute, 1986), the benefits include the support of cognitive and social development as well as facilitation of communicative competence.

Interviews are used to help students clarify an incident or confront an issue. Throughout the interview process, the teacher mirrors student comments regarding a specific incident. By acting as a facilitator and partner in problem solving, the teacher supports the student as he or she learns to confront issues independently. The teacher's stance in critical in these interactions. He or she must present a stance of warmth, responsiveness, and genuine interest in the student as an individual. The context in which the interview takes place must also support free expression of feelings, without judgmental comments by the teacher. The development of effective interviewing skills may require additional training and supervised experiences. Therefore, we suggest that teachers make use of consultants or other trained personnel when necessary.

Student-focused patterns of interaction within the activity phase of an instructional event may be difficult for some teachers to support or implement. Schools often emphasize independent work and a quiet classroom environment. The value of "on-task" behavior has been ingrained into our notions of student learning. The activities in Section Five suggest that interactions such as reciprocal teaching, class meeting, writer's workshop, peer collaboration and interviews are effective means of helping students become self-directed, self-regulated learners. As teachers, we probably need to consider modifying our definition of "on-task" behavior to include more conversational interactions around some data/materials/problem. Such shifts in thinking about classroom interaction are what we tried to present in Sections Four and Five (place-focused and student-focused activities).

REVIEW QUESTIONS

1. Select an instructional problem either in science or social studies. Describe how this activity could be completed by using cooperative learning as an instructional strategy. Contrast this with a

description of how the instructional problem would be addressed through the support of peer interaction (collaboration). Discuss the similarities and differences in the teacher's role as well as the students.

2. Certain types of activities seem to support peer interaction. Research examples presented in this chapter did not include any problems related to mathematics. Suppose students were presented with the problem of getting a houseboat down a small river from one city to another. Generate at least three ideas of how this problem could be legitimately included in an instructional event involving mathematics. What might be some benefits to using peer interaction as opposed to a more teacher-focused interaction?

3. Interviews may be used to support the student in an emotionally charged situation or to restore a strained student-teacher relationship. Briefly describe a situation in which an interview might be an important means for helping the student deal with a particular issue. Discuss reasons for selecting the interview rather than confronting the problem during a class meeting.

4. The teacher's interactional style in the interview process is critical to the successful use of the interview. Describe how the teacher's stance influences his or her interactional style. Briefly discuss how student variables might influence this interaction.

5. Interviews are used to help students confront specific issues. The teacher acts as a partner in the problem-solving process. Explain how this process differs from a "directive" approach, in which a teacher might directly intervene and instruct students in conventional behaviors.

APPLICATION ACTIVITIES

Given the emphasis on independent work activities in many school settings and the lack of acknowledgment of the value of collaborative interactions, it might be difficult to observe or participate in those activities in the classroom. Therefore, several options for activities are presented here.

A. Observation of Collaborative Interaction with Colleagues

The purpose of this activity is to observe collaborative interactions as you initiate a project with at least one of your peers. The project may be as structured as completing the review questions in this chapter to designing a set of science activities related to a specific concept. A less structured project may involve comparing interactions during writing periods across several classroom settings (e.g., each person in the group observes in a different setting).

As you work on this project, note the various roles of the group members. Are some individuals more actively involved in setting the direction of the project? Do some people assume the role of "onlooker"? Note any changes in roles as the project develops. That is, during the initial planning stages, some individuals contribute less, yet make important contributions to the project as it develops.

Finally, each member of the collaborative team should examine his or her own role in the interaction. Try to determine your role using the continuum described by Cooper and her colleagues. Describe how the role influenced your personal learning process (e.g., if you were more of an "onlooker," did you gain anything from this activity?).

B. Discuss Issues of Collaboration or "On- and Off-Task" Behavior with a Classroom Teacher

The purpose of this activity is to discuss several issues with a classroom teacher to determine the role of stance regarding student-focused activities. It might be helpful to interview a teacher whose class you have observed over a period of time.

Begin by describing initial impressions of the classroom environment. Does the teacher seem to value "on-task" behavior to the degree that little peer interaction is permitted? Are there certain activities during which interaction is encouraged? If possible, note the organizational influences on the teacher's stance. For example, do the school principal and other teachers value "quiet" classrooms? Or does there seem to be an acknowledgment that sometimes student learning might lead to an appearance of less teacher control?

Try to determine the teacher's stance toward collaboration through discussion. Summarize your comments with statements about the match between your classroom observations and the teacher's verbal descriptions of her stance.

C. Observations of the Interview Process

Some readers might have access to a classroom and have established relationships with students and the classroom teacher that would enable them to observe the interview process. The purpose of this activity is to observe an interview and tease out the factors that contribute to the success of the interview.

Briefly describe the specific incident that precipitated the use of the interview. Discuss the purpose of the interview (e.g., was it intended as "emotional first aid" or an exploration of a life event). Comment on features of the teacher's interactional style that seemed to facilitate the interview process.

Student-teacher relationships and the classroom environment heavily influence the interview process. If you have observed in the classroom over an extended period of time, comment on the teacher's relationship with this particular student. What was the student's role in the interaction? Describe the student's level of involvement in the interaction (e.g., was the student resistant to questions, was the student able to articulate thoughts and feelings about the incident). If possible, ask the classroom teacher to comment on the student's role in the interaction.

Summarize your comments in terms of the three components of the interaction: the student, the teacher, and the specific event or problem that was discussed in the interview. Describe how the student's comments determined the nature and direction of the interview.

REFERENCES

COLE, D. A. (1986). Facilitating play in children's peer relations. *American Educational Research Journal, 23*, 201–215.

COOPER, C. R., MARQUIS, A., & AYERS-LOPEZ, S. (1982). Peer learning in the classroom: Tracing developmental patterns and consequences of children's spontaneous interactions. In L. C. Wilkinson (Ed.), *Communicating in the classroom* (pp. 69–84). New York: Academic Press.

COOPER, C. R., MARQUIS, A., & EDWARD, D. (1986). Four perspectives on peer learning among elementary school children. In E. C. Mueller & C. R. Cooper (Eds.), *Process and outcome in peer relationships* (pp. 269–300). New York: Academic Press.

DAIUTE, C. (1986). Do 1 and 1 make 2? Patterns of influence by collaborative authors. *Written Communication, 3*, 382–408.

DELGADO-GAITAN, C., & TRUEBA, H. T. (1985). Ethnographic study of participation structures in task completion: Reinterpretation of "handicaps" in Mexican Children. *Learning Disability Quarterly, 8*, 67–75.

DE MAGISTRAS, R. J., & IMBER, S. C. (1980). The effects of life space interviewing on the academic and social performance of behavior disordered children. *Behavioral Disorders, 6,* 12–25.

DICKINSON, D. K. (1986). Cooperation, collaboration, and a computer: Integrating a computer into a first-second grade writing program. *Research in the Teaching of English, 20,* 357–378.

DYSON, A. H. (1987). The value of "time off task." Young children's spontaneous talk and deliberate text. *Harvard Educational Review, 57,* 396–420.

FORMAN, E. A. (1987). Peer relationships of learning disabled children: A contextualist perspective. *Learning Disabilities Research, 2*(2), 80–90.

GARNICA, O. K. (1981). Social dominance and conversational interaction-The Omega child in the classroom. In J. Green and C. Wallat (Eds.), *Ethnography and language in educational settings* (pp. 229–252). Norwood, NJ: Ablex.

GARVEY, C. (1986). Peer relations and the growth of communication. In E. C. Mueller & C. R. Cooper (Eds.), *Process and outcome in peer relationships* (pp. 329–345). New York: Academic Press.

JOYCE, B., & WEIL M. (1986). *Models of teaching* (3rd ed.). Englewood Cliffs, NJ: Prentice Hall.

KAHN, R. L., & CANNELL, C. F. (1957) *The dynamics of interviewing: Theory, technique, and cases.* New York: John Wiley.

MORSE, W. C. (1980). Worksheet in life space interviewing. In J. J. Long, W. C. Morse, & R. Newman (Eds.), *Conflict in the classroom* (4th ed., pp. 367–371). Belmont, CA: Wadsworth.

Project STRETCH, (1980). *Peer tutoring.* Northbrook, IL: Hubbard.

REDL, F. (1959). The concept of the life space interview. *American Journal of Orthopsychiatry, 29,* 1–18.

REILLY, M. J., IMBER, S. C., & CREMINS, J. (1978). The effects of life space interviews on social behaviors of junior high school needs students. Paper presented at the 56th International Council for Exceptional Children, Kansas City.

RESNICK, L. B. (1987). Learning in school and out. *Educational Researcher, 16*(9), 13–20.

ROGERS, C. (1982). *Freedom to learn for the 80's.* Columbus, OH: Charles E. Merrill.

SHEA, T. M., & BAUER, A. M. (1987). *Teaching children and youth with behavior disorders.* Englewood Cliffs, NJ: Prentice Hall.

STODOLSKY, S. S. (1984). Frameworks for studying instructional processes in peer work-group. In P. L. Peterson, L. C. Wilkinson, & M. Hallinan (Eds.), *The social context of instruction: Group organization and group processes* (pp. 107–124). New York: Academic Press.

VYGOTSKY, L. (1972). *Mind in society.* Cambridge, MA: Harvard University Press.

CHAPTER ELEVEN

"Walkin' What We Talk": Developing an Agenda and Describing Patterns in Classrooms

INTRODUCTION

The "language of practice" of a profession refers to the models of thinking and acting employed by practitioners to accomplish the tasks at hand effectively (Yinger, 1987a, 1987b). In learning the craft of teaching, the language of practice describes the interactions which occur in the complex classroom context. First-year teachers are quick to criticize teacher preparation programs that treat structuring classrooms as an "if-then" proposition. Rather, teachers are confronted with myriad "it depends" answers, in which a strategy effective for one student is not effective for another, where students represent diverse cultures, abilities, skills, and motives; where school contexts vary greatly; and where fellow-teachers are not necessarily involved in mutual support.

The approach presented in this book will, we hope, reduce the all too common baptism by fire into the complexity of life in classrooms. Through examining classroom interactions, teachers will begin to develop a stance that permits them to confront classroom complexity and design instruction that facilitates learning.

This chapter varies in format from the ten that precede it. In this chapter, we will review each of the major premises in the book.

After the brief review, we will, as the students' in one of our teacher collaborator's classrooms say, "walk what we talk." We will provide examples, from our work with teachers, which demonstrate the concepts presented. We will conclude the chapter with comments about key issues presented in the text as they relate to teacher stance.

OBJECTIVES

After completing this chapter, you will be able to:

1. Describe the issue of stance in classrooms.
2. Discuss the complexity of classroom environments and the multiplicity of variables considered in classroom structures.
3. Discuss developing an agenda for classroom management in practice in classrooms.
4. Recognize patterns of interaction as they appear in classrooms.

Objective One: *To Describe the Issue of Stance in Classrooms*

A teacher's stance encompasses his or her personal posture toward self and others, as well as theoretical orientation and instructional management techniques (McGee, Menolascino, Hobbs, and Menousek, 1987). As we discussed earlier, the literature has explored the relationship between teacher's stance and student-teacher interactions. Rohrkemper (1984) contrasted the socializing role of the classroom teacher and students' social perceptions of the teacher, classmates, and themselves. Marshall (1987), in a qualitative study exploring the conceptualization of teachers' motivational orientations and teacher strategies to support motivation to learn, contrasted teacher management and lesson framing statements in a learning-oriented, work-oriented, and a work-avoidance oriented classroom. Recently in their observations of teachers' interactional styles, Evertson and Weade (1989) described the efficacy of a classroom management style that elicited and supported student participation. The effective teacher provided explicit rationales for activities, set and followed consistent routines for classroom interaction, and maintained sensitivity to student needs in relation to the difficulty level of the lesson content. In each of the studies mentioned, the teachers' stances (as noted primarily through observations of interactional styles) clearly affect students' opportunities to engage in learning activities.

To study the relationship between stance and teacher-student interactions further, Bauer, Lynch, and Murphy (1989) scrutinized field notes of over fifty hours of observation in a fifth and sixth grade classroom of students with behavior problems. In view of studying the relationship between the teacher's expressed stance and management patterns, we collected data which provided insight into the teacher's perceptions of her philosophy of pedagogy. This data was collected after the conclusion of the school year, with the teacher naive to our questions of stance. During an interview, the teacher's basic goals of interaction and desired classroom orientation were recorded. These statements were scrutinized for patterns, and three categories of statements emerged: (1) each individual is responsible for his or her actions; (2) each student is special and has strengths; and (3) each student should be dealt with at his or her level.

In this study, the philosophy and self-management orientation the teacher expressed was demonstrated in her behavior. For example, the teacher's belief that each individual is responsible for his or her own actions was demonstrated behaviorally as she encouraged students to control personal behaviors and accept ownership of the effects of their actions. Her recognition of individual uniqueness and strengths was demonstrated by her nurturing support, social reinforcement, and intimacy in conversation with students. Finally, her expressed goal of working with each student at his or her own level was demonstrated by dealing with individual situations, at times recognizing the need for encouragement, and at other times increasing demands.

These studies not only provide illustrations of effective and less than effective classroom management techniques/styles of interaction, but also demonstrate the tremendous impact of teacher stance on classroom interactions. In addition in the Bauer, Lynch and Murphy study, the teacher's well-defined and clearly articulated agenda for classroom management emanates from her stance (as noted in Chapter Three). Thus, the teacher's stance has a profound effect on the teacher's actions and roles in the classroom. In Chapter One, we noted that teachers assume many roles such as decision makers, design professionals, improvisors, researchers, and master planners as they attempt to create and maintain environments which invite students to learn. We also observed that classrooms are highly complex environments in which teachers, students, and subject matter cointeract. A teacher's stance guides decision making and design processes necessary in the planning of instruction and permits the improvisation which evolves from the interactions between students and the data/subject matter or instructional problem.

Objective Two: *To Discuss the Complexity of Classroom Environments and the Multiplicity of Variables Considered in Classroom Structures*

Tattum (1986) contends that classroom management is complicated by the need to allocate time, space, and materials as well as coping with student behavior. Our students have reported to us on the ways that they manipulate these variables to structure interactions in their classrooms. As you read through these examples, note how the teachers' (our students') stance influenced how they designed and organized instructional activities to facilitate learning.

One teacher described structuring the classroom to initiate a week-long unit on space. On the first day of the project, the students' attention was drawn to the chalkboard that always relays a daily message entitled "Today's News." On this particular day, it said, "Today we will talk about Space." In addition, a plain bulletin board was covered only in black paper. Initial discussion about space took place during the social studies period in which students generated ideas related to space. On the second day, the students were still curious about the blank bulletin board. The teacher read from a book about space and asked the students if space was empty, like the bulletin board. From the resulting discussion, the students planned and produced objects and pictures to represent what was "in space" and completed the bulletin board. Through managing the noninstructional variables of a simple written announcement and a bulletin board, the teacher implemented student-focused activities.

In another example, a teacher reported on the daily "setup" which supports the students' behavior in the classroom. For example, the given rule is that to work on the water table, you must wear a smock. To manage the number of students at the water table, only three smocks are available. Students are cued to put the large beads on one string and the small ones on another, by having two or three beads already strung. Two pillows on the floor and a book implies a sharing activity.

In another situation, which actually surprised both the teacher and the authors, furniture provided a cue to the students about the behavior. The teacher used Writing Workshop, and had the students do their sharing in yellow chairs at the front of the room, which were in the room expressly for that purpose. After a field trip during which the students demonstrated less than conventional behavior, the teacher asked the students to write about their behavioral goals. She then moved the students to the yellow chairs for discussion of the goals. The students moved directly into the patterns that they had established for Writing Workshop, making the same comments, such as "I like what you wrote, but I think you need to add something" or

"I don't think that was too clear. Could you say it another way?" The students were taking their cues for the discussion not from the teacher, but from the setting.

Classrooms, then, are complex, not only because of the patterns of interaction which take place in them, but because of the wide range of variables which must be managed. Students take cues from the materials, furniture, time of day, and even more subtly, teacher position in the classroom. In addition, through observing how teachers manipulate variables such as time, space, and materials, the teachers' stance can be demonstrated. For example, as the teacher initiated the unit on space, she structured the instructional activity to provide maximal student input (i.e., through the use of a student-focused interaction) which furthered interest in the topic. In the second example, through carefully structuring the environment (e.g., cues at the water table), the teacher supported student behavior by facilitating independence from teacher direction and control. Although the furniture provided the cue for interactional patterns evident in the third example, the teacher's stance (established through other interactions such as Writer's Workshop) allowed this type of interaction to occur. The actions displayed by these teachers illustrate their facilitative stance which encourages student engagement in the instructional activity and supports students as they learn to regulate their own behavior.

Objective Three: *To Discuss Developing an Agenda for Classroom Management in Practice in Classrooms*

In Chapter Three we described a framework for developing an agenda for classroom management. The framework was designed to assist teachers as they worked through problems or instructional issues presented by students who demonstrate challenging behavior. One of the teachers with whom we work provided the following illustration of the use of the framework to plan activities and design interactions which supported student learning.

The student who was demonstrating a challenging behavior was a 7½-year-old black male student in second grade. Billy had reportedly demonstrated a wide range of "behavior problems" in school, including hyperactivity, fighting, impulsivity, and having an "attitude." He had been medicated for hyperactivity in the past, but was not receiving any medication at this time.

The first step in applying the framework for developing an agenda is to *describe the behavioral issue or instructional question.* Two main issues emerged through the initial description. The first of these is reported by the teacher as making noises in the classroom.

Billy would mutter and talk to himself, "beat boxing" (i.e., making noises similar to the background sounds in "rap" music), moaning, groaning, and dry spitting. These noises were made loudly and were reported to the teacher as distracting. The students complained that they couldn't study and learn, and the teacher complained that she couldn't teach. In an attempt to decrease the disruption, the teacher removed Billy from the class and had him complete his work in the third grade classroom next door, hoping that the "big kids" in third grade would intimidate him to be quiet. However, as the removal into the third grade classroom was used more frequently, Billy gradually increased the volume and frequency of his noises until he also disrupted instructional activities in the third grade classroom.

The behavioral issue of making noises was compounded by what the teacher reported as a second issue: Billy's "attitude." When reprimanded, he would respond "so what" or pout and withdraw. Within several minutes, his noises would become louder.

The teacher's perception of the issue was not quite clear. She questioned whether Billy was in complete control of the noises. When initially reprimanded, he would become quiet, then start making noises again within seconds. The teacher felt that the noises may not be attention seeking, in that Billy didn't even appear to realize he was making them. The noises, however, became louder after he was reprimanded.

Interviewing Billy (i.e., checking the student's perception of the issue) provided little insight. Billy indicated that he knew he was making noises, and that they were disturbing to others. When asked if he could develop a plan to decrease the noises, to help him be quiet so other students and he could learn, he shrugged his shoulders. Billy's mother indicated that Billy makes noises at home usually when excited (such as during a board game or using the computer). His mother agreed that the noises have become a significant problem. She stated that when she asked Billy about the noises, he gave one word answers, said "I don't know," and looked very solemn and sad.

In following the second step of the framework, *analyzing the issue or instructional question*, an antecedent-behavior-consequence chart was developed. Two incidents are depicted on the ABC chart in Table 11.1. At this point, teacher, student, task, and setting variables were analyzed.

Teacher Variables. The teacher's expectations for her classroom included quiet, cooperative behavior from the students. When cooperation was not apparent, she became frustrated and upset. The teacher reported that Billy was a bright boy who could complete his work if he paid better attention and didn't disrupt the class. She

TABLE 11.1 Antecedent-Behavior-Consequence Chart for Billy's Noises

ANTECEDENT	BEHAVIOR	CONSEQUENCE
Sample 1		
Teacher begins to discuss reading assignment.	Billy vocalizes to self.	Teacher reprimands Billy for noises.
Billy is reprimanded.	After two seconds of silence Billy begins to beat-box.	Teacher again reprimands Billy for noises.
Billy is reprimanded.	Billy states out loud, "I don't wanna read."	Teacher praises all other students for reading quietly.
Teacher ignores Billy; praises others.	Billy talks loudly, voicing dislike for teacher and activity.	Teacher sends Billy to hallway to sit in chair.
Sample 2		
Seatwork papers are distributed.	Billy looks at worksheet and talks to self.	Teacher reminds Billy that others are trying to work.
Teacher reminds Billy to be quiet.	Billy moans, groans, and spits.	Teacher reprimands Billy more loudly, saying "No one else is making noises, Billy. Why do you have to?"
Teacher asks Billy why he has to make noises.	Billy becomes silent.	Teacher resumes quiet monitoring of seatwork.
Quiet monitoring is resumed.	Billy starts to beat-box and rap his pencil on desk.	Teacher sends Billy to third grade class next door to finish his work.

perceived the behavior as out of Billy's control and, therefore, even more frustrating.

The communication patterns in the classroom were more reactive than proactive. Billy was reminded to keep quiet after making noises, rather than being told to be quiet in anticipation of a quiet worktime.

In addition, cultural issues emerged. The teacher is white and from a middle-class background. For religious reasons, Billy does not participate in holiday and birthday celebrations, nor does he have toys considered by his religion as disrespectful, materialistic, or frivolous. The teacher reported that she didn't understand Billy's home life or religion.

Billy also challenged the teacher's expressed beliefs about teaching and learning. Her belief system obtained through interviews suggested that when presented with good teaching, children are motivated to learn. She struggled with understanding Billy, who appeared disrespectful and unmotivated. She repeatedly stated that she just does not understand "kids like Billy." With eleven years of teaching experience in a white, suburban, middle-class private school, the teacher appeared to experience distress in the inner-urban school in which she was assigned.

Student Variables. Billy's expectations were quite different from those of the teacher. He appeared to believe that his noises are not offending. At times he pointed out and argued that others were making noises too. When sent to the hall, he often muttered "no fair." The communicative intent of the noises are difficult to ascertain. Although they may be, in part, a protest and a control issue, it is possible that the noises began as self-regulating behaviors, such as talking to oneself when completing a complex task.

No known changes in Billy's life patterns have occurred. Billy lived with his mother, but saw his father when he was "in trouble." Cultural issues again emerged. Billy frequently participated in "messing," which led to frequent fights and displays of power. This style of interaction, referred to by Billy and his peers as "just messing" when interrupted, was considered inappropriate by the teacher. In view of learning styles, Billy seemed to work best with background noise. When there is none available in the classroom, Billy may have been creating his own background noise.

Billy has a noted strength in his pleasant social patterns outside of the classroom. When he accidentally bumps or offends another child, he apologizes and shows true remorse. Billy is quite physically attractive and can be very animated and happy. A weakness identified by the teacher was his ability to "rub authority figures the wrong way" by his disrespectful attitude.

Developmentally, Billy, 7 years old, presented many of the social behaviors of a 4-year-old. He was impulsive, moody, and easily frustrated. He talked back, often challenged authority, and tried to push limits. Behaviors seen as a phase in a 4-year-old are perceived as disrespectful in Billy. Part of the issue may be Billy's immaturity and lack of learning more conventional school behaviors.

Task Variables. Billy made noises most frequently when given independent work. Billy expressed that he "hated" books and disliked math. His mother reported that he objected to going to school daily. The teacher's perception was that the materials and activities were challenging but not difficult or out of reach. Academic progress had been observed since the beginning of the school year.

Billy appeared disinterested in the instructional content when noises occurred. During gym, occupational therapy time, recess, or lunch, noises did not occur.

Setting Variables. Peers seemed to contribute to Billy's challenging behavior. At times they objected, at other times they encouraged him. Noises did not occur in one-to-one settings, or for other adults such as the gym teacher. Billy was quiet and cooperative during individual instruction but made noises during group discussion or teaching. Positive peer interactions occurred at recess, during one-to-one instruction, or during small reading group.

From this review of the teacher, student, task, and setting variables, several hypotheses were generated. The issue may be a control issue, or Billy may be commenting on his lack of interest. Since he is not interested in the instructional content, he may be trying to tell those in control (his teacher) that even though she is nominally in control, he has the final say and can therefore show his control by not following all of the rules. The control issue may be exaggerated by cultural differences between Billy and the teacher.

Another hypothesis is that the behavior is attention getting. In one-to-one settings and in playing with peers, Billy received attention and did not make noises. Left alone, he made noises. Lack of maturity and lack of learning more conventional school behaviors may also be an issue.

In view of communicative functions of Billy's behavior, the noises may have served to request affection, attention, social interaction, or play. They may have served as a protest against the type and amount of work. In addition, he may have been using self-talk to regulate his own behavior.

The next in the framework is to *generate hypotheses and define an agenda to develop more conventional behaviors.* The agenda selected after completing the earlier steps of the framework was to address the "noises" as an attention seeking behavior. The agenda targeted more conventional behavior to be reinforced in attempts to make the noises incompatible. Positive programming would be encouraged for conventional equivalents, with the teacher pointing out and praising Billy for being quiet, rather than calling his and the class's attention to noises. In addition, setting variables were

managed. Billy was allowed and encouraged to talk and share in peer
tutoring and small group collaborative learning activities. Positive consequences would be provided for quiet, on-task behavior. In addition, the
teacher would talk with Billy about his life, give him additional individualized time, and interpret and reconstruct his behavior for him.

The final step of the framework involves *evaluating and modifying the agenda.* The teacher provided opportunities for positive interaction through cooperative learning activities and peer tutoring. She
also gave Billy attention. It is interesting to note that the teacher
reported several positive days followed by one day of the challenging
behavior. Rather than "give up" the strategies, she was encouraged
to continue with this agenda. Through careful evaluation, the teacher
noticed significant changes in Billy's behavior. Besides impacting on
Billy's behavior through changes in the ways in which his teacher
interacted with him, analyzing the behavior reportedly helped the
teacher become more tolerant of the behavior. It was helpful just to
realize that Billy's behavior may in some way be reasonable or may be
traced to a specific source rather than the result of an "attitude."

This example clearly illustrates how the framework may be used
to contend with the complex issues presented by Billy's challenging
behavior. A teacher may assume the role of researcher and use the
framework to address a specific problem or breakdown in his or her
management agenda. However, as noted in Sections Three through
Five, the teacher may adopt a proactive strategy: through structuring
the classroom and designing activities to encourage student involvement and interest in the instructional interaction. In Billy's situation,
the instructional content and format (e.g., peer tutoring and small-
group collaborative learning activities) as well as positive teacher
interactions and individualized attention were used to alleviate his
challenging behavior. A more proactive approach is suggested
through use of patterns of interaction to design instruction and structure classroom activities.

Objective Four: *To Recognize Patterns of Interaction as They Occur in Classrooms*

The use of patterns of interaction to design instructional activities
is grounded in the image of the teacher as an actor in a three-way
conversation between the teacher, students, and some instructional
problem. In contrast to a more traditional view of classroom management which suggests that "problems" often result from "inappropriate"
student behavior requiring teacher "intervention" or a discipline/control
perspective, using patterns may help teachers become more aware of
the many factors which contribute to classroom interactions.

In the text, patterns of interaction were presented in Sections Three through Five. However, the separation of patterns of interaction into practitioner focused, place focused, and student focused may appear artificial when considering the complexity of classroom activities. In practice, there appears to be a pattern-to-pattern flow which is guided or shaped by the teacher's stance. An example of this flow was discussed by one of our students, a kindergarten teacher.

The teacher's overall objective was to introduce the concept of size (more specifically, differences in size) using Cuisenaire rods (small unit blocks, graduated in size from one unit to ten units). These rods varied in color as well as size, that is, one unit blocks were beige, ten unit blocks were orange. Over the six days during which the materials were used, patterns of interaction varied.

During the first day, active participation from the students was sought, through *place-focused patterns*. While everyone was seated in a group, the teacher "dumped" a basket of the rods onto the floor. The children were asked to talk about the rods and describe their color and size. Children decided that the rods should be sorted by color, and each student took a color to sort them into sets.

The teacher instructed each child to take one block of each color. They were then directed to "see what they could do" with them. The students responded by making designs on the floor, collaborating and lining the rods up together, and making shapes. The whole group actively participated in manipulating the rods.

The second day was again *place-focused interaction*, but the students were given vocabulary for the rods. Students initiated stacking, which was commented upon by the teacher. The teacher's comments increased the stacking activity by the children, some cooperatively, some parallel, some independently.

The third day involved *student (or participant)-focused interactions*. The children came to the group with their rods and began to work with them without the teacher's direction. The teacher refrained from making any comments, and the students began to make "steps" by stacking the rods in various ways. Students modeled making steps, and after a comment from the teacher, children began to stack the rods from long to short. On the fourth day of working with the rods, the activities began to emerge as more *practitioner focused*. The teacher initiated the discussion by asking all the students to make steps, and discuss which is the longest and shortest rod. Students were asked to create steps using the teacher's model.

On the fifth day of the activity, the teacher began the instructional interaction without the rods. Students were asked about what they did yesterday, and the teacher built a model of the steps from their verbal directions. Students were then sent back to their tables and given more specific directions on how many rods to select. On the last day, the activity was again *practitioner focused*. Students were again requested to order the rods by size, and then represent the order in color by paper.

The teacher suggested that each instructional interaction (lesson) was comprised of three parts: (1) review and modeling, (2) practice, and (3) review. The teacher contends that when she began to prepare the activities using the rods, she felt that her presentation would be more teacher (practitioner) focused. In practice, however, the lessons seemed to move naturally from place-focused, to student-focused, to practitioner-focused patterns of interaction. During the student-focused lessons, the students seemed to want to know more explicit information, which emerged into teacher-focused activities.

This pattern-to-pattern flow was facilitated by the teacher's stance. A teacher whose stance is more directive and less flexible might have planned a series of activities and followed those plans with little regard for students' reaction to the lesson presentation. In contrast, the teacher in this example allowed her students to guide the interaction. As she reviewed the entire instructional sequence, the teacher recognized her role as designer and improvisor. She "choreographed" key components of the instructional activity to invite her students to discover differences in size using the Cuisenaire rods. That is, she provided activities which enlisted the active participation of her students. The teacher capitalized on students' ideas and carefully guided the interaction through her support of cooperative learning and peer interaction. Through her facilitative interactional style, a smooth pattern-to-pattern flow resulted in a high level of student interest in the content (in this example, differences in size). As important as content, the students experienced the joys of discovering and sharing ideas. The improvisational interaction based on student reactions to the instructional problem supported student learning of content and facilitated their development of communicative competence.

SUMMARY COMMENTS

The focus of this text was to provide information regarding a different view of classroom management issues. Recognizing the complexity of the classroom context, we attempted to share our view of teachers as observers/students of classroom interaction. Several key issues were raised: the acknowledgment of the role of teachers' communicative competence and match with students, the importance of communication and application of routines, and the impact of communication styles and cultural differences on student participation in instruction. We hope that through the discussion of these issues, the reader has begun to develop his or her own stance.

Examples from our work with students suggests that a facilitative stance assists teachers as they deal with the complex classroom context as they confront the complexities of the classroom. The most effective practitioners we've observed are "students of classroom interaction" who may be at various places in their development as facilitative teachers. They design instructional activities to meet specific objectives and capitalize on opportunities for learning as they improvise based on the participants' interaction with the data/material/problem. Their classrooms are truly "learning places" both from the participants' (students) and practitioner's perspective.

We hope that this text provided the support necessary to assist the reader in his or her development (or perhaps recognition or reexamination) of stance. We invite the reader to "wonder" about student learning through observations of classroom interactions and continue to be surprised by learners. We hope that as you structure your classrooms using patterns of interaction or use the agenda presented to address instructional issues, your classrooms can become more like "learning places" (Marshall, 1988).

REFERENCES

BAUER, A. M., LYNCH, E. M. & MURPHY, E. S. (1989). *A teacher's stance: Building a self-management orientation in a classroom for students with behavioral disorders.* Unpublished manuscript, University of Cincinnati.

EVERTSON, C. M., & WEADE, R. (1989). Classroom management and teaching style: Instructional stability and variability in two junior high English classrooms. *Elementary School Journal, 89,* 379–393.

MARSHALL, H. (1987). Motivational strategies of three fifth-grade teachers. *The Elementary School Journal, 88,* 135–150.

MARSHALL, H. H. (1988). Work or learning: Implications of classroom metaphors. *Educational Researcher, 17*(9), 9–16.

MCGEE, J. J., MENOLASCINO, F. J., HOBBS, D. C. & MENOUSEK, P.E. (1987). *Gentle teaching.* New York: Human Science Press.

ROHRKEMPER, M. M. (1984). The influence of socialization style on students' social cognition and reported interpersonal behavior. *The Elementary School Journal, 85,* 245–275.

TATTUM, D. P. (1986). Consistency management—School and classroom concerns and issues. In D. P. Tattum (Ed.), *Management of disruptive pupil behavior in schools* (pp. 51–68). Chichester, England: John Wiley.

YINGER, R. J. (1987a, October). *The conversation of practice.* Paper presented at the Reflective Inquiry Conference, College of Education, University of Houston, Houston, TX.

————. (1987b). Learning the language of practice. *Curriculum Inquiry, 17,* 293–318.

Our special thanks to Tina Constanzo, Sandy Engel, Krista Mendenhall, Sue Murphy, and Carol Scheerer for permitting us to share their classrooms and interactions.

Glossary

The chapter in which each term initially occurs is indicated in brackets [ ].

activity   a segment of classroom time with an identifiable focal content or concern and program of action [4]

advance organizers   statements that briefly describe and set student expectations for the activity about to begin [5]

agenda   operational classroom plans, including activity structures, routines, and other interactional elements [3]

allocated time   the amount of time scheduled for an activity [4]

behavioral principles   rules governing behavior [7]

behavioral procedures   teaching and behavior management techniques based on behavioral principles [7]

class meeting   a group discussion regarding class-related personal, group, or academic problems [9]

classroom management   teacher activities that establish and maintain an effective instructional and learning environment; includes managing time, space, materials, records, and student behavior [1]

closure   the final, summarization phase of classroom activities [5]

cognitive behavior modification (CBM)   strategies that assist students in developing self-control [7]

communicative competence   communicative knowledge that allows individual members of a cultural group to interact in ways that are both socially appropriate and strategically effective [2]

contingency contract   an arrangement between teacher and student that designates how an individual is to behave and the consequences for the change

conventional   the degree to which the meaning is shared or understood by the social community [3]

cooperative learning   grouping students to achieve a shared goal [4]

correctives   learning activities designed to remediate specific errors [6]

demonstration   enacting all or part of the task or skill to provide a model for others [6]

dialogue   collaborative interaction carried out through language [5]

direct instruction   a teaching model that emphasizes the teacher's role in classroom organization and use of time [6]

directive   a management style in which activities are initiated and controlled by the teacher [2]

discussion   dialogue among a group on a specific topic or question [8]

engaged time   the amount of time in which students are interacting with material of at least moderate difficulty [4]

extinction   discontinuing or withholding the reinforcer that has been maintaining a behavior [7]

facilitative   a management style in which teachers use statements, encouragements, and expansions in their interactions with students [2]

feedback   information regarding performance [6]

guided practice   supervised rehearsal, drill, and practice [6]

if-then statements   statements of expectations put in the form of a contingency, for example, "if you complete your assignment, then you may have free time" [1]

inductive thinking   reasoning from parts to the whole, or from specifics to the general [8]

in-flight decisions   decisions that are made during the activity itself, in contrast to planned, premeditated decisions [1]

inquiry   identifying, formulating, and working toward the solution of a problem [8]

interactive decisions   decisions that are made during activities as a result of the interaction of student, teacher, and materials or content [1]

interview   a pattern of verbal interaction that is initiated for a specific purpose and focuses on specific content [10]

language of practice   the models of thinking and acting employed by practitioners to accomplish the tasks at hand effectively [5]

mastery learning   a model of teaching that emphasizes increased learning opportunities and individualization of time allotted [6]

nondirective interview   an interview during which the adult facilitates student exploration of ideas through reflective listening [10]

order   a state during which students are following the program necessary for classroom events to proceed [2]

participant   one assuming the role of learner [5]

participation structures   the communicative or behavioral demands placed on students, including when and how to speak, listen, initiate and maintain an interaction, and lead and follow discussions [3]

peer collaboration   a pattern of interaction in which peers work together toward the same goal [10]

peer tutoring   activities in which students assist other students in learning

place   the data, task, problem, material, and social issue with which the participant and practitioner are dealing [5]

pow-wow   a group meeting model focusing on individual goal development [9]

practitioner   one assuming the role of teacher [5]

preparation   the initial "setup" phase of classroom activities [5]

reciprocal teaching   an instructional procedure that involves a dialogue between teachers and students for the purpose of constructing the meaning of a text [9]

reinforcement   responses that increase behaviors [7]

routines   shared, cooperative, social scripts that automize and facilitate the activity by reducing the cognitive complexity of the classroom [1, 4]

rules   statements of limits; explicit constraints

scaffolding   the use of supportive cues and prompts that are gradually faded as the participant becomes more independent [5]

scripts   a series of experienced-based expectations about the ways in which events occur [4]

self-instruction   a strategy or series of steps to guide students through a specific task [7]

self-monitoring   systematically monitoring (assessing and recording) one's own behavior

self-regulated learning   student management of cognitive abilities and motivational effort in a way that learning is effective, economical, and satisfying [7]

stance   style, orientation, and attitude toward self and others that guide interactions [1]

stimulus change   changing the student's environment so that the behavior no longer occurs [7]

token economy   contingent management systems that allow students to earn tokens that can be exchanged at a later time for specific reinforcers [7]

wait time   the amount of time between student-teacher interactions [5]

writing workshop   a style of instruction in which writing is treated as a laboratory or studio subject [9]

INDEX

A

ABC chart, 47–48, 208, 209
Academic attack strategies, 136
Academic task structures, 40
Acoustics, classroom, 75
Action agenda, 10
Action system, 112
Activities
  defined, 67
  routines to structure, 67–69
  student-focused. *See*
    Student-focused group
    activities
  teacher-focused. *See* Direct
    instruction; Mastery learning
  See also Events management
Activity phase of classroom
  events, 87, 88, 89–94
  basic components of, 89–90
  instructional strategies or
    techniques during, 92–94

interaction patterns during,
  89–92, 112
Advance organizers, 88–89
Agenda for managing
  classroom, 10, 36–63
  conventional vs. appropriate
    view of behavior and,
    41–42, 54, 211–12
  direct instruction and
    mastery learning
    activities in, 110–11
  examples of situations
    needing, 36–38
  framework for developing,
    44–58, 207–12
  analysis of issues or
    concerns, 46–53, 208–11
  description of issue or
    concerns, 44–46, 207–8
  evaluation and
    modification, 55–58, 212